RAISING TWINS

What Parents Want to Know
(and What Twins Want to Tell Them)

Eileen M. Pearlman, PH.D.,
&
Jill Alison Ganon

HarperResource
An Imprint of HarperCollins*Publishers*

HarperCollins books may be purchased for educational, business, or sales promotional use. For information please write: Special Markets Department, HarperCollins Publishers Inc., 10 East 53rd Street, New York, NY 10022.

FIRST EDITION

Designed by Interrobang Design Studio

Library of Congress Cataloging-in-Publication Data has been applied for.

ISBN 0-06-273680-9

01 02 03 04 ❖/RRD 10 9 8 7 6 5 4 3

I dedicate this book to my family, with special thanks to
the twins in my life—my sister, Elaine, and my husband, Art.

— Eileen M. Pearlman

I dedicate this book to my grandmother, Ada Ganon,
and my great-aunt, Miriam—loving sisters and best of
friends.

— Jill Alison Ganon

CONTENTS

ACKNOWLEDGMENTS

We want to thank the following families for their generous participation in the preparation of this book. Special thanks to the twins and parents of twins who are represented in our "Twin Talk" segments for their wisdom, humor, and insight into twin life.

The Castillo family—Belen, Nazario, Alex, and Dave

The Coon family—Susan, John, Bradley, and Taylor

The Davis family—Mary, Mark, Erica, Chris, and Andy

The Kollantai family—Jean, Bernhard, Berney, Alexander, and the memory of their son and brother Andrew

The Leavitt family—Lauren, Todd, Julia, Chloe, and Eliza

The Meneghin family—Sonia, Gary, Marco, and Dino

Suzanne Pierre, Wendel DePieza, Tsedal, and Tamir DePieza

The Register family—Kathy, Steven, Nathan, and Brian

Diana Taylor, Bernard Weiner, Amaro, and Hermes Taylor-Weiner

The Timiraos family—Carol, Vince, Nick, and Alex

The Tolentino family—Lana, Francisco, Lanita, Francisco, Lanaii, Laticia, and Miguel Angelo,

Juliette Tuakli, MD., Eyi, and Yetsa Tuakli-Wosornu

The Vane family—Deborah, Gregg, West, Robin, and Katie

Kathy Young, Tim Ganon, Sydney, Ben, Morgan, and Margo Ganon

We offer our grateful thanks to the following people for their time, interest and support of this project:

To Jean Kollantai, founder of the Center for Loss in Multiple Birth, Inc. (CLIMB), for her devoted work in support of families of multiples, and her thoughtful notes on Chapter Twelve of this book.

To Philip Holthouse for his wise words on financial matters.

To Melani Eaves and the San Gabriel Terrific Twosomes Mothers of Twins Club for inviting us to their meeting and introducing us to such great twin families.

To the members of the Parents of Surviving Twin's Support Group—Lori Conway, Debi Garlick, Laura Hanaford, Sandy Lee, Kathy LeVay, Tracy Milstead, and Nadia Scott for their strength and commitment to their families.

To Lynette Glover for being a real pal to the sister of her real pal.

To Dr. Juliette Tuakli for her brilliant referrals.

To our agent, Angela Rinaldi, for her dedicated work on our behalf.

To Tricia Medved for once again reading a proposal and seeing a book.

To Greg Chaput for patience, enthusiasm, and a caring editorial eye.

To Marge at the Busy Key for many hours of transcriptions.

To Art Pearlman for his insight and support.

To the extended Pearlman family for their encouragement and ongoing support.

To Joan Ganon for always being there.

To David Arnay and Miles Ganon Arnay for surviving another book.

Dr. Pearlman wishes to thank all the multiple birth families she sees in her practice for sharing their wisdom and enriching her professional life.

INTRODUCTION

$\mathcal{A}$s we prepare this book for publication, a new report by the National Center for Health Statistics, "Trends in Twin and Triplet Births: 1980–97," confirms that the rate of multiple births is skyrocketing. The report tells us that from 1980 to 1997 the number of twin births in the United States rose 52 percent (from 68,339 to 104,137). Even more astonishing is the increase in multiple births to mothers in their forties: The twin birth rate rose 63 percent for women between the ages of 40 and 44 and rose almost 1,000 percent for women from 45 to 49 years of age.

More and more children will grow up knowing twins and having twins as friends and neighbors; more and more teachers will have at least one set of multiples in their class each year; more coaches will have twins on their teams; more pediatricians will have twins as patients; more parents will face the prospect of raising children who are multiples; and finally, more children will grow up experiencing the unique joys and challenges of the twin relationship.

Raising Twins is a guidebook for the increasing number of mothers and fathers who set out to have a child and hit the jackpot with twins. This book applies a developmental approach to parenting twins as well as triplets and higher order multiples from toddlerhood on through adolescence and young adulthood.

Why a developmental approach? The answer, as it applies to this book, is very simple—we believe that an understanding of the cognitive, emotional and physical development of twins will be useful not only when your children are very young, but also through the mostly uncharted territory of their older elementary through teenage years.

We start our developmental exploration at the very beginning, with twins not yet born, sharing the intrauterine environment. But this is not a book about twin pregnancy, nor is it a book about raising your infant twins. We include our discussions of very early development because we believe they contribute to a richer understanding of your twins' toddlerhood, childhood and adolescence.

We're very pleased to include many chats with twins throughout this book. These Twin Talk segments feature interviews with twins who range in age from 5 to 21. We gave our twin subjects cameras and asked them to photograph each other. We've included many of those pictures and added a few others from family albums. While we could have included conversations with many twins, we chose to use multiple interviews with a core group of eight sets of twins so that you would have an opportunity to get to know them as they make their appearances throughout the book. *We hope parents will read this book with their own twins*—and begin their own "in house" dialogues about sharing, fighting or even advice to parents about raising twins. We've included an epilogue that features several more interviews as well as a few additional talks with other twins on new topics. We hope you enjoy getting to know these twins as much as we enjoyed our meetings with them.

While our approach is developmental, this is a topic-driven book. Whether you are a seasoned parent of one or more singleton children, or your twins have made you a first-time parent, multiples have a significant impact on the life of your family:

- How will you handle school and class placement?

- When is it good for twins to share, and when do they need their own toys, friends or time with you?

- How can you help your twins to become individuals while supporting their twin bond?

- How can you love your twins equally, though not the same?

- What do you do when twins mature at very different rates?

- What do you do when twins mature at the same rate but have very different needs?

We hope that parents who are "in the trenches," dealing with the daily challenges of raising sound, healthy, individuated twins, will use this book on an "as needed" basis: Parents with preschool-age twins might want to read a little bit about developmental issues for three- and four-year-olds in Chapter Two, "Twin Development," and then skip to Chapter Nine, "Schooldays," for an overview of the issues relevant to their twins' educational needs. New parents of twins will find it useful to thumb through Chapter Three, "Being the Parent of Twins," where they will find many suggestions for strengthening their couple relationship as they work together to make a home for their children. Chapter Ten, "Teenage Twins," will provide practical tips for seeing twins through the three stages of adolescence. We've also included a chapter dedicated to the discussion of numerous twin myths. Naturally, we could not include every myth we've heard—that would be another whole book—but we have chosen to include many myths that are frequently discussed. Think of *Raising Twins* as a friendly reference book that is there for you and your twins when you need it. We like to imagine that it will live on your nightstand, where it will rise to the top of the pile of books every now and again for many years to come.

Some final thoughts: The focus of this book is twin specific, but we hope families with higher order multiples will also find it useful. As you read *Raising Twins* you'll notice that we alternate the use of gender descriptive pronouns throughout the book—his or hers, he or she. We do this to avoid the very distracting and awkward use of his/her and he/she throughout our text. It is also worth noting that we have chosen to describe twins as "identical" and "fraternal" throughout the book because those are the terms you and your twins will hear and use out in the world. We realize the corresponding terms *monozygotic* and *dizygotic*, which we describe and discuss early in the book, are more scientifically accurate, but we've yet to hear a mom tell us she was approached in the mall and asked if her twins were monozygotic or dizygotic.

RAISING TWINS

"*Twins means playing and reading together. Living together, walking together, and riding together. That's all.*"

—Brad, 5-year-old fraternal twin boy

THE BIOLOGY OF TWINNING AND TWIN DEVELOPMENT IN UTERO

TYPES OF TWINNING

When done the old-fashioned way (that is to say, in a candlelit room, without the presence of a laboratory technician), a man's sperm meets a woman's egg (ovum), and the fertilized ovum enters the uterine cavity and is implanted there. The cells then begin to differentiate. Some form the placenta, while others create the sac made up of two layers: an outer layer (the chorion) and an inner layer (the amnion) in which the embryo (the stage in human development between the ovum and the fetus) will reside throughout its gestation. The cells will continue to develop until the embryo becomes a fetus after 8 weeks gestation. Approximately 28 weeks later, the fetus, now a baby, is delivered into your loving family.

In order for twins to occur, two embryos develop simultaneously in a woman's uterus. If we translate the statistics below into the likelihood of a woman in the United States giving birth to twins, we come up with a figure of approximately 1 in 39 being doubly blessed in the delivery room.

If you are the parent of twins, the great majority of you know that you have given birth to two children who developed in the uterus at the same time from the same impregnation. But that is just the very beginning of the story. Twinning actually occurs in one of two ways, resulting in either *dizygotic* (fraternal) or *monozygotic* (identical) twins. The diagram below should make the fundamental biological difference between the two types of twinning very clear.

Twin Biology

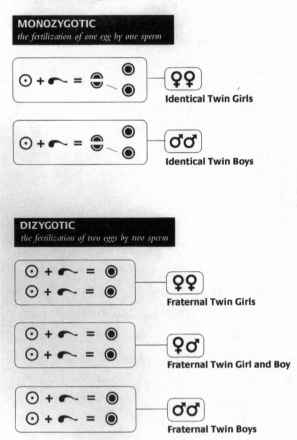

Dizygotic and Monozygotic Twinning

Dizygotic twinning occurs when two different ova, occurring from two separate follicles, are fertilized by two separate sperm. Dizygotic twinning accounts for approximately two thirds of all twin births. Dizygotic twins each have their own separate placenta, as well as two chorions (dichorionic) and two amnions (diamniotic). Sometimes the placentas are implanted close together and may fuse, thereby giving the appearance of one placenta, when in actuality there are two. If the determination of zygosity is performed by a cursory look at the placentas, an inaccurate diagnosis may be given. Dizygotic twins share the same degree of genetic similarity as any two siblings born at different times to the same set of parents, except for one major difference—dizygotic twins share the same intrauterine environment for approximately seven to nine months. This closeness and sharing from fertilization to birth and after creates an important bond to many dizygotic twins.

There are several factors that are believed to influence dizygotic twinning, though no one of these can be said to be its single cause. The following are some causes of dizygotic (fraternal) twinning:

- *The use of infertility technologies, assisted reproductive technologies (ART).* The use of the latest infertility treatments has greatly increased the chances of having multiples. When irregularity in ovulation is suspected as a cause of infertility, a woman may be treated with medication, such as Pergonal or Clomid, designed to stimulate the development of multiple follicles within her ovaries. In turn, these follicles may produce multiple eggs, resulting in a greater likelihood of twin or higher order multiple pregnancies.

  Technologies that transfer eggs into the uterus or fallopian tubes, such as in vitro fertilization (IVF), gamete intrafallopian transfer (GIFT) and zygote intrafallopian transfer (ZIFT), can produce dizygotic multiples. On occasion, the ovum splits and may result in monozygotic twinning.

- *Women delaying the start of their families.* With an increase in maternal age, there is more likely to be an increasing secretion of follicle stimulating hormone (FSH), which leads to ovulation of two ova, thereby producing

COMPARING THE RATES OF DIZYGOTIC AND MONOZYGOTIC TWINNING IN THE UNITED STATES

The rate of *dizygotic twinning* **is approximately 21.9 per thousand and is known to be influenced by factors we've described, such as infertility treatments, maternal age, genetic, ethnic and racial predisposition, and environment.**

The rate of *monozygotic twinning* **is approximately 4.0 per thousand. It is consistent throughout the world's many different cultures and geographic locales and does not appear to share any of those influences that help to explain dizygotic twinning.**

dizygotic (DZ) twins. Women between the ages of 35 and 39 have a greater likelihood of having multiples than younger women.

- *Genetic factors.* There is a genetic predisposition for dizygotic twinning—that is, the tendency to release more than one egg at a time. This tendency can be inherited from either the mother's or the father's genes. Since only women can produce eggs, this genetic predisposition displays itself on only the mother's side.

- *Racial factors.* Dizygotic twinning among the numerous races living in the United States varies considerably.

   Blacks: 25.8 per 1,000 births

   Alaskan natives: 24.9 per 1,000 births

   Caucasians: 19.6 per 1,000 births

   American Indians: 18.8 per 1,000 births

   Japanese: 17 per 1,000 births

   Hawaiians: 15.3 per 1,000 births

   Filipinos: 13.2 per 1,000 births

   Chinese: 11.2 per 1,000 births

Access to infertility treatment is closing the gap among the races with regard to the rate of dizogotic twinning.

- *Mothers of dizygotic twins are usually taller and weigh more than mothers of monozygotic twins.*

- *Women who have given birth to dizygotic twins have increased levels of FSH.*

- *Seasonal fluctuations.* It has been reported that the length of daylight may affect the production of follicle stimulating hormone (FSH). Some countries in the northern hemisphere, where there are long summer days, such as northern Finland and northern Japan, have higher dizygotic twin conceptions during the month of July. But there is no consistent evidence.
- *Nutrition.* Malnutrition decreases the twinning rate. During difficult economic times, such as those caused by famine, there tends to be more malnutrition and lower dizygotic twinning rates. In Yoruba, where the twinning rate is high, their diet (yams) may cause stimulation of the follicle stimulating hormone (FSH).
- *Environment.* Some reports say that toxic substances in the water and food supply can affect the production of sperm and decrease dizygotic twinning. On the other hand, in regions that have high levels of polychlorinated hydrocarbons, there is an increase in twinning, leading some to believe that there may be some "estrogen-like effects" in some pollutants.

Monozygotic twinning is the result of one egg being fertilized by one sperm, which then splits into two separate zygotes (embryos) some time within the first 14 days after fertilization. The earlier the split, usually before implantation (first five days), the more likely the occurrence of two separate placentas. Each placenta has one chorion (outer membrane) and one amnion (inner

UNIQUE CLASSIFICATIONS OF DIZYGOTIC TWINNING

SUPERFECUNDATION
Fertilization of two ova that are the result of two or more acts of sexual intercourse during the same menstrual cycle.

SUPERFETATION
The fertilization of two ova from successive menstrual periods within a short interval.

membrane). We call this dichorionic/diamnionic twinning. If the splitting of the fertilized egg occurs later, between day 5 and day 7, there will be one chorion (monochorionic) and two amnions (diamnionic). This condition is described as fused placentas. When splitting occurs after day 8, those embryos share one placenta containing one chorion (monochorionic), and one amnion (monoamnionic).

The birth weights of monozygotic twins may vary more than dizygotic twins. This may be due to their different position and different nutritional connection in the womb. As they continue to grow after birth, their weights will become more similar. Making a determination of twin zygosity at birth would be inaccurate if only the birth weight and number of placentas were used.

Monozygotic twins are genetically the same and are always the same sex and have the same blood type. They are very similar in their physical appearance, intellectual abilities, temperament and so on. Due to their many similarities, monozygotic twins tend to have a close relational bond. It is important to note that as much as monozygotic twins look alike, they are *NOT* "identical." They each have their own personalities and exhibit differences in most traits. The factors that cause monozygotic twinning are still unknown.

Some monozygotic twins are referred to as "mirror image" twins. This is believed to be due to the later splitting of the zygote. The name "mirror image" evokes the opposite manner in which one's image is seen when looking in a mirror. Opposites may be seen in hair whorls, handedness, dental features and other bodily features.

Conjoined twins (sometimes referred to as Siamese twins) are physically joined together. The incidence of this type of twinning is very rare, and there is no clear etiology (cause) surrounding it. The most common theory is that conjoined twins occur when the fertilized ovum is delayed in splitting.

There is some evidence to suggest a third type of twinning called "polar body twinning." An oocyte (an egg before maturation) divides, becomes a polar body and then is fertilized along with the original egg. The result may be a set of twins who have the same genes from their mother and half of the genes from their father. The only way to know for sure if your twins are "polar body twins" is to have a DNA test performed.

Identical female twins may be affected by a process called "lyonization." Males receive one X chromosome from their mother and one Y chromosome from their father (XY). Females receive one X chromosome from each their mother and father (XX). Approximately six to eight days after fertilization, during implantation, one X chromosome in each cell becomes inactivated. There is a possibility that the same chromosome does not become inactivated in both female twins. This can cause a difference in their traits.

Triplets and Higher Order Multiples

Triplets or higher order multiples—quadruplets, quintuplets—can occur with one, two, three or more eggs. Triplets can result from the following: Three eggs are fertilized and result in trizygotic triplets (TZ triplets). With two eggs, one egg may split after fertilization and one egg does not, resulting in a monozygotic pair of twins and one dizygotic triplet. Rarer still is the splitting of one egg three times after fertilization, resulting in monozygotic triplets (MZ triplets).

KNOWING THE ZYGOSITY OF YOUR TWINS

It is important to know the zygosity of your twins for the following reasons:

- *Medical concerns.* In the case of a medical situation requiring a blood transfusion, monozygotic twins

VANISHING TWIN

With the recent advent of transvaginal ultrasound, there has been an increase in the number of multiple gestations being observed. Expectant parents may undergo their first ultrasound during the first trimester and discover there are two or more embryos. When they return for another ultrasound, after the first trimester, they may find only one fetus and the disappearance of the other. One embryo may have been resorbed by the mother or spontaneously aborted, leaving little or no trace of its existence, thus the name "vanishing twin."

share the same blood type and can aid in the transfusion. Also, some monozygotic twins, who are matched for a particular organ, may be able to aid their twin when an organ transplant needs to be performed.

- *Physical and emotional understanding.* Monozygotic twins are very similar in many areas, such as their intellectual and physical capabilities. When identical twins are exhibiting noticeable developmental or emotional differences, this may be a clue to parents to investigate the causation of this difference.

Dizygotic twins vary in many ways, such as their physical, cognitive and emotional development, performance and interests. Parents who expect their twins to be the same may put undue pressure on their twins. Recognizing their areas of differences and similarities will aid in their self concept and acceptance.

Determining the Zygosity of Your Twins

Nancy Segal, a twin researcher, noted in a 1984 study that it was not unusual for parents to mistakenly identify their identical twins as fraternal. Certainly, statistics tell us that there are more fraternal twins than identical twins, but are all parents who believe they are the parents of fraternal twins correct?

In the past, examination of the placenta was one way doctors determined the zygosity of twins: one placenta meant identical and two placentas meant fraternal. Yet as we stated earlier, we now know that assumption may be inaccurate. Early splitting identicals may have two placentas, and fraternal twins may have their placentas so close together that they become fused. In some cases, a skilled and experienced pathologist, examining the placentas closely, may provide an accurate diagnosis of identical or fraternal. Today, modern technology provides very accurate methods for determining zygosity. The first two methods provide the most accurate results:

- *DNA fingerprinting.* The comparison of blood samples identify unique genetic patterns (DNA) used to determine the zygosity of multiple birth infants and adults.

- *DNA–Buccal cells.* Special swabs and brushes are used to scrape the inside of the cheek to remove cells that can then be mailed to a laboratory and analyzed. Identical twin's cells will match, and fraternal twin's will display differences. This test is less costly than DNA fingerprinting through blood samples.
- *Blood group.* Red blood cells are examined for several factors in addition to type (A, B, O) and RH positive or negative.
- *Physical appearance.* The determination of zygosity may be aided by observing many characteristics such as height, weight, color of eyes and hair and so on. Many identical (MZ) twins show a discrepancy in their weight and length at birth, and many fraternal (DZ) twins show a similarity.

TWINS IN UTERO

In the next chapter we are going to discuss twin development from birth through adolescence. Yet the influences of the intrauterine experience are also important to anyone seeking a comprehensive understanding of twins. It seems reasonable to assume that the unique nature of the twin relationship begins with their immediate and constant exposure to each other within the womb. By the time they reach 16 to 20 weeks of gestation, your twins are responding to each other through the placental membrane that usually separates them. You may be able to observe them kicking at each other during an ultrasound exam. By the twentieth week, at a typical weight of at least one pound each, they are interacting frequently and elbowing each other for space. Their periods of sleep and wakefulness may or may not coincide. A pregnant mother may feel as many as eight extremities moving at one time. By the beginning of the twenty-seventh week they are hearing not only their mother's heartbeat, but each other's as well.

Birgit Arabin of the Ziekenhuisk, the Netherlands, presented a paper at the International Society for Twin Studies (ISTS) in Helsinki, Finland, in 1998, where she showed documented ultrasounds of twins in the uterus engaged in different forms of "contacts" with each other. At the end of the seventh week, twin fetuses exhibited reflexive response to touch. At first the response was to move away from a touch on the cheek; afterward some moved toward the touch. This differs from singleton pregnancies where the only touch is caused by itself and is usually only on the facial area. She observed different forms of "interfetal communication" in which twins touched each other with their feet and hands, as well as their lips.

There is also a fascinating study by Italian psychoanalyst Alessandra Piontelli. Dr. Piontelli used ultrasonic observations beginning at the eighteenth week of gestational age and continuing at monthly intervals to the end of the pregnancy. These observations were followed up with weekly assessments for the first year of the twins' lives and then annual exams throughout early childhood. The twins in her study typically occupied different positions within the womb—with one usually staying on one side and the other on the opposite side. She also discovered the character of the two placentas was frequently different—for example, where they were attached and the thickness of the placenta itself. The placement of the umbilical cords also tended to be distinct from each other. The majority of the twins she observed were separated by a dividing membrane and therefore inhabited two different embryonic sacs, each of which had its own unique environment. Presumably the combined effect of these different environmental conditions yielded different intrauterine sounds, motion and tactile sensation for each twin. This demonstrates the separate intrauterine conditions that exist for each twin.

Dr. Piontelli also noted differences in the individual temperaments of the twin couples she observed. This is important because it tells us that regardless of zygosity, every twin has a preferential posture, as well as specific activities and unique repetitive patterns of activity within the womb. The frequency and style of bodily movement in utero was highly individualized. The study goes on to describe a variety of individual reactions of each baby toward his or her twin. In some twin couples, she found little or no interaction—for example, when one moved, the other showed no reaction. In other cases, she described "activity con-tact"—if one baby made contact, the other one would react. There appeared to be an ongoing dance of response and withdrawal. She noted in her study that some individuals within the twin couple searched actively for contact, while oth-ers remained neutral or made contact only as a response. Dr. Piontelli also described styles of contact from gentle mutual affectionate stroking of each other's cheeks, to more aggressive, almost territorial physical interaction. Dr. Piontelli's study concluded that each twin couple she observed established a way of relating that seemed to remain fairly consistent throughout their intrauterine relationship and on into early childhood.

"The whole world is going to treat your twins like they are one person. You, as parents, need to let them know they are individuals in your eyes and that you love them both for who they are."

—Dino, 21-year-old fraternal twin

TWIN DEVELOPMENT

A FEW WORDS ABOUT DEVELOPMENTAL GUIDELINES

Any discussion of human development should always begin with the caveat that developmental stages are general guidelines meant to support your understanding of your children, not to make you worry that they are "not on schedule." As parents of twins, you face an additional challenge: a lifelong commitment to avoiding comparison, by looking at your twins as individuals. That won't always be easy. It may be helpful to realize from the get-go that there will be times that you do compare your children, both to each other and to their peers. But being alert to that tendency will help you to restrain it.

Consider this: If one twin's first steps are viewed as an extraordinary achievement when they occur earlier than is suggested in the developmental guidelines, how do you view the twin who doesn't manage to toddle across the room until a month after the guidelines say it is most likely? In the exhausting but heady first year of your twins' lives, it may be wise to recognize that neither achievement is in the center of the development charts, yet both are still in the range of normal.

Naturally, it is wonderful to watch your children cross each of their developmental thresholds, but you will do yourselves and your twins a tremendous service by keeping the following thoughts in mind:

- *All in good time.* Developmental guidelines are averages—don't use them as a yardstick to measure one twin against another. As you get to know your twins as individuals, you'll grow increasingly comfortable with each twin developing at an individual pace.

- *Use common sense.* You are likely to be the best judge of your child's general well-being. If you have a nagging concern that a twin is experiencing a developmental problem, talk to your doctor about it.

- *Human development occurs in fits and spurts.* Often, a child becomes enthralled by a new developmental achievement, such as crawling. This thrilling ability to locomote by herself is so exciting that she keeps practicing it, perhaps for weeks. Think of this naturally occurring developmental plateau as a refueling stop for a very busy mind and body. Sometimes a child may attempt to walk and all of a sudden return to the certainty of crawling. One day she'll try walking again and far surpass her initial attempt. Eventually she will be motivated to stand upright and the whole process will begin again.

In the process of providing a general developmental outline in this chapter, we will touch lightly upon many of the issues from sharing, to schooling, to making friends, that will be examined in detail later on. Your life as the parent of twins will be filled with many rewards and many challenges. Just remember that a little insight into your twins' development is a very handy tool to have in the parental tool kit. It will also help to keep you informed about what lies ahead.

This chapter will look at the specific age and stage development for non-twins and then will compare how twin development is similar to or different for that particular age or stage. Before we get into those developmental discussions, we'd like you to hear from two young men who have made their way from birth through adolescence and have some wonderful insights about their journey through life as twins and as friends. We hope you enjoy the first of many Twin Talk segments.

TWIN TALK

Jill Ganon
Dino and Marco, 21-year-old fraternal twins

THE TWIN RELATIONSHIP

Jill: It seems from our talks with twins that the older they are, the more aware and interested they become in their twin relationship. You are now in the same college, living together, and both want to become professional musicians. What thoughts do you have on how your twin relationship figures in your lives?

Dino: A lot. For me being a twin has always had a

Dino

Marco

big impact regardless of the environment. My parents have always been very conscious of not comparing us to each other. But even though we are fraternal twins, we look very much the same to everybody else, and it is like we have always been treated as the same person by people other than our parents. I can't tell you how many times I've heard, "One of you guys, whichever one, a twin. . . ." We are constantly compared, and we've always known that whatever one does, it is likely to reflect back on the other. You have to make a real conscious effort to not let that affect your relationship with your twin.

Marco: I think we're lucky in that we have a really good relationship. We graduated from high school in 1996, and between that class and the one before, we had at least five or six sets of twins. And most of them that I knew hated each other, but we got along really well. There was never an open rivalry. But I think there is some subconscious competition and you do want to do as well as the person you're comparing yourself to.

Jill: Why do you think your relationship is as good as it is?

Marco: Our parents had a lot to do with it, and also the fact that we were males and I think it's a lot easier to be twins and be males. We knew two sets of female twins in high school, one fraternal and one identical. The identical twins were both very pretty and I don't think it was that hard for them. The fraternal ones didn't always get on as well because one was just a lot prettier than the other. Society makes it tough for girls . . . having to look a certain way. An adolescent girl is held up to this ridiculous standard, and on top of that, as a twin she has to compete with somebody else. I think the fraternal girls had a hard time. I don't think they hated each other,

but it was definitely like they'd walk in the house and start bickering. I'd have to confess that to me it seemed that one girl was pretty and the other was homely. That must be hard. We look pretty similar, and we've never had a problem with that.

Jill: Can you talk about the idea of balance in your relationship?

Marco: I was actually born with a fairly rare heart condition. They still don't know a lot about this particular condition, so I have to kind of take it as it comes . . . year by year. So that was kind of a big thing for us growing up. I couldn't do sports or anything like that because of my heart, and I always wanted to do it. I was on a basketball team when I was in the fourth grade, but I wasn't allowed to actually play. I couldn't do all the running and everything like that. I would come to practice, and I really wanted to play. I remember when I was in middle school, especially being compared to Dino, it made me really competitive. You know they would have sprints and things like that in the PE classes. I would always try to win, and that continues to this day.

Dino: Marco is one of the most competitive persons I know. And because I was always around Marco, it was partly my job to make sure he didn't do stuff like that. It is still kind of in the back of my mind, and I'm always bugging Marco to make sure he's not going to do something stupid. I just always knew it wasn't safe for Marco to do this stuff. I think my parents also didn't want to burden me with having to look out for him, but I knew I had to stop him if his competitiveness was going to make him do something dumb. I really took it on myself.

Marco: Just the other day we were at a coffee shop and when the waiter asked us if we wanted something to drink, Dino says, "I'll have coffee and make sure his is decaf," 'cause I'm not supposed to have caffeine. Things like that. Sometimes it's a problem in that while I appreciate someone looking out for me, I can take care of myself. I also realize that sometimes I do stupid things, like push myself too hard. Sometimes I have to have him there to watch out for me. Actually, that brings up another point, which is that we've always sort of watched out for each other in different aspects of our lives.

Dino: There's kind of like a division of labor, because we still live together and I do watch over him, trying to make sure he doesn't do anything he shouldn't. He doesn't do it as much anymore, but when he goes in the gym, I'll say, "Did you lift too much?" or "Don't strain your heart." But on the other hand, he also knows that I'm really disorganized, so Marco will handle our bills and stuff making sure they get paid on time. We also kind of balance each other in the way we deal with frustrations. I direct everything outward and he directs everything inward. If somebody does something to Marco, he acts like it's his own fault. I'm always trying to draw his anger outward and get him to talk about it or try to look at it in what I consider to be a more rational way. Me, I direct my anger outward, but I have a tendency to get enraged really quickly.

Marco: That's like our father. I deal with things more like our mother.

Dino: So he will try to calm me down. I think we both suffer a lot for each other in as much as I will try to talk him out of beating himself up, and he'll try to talk me out of beating him up. *[Both laugh.]* Marco will say, "Calm down and try to be a little rational."

Marco: If he directs his anger at me for no good reason, I usually never yell at him. I just try to absorb it, so he can kind of get it out of his system. And we've always kind of been like that. There has always been this pattern where Dino was always more outgoing, and I was very shy. We dealt with everything that way. But it is kind of changing.

Jill: How is it changing?

Marco: I was always shy and I used Dino as a way to help me get into things—parties and things like that. It's always been easier for me to let him meet people, and then I sort of follow him. But I recently went away to work for a month without him. I spent a little bit of time figuring out who I was and trying to develop personally away from him. It really helped me when I got back, and I think it also helped our relationship. Now when something happens, I don't think about it in a competitive sense like I used to. I really am honestly happy for him, and I think it's because I have a much better sense of who I am and what I want to be doing.

Dino: Basically, I agree with what Marco said. There are all these issues—sometimes you want to get away from the person, you want to stop being compared, but for better or for worse you just can't. And you have to figure out how to just make the situation work. Sometimes that means removing yourself for a little while, and sometimes that means focusing on something else. My proudest moments are when I do something in which Marco is not involved. And I'm proud and I can show it to him. If it's something I'm really happy with and I can bring Marco to see it, that's probably one of the things I enjoy most.

Marco: I think we both think you've done something really well if your brother likes it. Because he knows you better, he's heard everything you do or seen everything you do, so if he likes it, it must be good, 'cause you can't fool him.

Jill: Have you given any thought to what it would be like to live separately?

Dino: I go through phases. I don't necessarily want us to live apart. Marco has been talking about going to New York for the last couple of years. One of the hardest things about living so closely is that whatever I do is almost always in reaction to what he does. Marco will get going with one thing or another and I feel I have to do it or stop doing it regardless of whether I want to do it or not. It is purely reactive on my part. Sometimes I think that living together makes it hard because there is nowhere to turn. You can't take refuge from it because there's always—I'll give you an example. Marco started working out, going to the gym. And within a month I just said, "I can't take this." I needed to go because I had all these fears that Marco was going to start looking really good and everybody would say, "What happened to you? Why are you such a stick of butter? Your brother looks great." So I started going to the gym. I don't always want to go, but I force myself. What I have been saying lately is that we should try living apart just within the city in two separate studio apartments. As much as sometimes I just want to get away from Marco and not be compared to him, I don't want to be that far away from him that we can't go see a movie. Like I said, he's the most important person in my life, so I would never want to have him out of my life. I think it would be really hard if he was living in New York and I was here.

Jill: Does your closeness remain constant or does it tend to fluctuate, either in response to getting older or perhaps as a result of circumstance?

Dino: We are very close to each other. I don't think we've ever violated each other's trust. Maybe there have been times by accident . . . but I don't think there has ever been a time when one of us has ever done something deliberately malicious to the other. I know that no matter what I say to Marco or however angry I get, or any stupid thing I might do—throwing a glass across the room or something like that—I'm always there for him and he's always there for me.

Marco: That's the wonderful thing about being a twin. I don't know how it is with other siblings, if they're really close, but with us it's you always have someone you can talk to about anything. We can sit and talk any time of the day or night about anything. And both of us can give each other advice on things. We trust each other's advice. We both have a deep understanding of what makes the other person tick. I think probably when I get married or have another serious relationship, it will be years before anybody will understand me the way that Dino does. They didn't grow up with me; they didn't have the same parents. We don't have to talk to communicate. I can always understand Dino's reaction to something, even if it's not the way I'd react. I can very easily put myself in his mindset just because we have such a deep understanding of each other.

INFANT DEVELOPMENT: FROM BIRTH TO EIGHTEEN MONTHS

Once a newborn leaves the intrauterine environment, she enters a world of sensation. She begins to learn about the world through a rapidly expanding sensory vocabulary of taste, touch, sight, hearing, and smell. Even though infants are able to hear for months before they're born, the most acute sensory experiences for very young babies are taste, smell and touch. At first, the young baby seeks her own comfort, intuitively rooting toward the breast for nourishment and preserving her energy in many hours of sleep each day. Between birth and two months the waking baby is sucking and clinging and crying and smiling.

Meanwhile, a baby is absorbing the extraordinary variety of sensory experience in the world around her. She feels warmth and cold; the sensation of the bath; the sounds of music and voices and the pets in the home; the excitement of visiting fam-ily and the calm of a quiet house. All of this is still on a sensory level.

Naturally, parents thrill to every new aspect of their baby's development. Between 8 and 12 weeks there are the wonderful moments of a baby's very early social smile—not yet because she is aware that there is someone to please, but sweetly and simply because there's someone out there at whom she can smile.

Between 20 and 24 weeks the baby becomes far more responsive to the advances of parents, siblings and extended family. She is beginning to vocalize, even using sound to attract attention from parents or siblings. Just as parents grow more in love with their baby each day, babies are beginning to be enthralled by the sights and sounds that surround them. They are sleeping more at night and are therefore more alert and prepared to interact during the day. They are learning to sit and are able to grasp an object held before them. A 20-week-old baby may smile at her mir-ror image, even though she may not be aware of herself. She may cry when someone leaves the room. By the time she reaches 24 weeks, she will vocalize at her mirror image and is now able to tell the difference between strangers and family members or other close caregivers.

As a baby's emotional life develops, between two months and six months, she enters a more symbiotic relationship with her parents. Emotionally, baby and mother are one at this point. Bonding and communication grow increasingly sweet for both parents as they rock and change and feed their infant. The baby makes her fundamental needs known, the parent responds, and in this wonderfully basic way, an attachment between baby and parent is formed. It is this early attachment that begins to forge a lifelong bond between infant and parents.

As she continues to grow, between six and eight months, she enters the first stage of the separation-individuation process: differentiating herself from her mother. Every mother has experienced it—your baby touches your hair, and it is as if she is trying to figure out, "What's me and what's not me?" As she continues to grow through her first few years, she begins to reach an understanding that she is indeed separate from her mother.

Between 10 and 16 months a baby starts to move independently and investigate the environment. She grows more interested in crawling and creating distance—both emotional and physical—between herself and her parents. She is becoming more aware of herself as a separate entity and more comfortable with that understanding.

YOUR TWINS: FROM BIRTH TO EIGHTEEN MONTHS

As the parent of very young twins, from zero to two months, you are dividing your attention between two babies. If your babies were premature, you may be spending a great deal of time with one or both of them in the hospital. This is an extremely hectic period for parents. At five to six weeks, your twins show an awareness of each other that is not likely to be present were two singletons of the same age to be placed in proximity to each other.

Regardless of the interaction that may be present between the twins themselves, many parents express concern that neither twin is receiving enough quantity or quality of their time to develop the bond that is so important between parent and child. There is no magical event that occurs enabling a parent to say, "I am bonded to my baby." Bonding takes time, and with twins it usually takes longer than with one baby. Let's face it—there are two babies to get to know. It takes time to learn their individual cries, expressions and coos. Once you are familiar with each baby, you will be hooked. This is the time for parents of twins to take advantage of any and all offers of help from extended family and friends. The parental instinct driving you to seek more individual time with your babies is a sound one. There are things you can do to give yourself the gift of one-on-one time with each of your twins. For example, while it may be very helpful to nurse your babies together, feeding time can also be an opportunity for individual baby time. This opportunity to gaze uninterrupted into your baby's eyes and to have her gaze at you is vital to establishing your relationship.

It is important to recognize that you are reacting to two babies who are very likely to have different temperaments and ways of relating to you. Try not to be too hard on yourself when you find yourself being particularly frustrated with one or the other of your twins. It is perfectly natural to fret if one baby is a fussy eater, just as you experience relief at your other twin's healthy appetite. You are a novice at this, so do yourself, your mate and your twins a favor—understand that you are doing the best you can, and know that while it may not be perfect, it will all be just fine.

As a parent, particularly if you are a first-time parent, you want desperately to meet all your baby's needs. This is an impossible feat even with one baby, and with two it is completely out of the question. But there is a method to the madness of parenting. The truth is that if every need of the young baby is met, there is no reason for that baby to emerge from that early, very sheltered environment. Some amount of frustration is inevitable and may be good. It is the balance of loving care and occasional frustration that propels your babies to want to cry out and communicate; to reach out and grab that toy; to crawl across the floor and climb all over the saintly family dog. Of course, extreme or prolonged frustration would impede growth. But by providing an environment where most of your babies' needs are met, you are giving your two babies just enough of the right stuff to enhance their development.

Next is the symbiotic phase—between two and six months—in which you and your twins are growing more in sync. In developmental terms, we say the baby and mother "become one" at this time. The time has come when you could walk into a room filled with noisy babies and immediately pick your child's cry out from all the rest. You still should not expect yourself to meet all the needs of your twins as quickly, or even as thoroughly as you would with just one baby to care for, but that is a natural consequence of the increased demands upon you as a parent.

This is a very physically and emotionally challenging time for the parents of twins, especially if your babies have very different temperaments. You may find that you relate more readily to one twin than the other, and even though that is perfectly natural, a lot of parents feel guilty about it. Some parents of twins will tend to bond more deeply to the baby who weighs less at this time, the manifestation of concern about the baby's heartiness and health. Other parents may relate more to the robust baby. You may find it helpful to know that these feelings of preference often shift back and forth between your twins over time, or that while you feel closer to one baby, your mate has established a similar bond with your other twin. Rather than chastising yourself or feeling guilty about these feelings, give yourself some credit for acknowledging them. This is the first step in sorting these feelings out, helping you to understand the feelings instead of acting them out. Also recognize that your way of relating to each baby represents a healthy impulse to see your twins as separate individuals.

During these months, each of your twins begins to show more and more signs of establishing their own personality. At around three months, when your twins are lying side by side sleeping peacefully, it is not unusual for one's thumb to be in the other twin's mouth. They do not yet have an established awareness of being separate from each other. By five to six months when singleton babies are just growing more aware of relating to the people around them, twins have already become more aware of each other. They recognize and are effected by each other, and you may find that at times being together has a quieting effect on both.

At around six months of age your twins may become attached to a transitional object. The transitional object is something that a child uses to comfort herself when the mother is not present. It is a reminder of the mother that soothes a baby or young child. This transitional object helps your baby deal with his anxiety when he becomes aware that he and Mommy are separate. It can be a blanket or an article of clothing or a stuffed animal. This transitional object may have been chosen earlier in an attempt to help the baby sleep or nap on his own. Often it has the comforting scent of the mother. Twins may also use each other as a transitional object. When Mommy and Daddy are not around, they feel comforted and soothed by each other's presence. Eventually, the singleton child outgrows his transitional object and puts or throws it away. For twins, if their transitional object is their co-twin, this is impossible, as their co-twin is simply not disposable. As such, they may continue to find comfort and support from each other as they grow older.

Between six and eight months, and continuing through the first three years of your twins' lives, there is a period of separation when your twins are starting to become more aware of themselves as separate from you. At around seven months your twins may really be taking notice of each other. You are likely to see them smiling, and if they happen to be sitting across from each other, they may play as though each is a mirror image of the other, not actually recognizing that they are distinct and separate beings.

By the time they reach 10 months, twins will begin to distract and console one another. When one is having a difficult time, the other one may try to provide a distraction by banging on an object or vocalizing with apparent concern or sympathy. At this age they may try staring at each other and generally offering some type of consoling behavior.

When they are 11 months old, their vocalizations become quite interactive. They'll go back and forth with one another in a very conversational way: One will talk, and then the other will talk. They may be making some babbling sounds, and it may go back and forth for minutes at a time. With non-twins, this kind of exchange usually doesn't happen until about 18 months.

When they reach their first birthday, some twins will seek and enjoy comfort from each other, while others may not seem to recognize the presence of their twin. These extremes of reaction can occur within a pair of twins. It is not unusual to see one twin of 12 to 24 months old waddle across a room to console her crying twin with the offer of a toy, while her co-twin chooses to remain aloof when the situation is reversed. Between 14 and 16 months, twins become quite aware when they are separated from one another, and their reunion, even just half an hour later, may be cause for absolute rejoicing and glee.

Many parents agree that some of the greatest fun begins at around 14 months as twins begin to consciously copy each other's actions. One of your twins will do something, like banging a wooden spoon on the floor, and the other finds this action completely irresistible and so the percussion duet begins, often provoking hilarity between them, and an Excedrin headache for you. As they get a little older, around

15 months, they grow very skilled at provoking each other at games, which grow increasingly complicated the older they get.

Twins tend to learn about the lifelong need for give-and-take earlier than their singleton counterparts. While other babies play side by side without interacting in what is called parallel play, twins are becoming socialized into playing with each other. They tend to grow acclimated to the almost constant presence of another person occupying their time and sharing everything from Mommy to a favorite toy.

This is the time that your twins may become so utterly wrapped up in each other that they are not even aware of anyone else being in the room—and that includes you and other siblings. One mother of teenage twins says she remembers feeling a little like the girl at the prom who wasn't asked to dance as her 18-month-old twins would get so engrossed in play that they ignored her. "It really took me a little while to realize that this was a *good thing*," she said, laughing. "It just sort of came as a shock that they were so capable of entertaining each other, but fifteen years later, I can tell you they are still keeping each other laughing, and it is one of the greatest joys of my life."

Between one and two years, non-twins are growing very aware of their own names and will also begin to clearly recognize "da-da" or "ma-ma" as being attached to their father and mother. Some twins recognize themselves when they're called by name, and some will answer to both names or even a combination of both names, such as Jim-Josh or Emma-Tess. Still others will not consistently respond to a name at all. This situation is exacerbated if twins have similar-sounding names, such as Tara and Sara or Tim and Lynne.

TODDLER DEVELOPMENT: FROM EIGHTEEN MONTHS TO THREE YEARS

An infant is very much dependent on her parents to move her from place to place and supply stimulation in the form of toys or physical play or conversation. Toddlerhood is the threshold defined by a baby's ability to be more upright and more mobile. Now all of a sudden she is able to go across the room under her own steam and pick up a toy that looks interesting, or overturn the plate of spaghetti that has been left unguarded on the dining room table. Though major child-proofing in the house should be complete by now, this is a time to fortify even further. Newfound locomotion fosters tremendous feelings of independence, and simply put, a child feels like she is the mistress of all she sees. Toddlers grow almost drunk with power at this age. They are learning to participate in their surroundings, and there is a clear motivation present when it comes to mastering physical skills.

At the same time, the young toddler does not yet have the cognitive ability or the vocabulary to form complex questions, so like countless generations of intrepid explorers before her, she is searching her ever-expanding world for new adventures and experiences. It is really one of the most extraordinary periods in all of human development, as a toddler simply absorbs the environment, without forming complex queries about what it all means. In many ways, when as an adult one attempts to practice meditation, it is a return to this precognitive state that we seek.

Along with the toddler's new found physical independence comes an independence of spirit (otherwise known as stubbornness) that makes for the first real testing ground of the parent/child relationship. Many 18-month-olds find it hard to respond to parental requests or to keep within reasonable bounds of behavior. They may pretend not to hear you call, preferring to be off on their own in another room. One mother described watching her 20-month-old son push a chair across the kitchen to within striking distance of a forbidden counter and then turn to her and say sternly, "Mama, go away now!" Toddlers are always trying to test their parents, and sometimes parents find a child of this age to be extremely strong-willed. Children of this age are easily overwhelmed by their own desire to experience as much as they can as fast as they can. Simple overtiredness and emotional immaturity combine with predictable results that sometimes lead to tantrums.

Between 16 and 24 months your toddlers are entering the stage of rapprochement: One moment they feel their independence—boldly going off on their own—

and then a few moments later, they become aware they are alone and quickly return to you for hugs and kisses. This is a time of push and pull. You can see why at around 18 months old, separation anxiety is at its peek. The child who wouldn't be bothered by your absence before is suddenly clutching at you and continually wants you in his sight.

At around two years old a parent may feel that things seem to smooth out and slow down for awhile. As with all developmental stages, this newfound tranquillity may come and go, but the two-year-old is feeling a bit more mature, and some of that almost desperate need to test parental control may subside. Parents are likely to describe life as being a little calmer, and a kind of equilibrium may settle in for a while. It is no coincidence that as the two-year-old grows more mature and comfortable with herself, she is less demanding and a little more capable of waiting for her needs to be met. There may be more compliance with parents' requests as a two-year-old acquires more language and works hard to apply her increased cognitive ability to express her feelings and desires. The use of the words *I* and *me* and the consistent ability to respond to her own name indicate that the two-year-old sees herself as an individual.

Enjoy this honeymoon period while it lasts, because at about two-and-a-half, many toddlers enter a stage where they become more rigid, often requiring very set routines around activities such as eating and bedtime The two-and-a-half-year-old is often a creature of habit and is very clear about wanting everything to be in its proper place. This is the time when the use of a transitional object can be very comforting for a toddler.

Toddlers experience a frequent push/pull between conflicting desires. One of the ways they learn who they are at this time is to push against someone, and that is frequently the parent. It feels like a crisis, but it's not. It is the child starting to feel more separate.

As they approach three years of age, they have more of an idea of object permanence. A child of this age is able to reason in the following manner: When something or someone is here, and I go away, it will still be here when I come back. That begins to translate into the understanding that when Mommy says that she's going away but will be coming back, *she will really return.*

At this age, the toddler grows very committed to the idea of choosing what she wants to eat or wear or play with. The only problem with this attempt at self-determination is that often *she has no idea what it is that she actually wants.* Offering a choice between two options may be helpful, but if that doesn't work, make the choice for your child and quickly move on. This is also a time when short negative sentences may make frequent appearances in your child's vocabulary. Don't be surprised when a simple statement such as "It's time for bed" or "Do you want more juice?" is met with an immediate "NO!" The use of language to fortify her position as the center of her own universe is a natural consequence of this very egocentric period in a child's development. She is experimenting with noncompliance.

As she grows out of this very egocentric stage and into the time when she begins to see herself as part of a community of family, friends or school mates, this infatuation with negativity will fade (at least until adolescence, but we'll get to that). As cognition grows and vocabulary continues to expand, toddlers will ask a lot of questions, such as "What's this?" or "What's that?" This is an ideal time to support language acquisition by responding in simple sentences, such as "This is Daddy's car" or "The cat is eating her dinner." Toddlers are very concrete and will derive a lot of support and comfort from a direct response to their questions.

YOUR TWINS: FROM EIGHTEEN MONTHS TO THREE YEARS

Your toddler twins face the great challenge of learning to share during an egocentric stage in their development. Sharing is not an innate trait of human or twin development. Your twin toddlers are not only saying "NO!" to you, but they are also saying "NO!" to each other. Sharing is learned through many hard lessons over a lifetime of experience and compromise. Your twins are learning this lesson earlier than the rest of the population. They must learn to share Mommy and Daddy; a favorite toy; the attention of a sibling; even the opportunity to be the first one into the bath. They're more aware of their co-twin as both playmate and rival. There may be frequent competition for your attention, and you are likely to notice a lot more physicality: actually pushing and pulling each other or acting out by yelling.

This is often the time when twins will start biting and fighting with each other. One of the most frequent concerns of exasperated parents is the twin (or twins) who bites. Typically, biting is a problem among toddlers because they do not yet have enough language to communicate their desires. They also lack the ability to cope with the frustration that follows when that desire is not met—or is not met fast enough. Toddlers are also learning about being separate from their twin as well as their parents. This is their way of learning "What is me and what is not me?" When you bump up against something or someone, it is definitely "not me."

Observation of non-twin preschoolers revealed that "mild to moderate conflicts" occurred *every three minutes* and "major conflicts" took place three times per hour. You can see where your skills in distraction and refereeing will come in handy. Many conflicts for twins at this age are very much exacerbated by their lack of language skills.

As you watch your babies turn into young children, they are watching each other. Sometimes the twin who has not mastered a skill will learn to do it by watching her twin. Your toddler twins' ability to imitate and copy skills or behaviors is typically more advanced than in a singleton child of the same age. In some ways they are also developing a kind of love relationship. Moments after some stormy confrontation, they will grow completely engaged in helping or consoling one another. If one of them is hurt or drops a toy and they're unhappy about it, the other will pick up the toy and give it to her twin. It is amazing to watch the seemingly contagious current of strong emotional feelings that wash over your twins at this age.

This is also the time you may observe one child being a little more dominant than the other, snatching toys from her more submissive twin who may look bewildered and do nothing, or may cry but fail to take any action. As challenging as this time is for your twins, the greater challenge may be yours as you try to figure out when and how to intervene and when to observe from a distance and let them sort things out on their own. While we'll discuss these issues later on in detail, it is useful to realize that the twin who appears to be more submissive has her own strengths and abilities that may be subtle but are present nonetheless. Naturally, you must step in if one twin is physically hurting the other, but when possible, let them sort out their spats on their own. And don't be surprised when the child who appears submissive makes a developmental leap in language or motor skills and surges into dominance for awhile.

Often, when you ask an adult twin what it was like to be a twin growing up, they tell you, "It was just 'normal.' There were always the two of us, and it was the only life we knew. . . ." While your toddlers may sometimes be at odds with each other as they try to establish themselves and claim their own turf, they also have the benefit of always having a playmate available. This is the age that your toddlers may first begin to start working as a team. And this theme of twins as teammates will resonate in different ways throughout their lives. Sometimes this team relationship will exclude parents, other siblings and even friends. Believe it or not, it is not unusual for a mother of three-year-old twins to feel like they are "ganging up" on her or excluding her (or another sibling) from their private world. As many parents will tell you, that ever-present playmate is often a co-conspirator. Your toddler twins may tend to get into an awful lot more mischief than the singleton child could imagine.

One mom described walking into the bedroom shared by her toddler twin boys as they were gleefully tearing down the new wallpaper next to their cribs. They were taking turns and mimicking each other as they had a rip-roaring good time tearing the paper off the walls. It was clear that they were inciting each other to greater and greater mayhem—one did it while the other laughed, and then they switched roles, growing more amused with each other's antics as the wall turned into a disaster zone. Because they're both at the same cognitive level, there is no way that one of them is going to police the other and say, "Hey, we're not supposed to do this." It is a kind of toddler free-for-all.

This is also a time when your twins may be developing that verbal shorthand that you may have heard described as "twin language" or the "secret language of twins." Since twins spend so much time in each other's presence, they tend to mimic one another. When one says the word *juice* and it comes out as *ju*, the other will mimic it. They will reinforce each other's use of the improper word, which will become words. Parents need to ignore the improper language and model the proper word: "You want juice."

After many months of dealing with the often divergent needs of twins as babies and very young toddlers, many parents feel relieved when their toddlers begin to get really focused on playing with each other. But as your twins get closer and closer to preschool age, it is a great idea to make sure they have the opportunity to learn how to socialize with other children. This is especially valuable because it encourages verbal communication outside the small circle of the family and the even more exclusive club of just the twins themselves. By broadening their social world and exposing them to the ways in which other children play, you are laying the groundwork for a positive preschool experience.

PRESCHOOL DEVELOPMENT: FROM THREE TO FIVE YEARS

Three-year-olds are very social creatures. They are once again interested in conforming to what is asked of them, as well as to the social situation they perceive on their own. They have arrived at another developmental plateau. Give and take is a little easier for them, and their interest in and ability for cooperation makes for another period of relative calm. Three-year-olds are often eager to please parents as well as playmates. They're becoming more and more social and are starting to be able to make more friends. This is an excellent age to think about starting your twins in preschool.

Children at this age are integrating skills at an accelerated rate. Their physical abilities facilitate increased socializing, and their growing understanding of themselves as members of a social community support emotional maturity and an increased dependence on language to communicate.

Language development is really taking off. This is an age when parents begin to see a three-year-old's ability to delight in little repetitive word plays and shared jokes. That sense of "I" is becoming more and more defined at three years old. They really know who's "me" more than who's "other." They can even combine themselves with someone else and begin to use the pronoun "we."

The three-and-a-half-year-old returns once again to asserting her will. It's a little harder for her to be compliant, and parents may be disappointed to discover that established routines such as bath and bedtime are again being questioned. The child who went sweetly to sleep after a story is insisting on another story and another—it is a return to the battle of wills. And for the first time, parents hear their children's concern about how they *feel* about them: *Mommy, do you still love me even though I spilled the milk? Why did Jenny play with Lisa instead of me?* Feelings, their own and others', are beginning to matter more, and they're able to listen to and absorb simple, reassuring explanations about abstract feelings: *Yes, I still love you. Wouldn't you still love me if I spilled my milk?*

Between three and five, they begin to get attached to other people and will have pals for whom they show great affection. This is a time that some children exhibit imaginary playmates. A four-year-old is becoming a little bit more intuitive and imaginative with toys and playmates. There's a lot of dressing up and pretending to be Mommy or Daddy or a fairy princess. They really begin to refine their motor skills, such as kicking, catching a ball and throwing skills.

Verbally, they are also showing a little bit more of their feelings. They yell if they're angry, or express sadness if they're upset or sad. They begin to use language to express more of their emotions, so there is a greater opportunity to resolve conflict with parents, siblings or peers. This is a time when children become more outgoing. There is a tendency to swagger or boast and be generally delighted with themselves.

YOUR TWINS: FROM THREE TO FIVE YEARS

This is typically the time that twins enter preschool, which means you are faced with the questions of choosing a school and also deciding whether to separate the twins in school. Some schools separate twins as a matter of policy, and some do not. It is probably best that your twins be given the chance to begin their classroom experience together. They are already coping with separating from you and will draw comfort from being together. This is not necessarily to say that there are benefits to their eventually being placed in separate classes. When that separation does take place, you, your twins and their teachers will all need to be a part of the decision-making process. This is one of the most complex issues you'll face as the parents of twins, and we'll discuss it thoroughly later on.

Just as your twins gain a lot more exposure to the world around them, you see a lot more of them in the context of their non-twin peers. There is an additional temptation to compare your twins by the yardstick of how they measure up to their new friends. One of the first things you may notice is a difference in their language skills. Language acquisition and use may be a little slower for twins than it is for non-twins, particularly for boys. Delayed language in boys may be due to factors such as the impact of the complications of prematurity on male infants. A study done in Australia found that on average, 30-month-old twin boys are as much as eight months behind the expressive language skills of their non-twin peers and six months behind in comprehensive language. But at the same time, their speed of language response may be a little faster, perhaps because they are used to having to compete for your attention. You may find that non-twins have relatively greater clarity in their spoken words than your twins do. Remember that your children have been developing their linguistic shorthand by mimicking and learning from each other. Sometimes their "secret language" is simply the use of incorrectly pronounced words, often with missing consonant sounds. Even as adults, twins often seem to have their own spoken shorthand. They use an abbreviated language—why finish a sentence when their twin already knows what they are going to say?

But for your young twins, exposure to other children will tend to have the effect of supporting and enhancing their language skills.

At this age it is typical for parents to begin to recognize more distinctions, especially in boy/girl twins. One may be more verbal; one may be fairly easygoing while the other is more reactive; there may be real differences in attention span. Try to anticipate that your twins are processing their expanded world as individuals and are not likely to accomplish new skills in lock-step. Now is when you may see the glimmerings of the artist in one and the athlete in the other. The only thing you can say for sure at this age is that anything is possible. Looking at them as individuals and accepting them for who they are is really important at this time. They may be imposing pressure on themselves, either to catch up or even to hold themselves back. There is also the possibility that they will grow more and more similar in temperament in these years. The best advice for you as a parent of preschool-age twins is to step back and observe.

EARLY ELEMENTARY DEVELOPMENT: FIVE TO EIGHT YEARS

The five-year-old is riding a wave of confidence derived from her generally increased skills in all areas. The shift to kindergarten from preschool is demanding, particularly if a child is moving on to a different school, but most children are up to the challenge. The brand-new kindergartner is a pretty sturdy little person: friendly, not overly demanding, and usually very interested in pleasing parents, teachers and new friends. Reading and math readiness is improving, and intellectual curiosity is more easily expressed. Large motor coordination continues to mature as they begin to skip and jump. The mastery of fine motor activities, such as tying their shoelaces and writing their alphabet, provide tremendous inner satisfaction.

At five-and-a-half, there is another developmental plateau. The novelty of the new school experience gives way to many complex social and intellectual situations. The flexibility of the five-year-old seems to disappear, and parents may once again be confronted with their child's preference for routine. This need for established rituals coincides with increased personal responsibilities. Age five is also a time of emotional extremes. An "I love you" expressed to a friend can turn quickly to "I hate you" at the simplest infraction.

The five- to seven-year-old is washing herself and brushing her own teeth and choosing her own clothes and dressing herself. She likes "being in charge" and may balk when her decisions are questioned. But children at this age are real communicators and will usually use their language to communicate anger or frustration.

One very satisfying developmental threshold is the child's ability to respond to correction: When a mother or father says something to them, they're able to listen more and not be angry and upset or have a temper tantrum. They are more and more able to contain and process their feelings.

This is also a time that children begin to ferret out the differences between their parents. They know very well who is the soft touch when it comes to reading an extra bedtime story and who is the firmer disciplinarian. At this age, Mommy and Daddy are sometimes interchangeable—sort of an "either port in a storm" attitude. But this is also a time when a little girl may want to cuddle up with Daddy and a boy will seek special attention from his Mom. Boys may begin to be a little competitive with their dad at this time as they eagerly assert their own competence.

As children move through these early elementary years, they form more and deeper relationships with their peers. They're becoming a little more independent of their parents—testing the waters for their own ability to survive without constant and immediate access to Mommy and Daddy. Where until now parents have been a sort of buffer zone for conflict resolution, children grow increasingly able to let conflicts subside on their own. As their emotional maturity grows, they learn that it is sometimes all right to let feelings stay inside instead of always acting them out.

These years are rich in fantasy. Parents, siblings and friends may be drawn into extended fantasy play. Fantasy is also a tool for helping to dispel anxiety. The seven-year-old may know very well that there is no monster under the bed, but she still is able to convince herself that it *might be there* and need Mommy to make sure her room is monster-free.

TWIN DEVELOPMENT: YOUR FIVE- TO EIGHT-YEAR-OLD TWINS

Supporting your twins as they try to balance their dependence upon each other and their independence from each other is a great challenge. Preschool is kind of a dress rehearsal for the beginning of your twins' lives as students. Now they've made it to the big time—kindergarten! This is a great time to remember one of the most useful of all parenting tips: Observe, observe, observe. Try not to be wed to a particular strategy regarding your twins' class placement. There is not necessarily a "right way" for twins to make their way through school. As with all children, a move to a new school is a very vulnerable time. Your twins will again be dealing with separating from you and might benefit by starting off in the same class. Kindergarten is a wonderful opportunity to begin to assess the learning styles of each of your twins; observations made now will be very useful in making decisions about class placement a little further down the road. There is plenty of time to make the shift into separate classes a little later on. It is important to note, there are some twins who do well in separate classes right from the start.

The deepening friendships that are a big part of development at this age are even more complex for twins. You probably arranged some play dates back in preschool and got your first taste of the elaborate nature of your twins' social lives. Do you have one child come over to play with your two children? Or does each of your twins get to have their own playmate come over? What about when the mother of a singleton arranges a play date—can she (and her child) handle having both your twins or would she prefer that only one child visits? While we'll talk about this in depth later on, it will be useful for you to remember that the individual nature of each of your twins will be an important deciding factor in the way you help to support their social lives. Learning about friendship is vitally important in these years, and that includes your twins' friendship with each other.

PREADOLESCENT DEVELOPMENT: FROM NINE TO TWELVE YEARS

Preadolescent children are developing a stronger sense of self. This is accomplished in no small part by sizing themselves up in comparison to their peers. They're taking tremendous satisfaction from their friendships, and both boys and girls are very concerned with their relative ranking in the pecking order. Girls begin to show their interest in the fine details of interpersonal relationships now and can be very supportive or quite damaging to each other. Preadolescent girls are developing ahead of boys, so in boy/girl twins, this may be a time that a girl is taller and heavier than her twin. Some girls begin to menstruate during these years and show an escalating awareness of the opposite sex. This is in direct opposition to boys who remain fairly clueless and are likely to show more interest in sports than in talking to or about girls. Boys and girls will tend to become more private about their bodies, clearly expressing a desire for privacy, particularly when dressing.

The arc of their physical development continues its upward curve as they become more and more active and competent. Team sports may be an important part of the lives of boys and girls. Physical activities such as bike riding, swimming or jumping rope become joyous modes of self-expression and confidence.

The preadolescent child is eager to learn new skills and demonstrate competence in them. That goes for everything from sports to using tools. They love to produce concrete results, and their artwork grows more reality-based. Whereas the younger child draws human figures that frequently have very large heads—a symbolic representation of their egocentric stage of development—the preadolescent is experiencing a more global period of development and is very interested in drawing correct body proportions and mastering techniques of realistic drawing, such as perspective and shadowing.

Children at this age are often daydreamers, and they may even reflect on their daydreams for extended periods of time. The increasingly sophisticated cognitive skills of preadolescence enables them to go beyond the "black or white" thinking present in younger children. A strict teacher who might earlier have been perceived as "bad" might now be seen for some of the good qualities she has to offer: She may be strict, but at least she is fair.

These children are able to concentrate more, organize themselves more, and do more of their schoolwork on their own. They're becoming more self-regulated and more independent.

The language skills of the preadolescent are fairly sophisticated. They are able to form, express and defend their opinions with the ideas behind them. Language is used in a more global way: to identify them as part of a peer group and also to express the full range of human emotions. Their fluency supports debate, and they grow increasingly interested in taking sides in discussions among friends, within the family or in the classroom.

TWIN DEVELOPMENT: FROM NINE TO TWELVE

The pecking order that engages all children in this developmental stage is of extreme interest to twins. But their involvement is likely to extend beyond their peer group to include classifying each other. Many twins really work at staking out their turf, saying who is best at this and who excels at that. This focus can become very detailed, as in "I got nine right on my spelling test and you only got eight." Other twins are not so outspoken and keep their comparisons to themselves. Even as they place each other under the microscope for close inspection, they continue to enjoy each other's company. But from this point on, their world is getting bigger and bigger, and they are likely to develop intimate friendships with others and grow less mutually dependent. Of course, this rarely happens to both at the same time, so the challenge to parents is to provide support when one twin is reaching out to friends and the other feels left behind.

This is a time when the different issues that are going to affect identical and fraternal twins may grow more obvious. Fraternal twins may become less alike in their size and general appearance, particularly boy/girl sets. Same sex twins will start comparing their looks. Identical twins will look at minute details, such as who has more freckles on their nose or an extra fraction of an inch in height. Identical twins may have similar interests in hobbies, sports and extracurricular activities. But they may also be trying to figure out whether they want to be together or apart as they pursue their new interests. With any sets of twins, you are now deep into the car pool chronicles as you work with other parents to shuttle your children around from Little League to ballet to scouting and swim lessons.

Around this time, twins become very aware that they are no longer the center of the universe. The attention they've grown accustomed to simply for being twins may diminish significantly, a natural consequence of branching out in different directions in their expanding world. This may be the first time they are meeting new friends away from the actual physical presence of their twin. Now that they're older and more established, the novelty of their twinship has faded a bit, and peers are genuinely attracted to them as individuals. Each twin needs to develop the social skills to enable them to stand on their own out in the world.

This is a time when they want to be seen as separate and get very frustrated with people calling them by each other's name. They want to be seen more as individuals and not as "the twins." Yet this process of separation is not a smooth one. The push/pull of your twins' dependence on each other can make for volatile emotions in these years. You may find that your twins will grow extremely determined to be more like their peers and not stand out. They are also increasingly aware of other people's feelings, particularly their friends, and will not want to alienate them.

As important as friends have become, you as parents are vitally important to your twins as they look to you to help them to model their behaviors and gender identity. These can be demanding years, and you'll find yourselves treading lightly as you support your twins in their daily balancing act. Boys are very concerned with their physical performance and competence, yet you may have two boys with extreme differences in ability. In any twin combination there may be one child who is excelling academically and another who is having a tough time with school. Your challenge—*and it is huge*—is to support both, figuring out how to recognize one without diminishing the other. Nobody said it was going to be easy.

As your girl twin gets closer to full-blown adolescence, she may begin to withdraw a little bit from the cuddling with Daddy she sought as a little girl. Girls will tend to bond a little bit more with their mothers now, and the boys will tend to identify with their dads, eager to do "guy stuff." You may be able to take advantage of this closeness to the twin of the same gender by sharing an interest in a hobby or new activity. This can be extremely helpful if one twin is feeling left out because the other is focused on a new friend.

ADOLESCENT DEVELOPMENT: FROM THIRTEEN TO SEVENTEEN

The unrelenting surge toward adulthood is at full throttle by now. Physical development is well under way, and there is a deepening desire among teens to establish their own identity. They try on and cast off a series of images in these years. Where hobbies and interests were fairly flexible in preadolescence, young people at this stage of development are more selective about everything from hobbies to clothing to friends. Whereas earlier they were friends with just about everyone, now they're trying to find friends who really engage them or share similar interests.

Both boys and girls are showing real interest in the opposite sex. And instead of the sort of rotating crush that changed daily in the younger adolescent, the older adolescent tends to really fall for a particular love interest. This is also an age for doing what looks to parents like a whole lot of nothing, but there is actually a lot of thinking going on—fantasizing, daydreaming and trying to understand relationships with friends and family members.

Being the parent of an adolescent requires an awful lot of listening. It should not really be the goal of a parent to fix things for their adolescent children.

Teenagers say all the time that they just want their parents to listen to them and not to try to solve their problems. The days of being able to "make it all better" have passed. Parents should now be helping their adolescents develop healthy mechanisms for sorting out their interpersonal problems and coping skills for dealing responsibly with day-to-day living.

Where preadolescents want desperately to be accepted by their whole peer group, teenagers are looking beyond that blind need for acceptance and want to be liked for their values, for their person, for the way they think about things. They're becoming more and more discriminating about their friends. It's still important to be popular, but now they're in high school and they're starting to think more about college and the future and what their life is going to be like later on.

Older teens are less susceptible to peer pressures, and some are more willing to listen to their parents. Their cognitive skills are quite sophisticated now, and they can sometimes go back and forth in a discussion or even in an argument without losing control of themselves. There may still be issues around independence, but they are less charged. Before it was a sort of pack mentality; now as older teens, they're dating and learning about more mature one-on-one relationships.

YOUR TWINS: FROM THIRTEEN TO SEVENTEEN

Adolescent twins are likely to have their own social lives. That is not to say that they don't share some friends and sometimes attend the same parties, concerts or school events. But the selective adolescent is defining herself by her friends and her interests, and there may be less time for her twin. This may be a little harder for identical twins. Sometimes identical twins reach adolescence without having built steadily toward negotiating their separate identities. Their need for each other may have overwhelmed the developmental impulse toward individuality. The result is adolescent twins who are drawing even closer together and fearing being apart. This is why it is so important all along to see your twins as individuals and support them in seeing themselves that way.

But this journey toward independence can have its rough patches for any set of twins. It may be the first time for both of them that a good friend is hearing the intimate thoughts they used to share only with each other. Willingness to turn to another person is a necessary developmental step. Twins need to grow up and form trusting, intimate relationships beyond the twin bond. This may happen to both twins at the same time, in which case you as parents are left consoling each other, wondering where the years have flown. Or it may happen for only one twin at a time, resulting in some hurt feelings and long, sulky evenings on the home front. The days when you could make it all better have long since disappeared. Nevertheless, you can talk to the twin who is feeling left out about the fluid nature of the twin relationship. Remind her of an earlier time when "the balance of power" may have been reversed. Perhaps the healthiest advice to offer is to try not to take it personally.

You may find that after one twin has asserted her independence from you and her twin, she will return to the nest for "refueling." Suddenly the twin who has been too busy for family for the past three months is hanging around at home. However independent she may have appeared, there is a need to check back in and make sure that everything is as she remembered. Of course, this may be the time that the other twin is likely to assert her independence and the cycle begins again. As always, try to listen sympathetically and not feel compelled to solve the problem.

⧄

Chapter 3

"I had no twins in my family. We didn't use any fertility drugs. It's something that just happened, and I was shocked. I have a daughter who is two-and-a-half years older than my twins, and I was looking forward to having a second child and an easy childbirth. I knew what it was like. My husband was in Europe when I had an ultrasound at three months. First they told me they saw two heads. I was in a panic. . . . I thought I had a deformed child. Then they said, 'You have twins.' I probably cried the whole rest of the week. I didn't want twins. My husband was in Belgium, and he called me about two days later, and I said, 'Guess what?' I told him on the phone we were having twins. And he said, 'We can deal with this.' I immediately felt much better knowing that he felt that way."

—Mary, mother of 7-year-old identical boys

BEING THE PARENT OF TWINS

DOCTOR, COULD YOU PLEASE REPEAT THAT?

*E*very parent has a story to tell about how they found out they were going to have twins. One dad in his thirties got the call on his cell phone just before boarding an international flight. The stunned dad-to-be shared the news with the airline attendant when he checked in. Shortly after the plane was in the air, the pilot announced over the public address system that a passenger on board had just learned that he was to become the first-time father of twins. Everyone burst into applause, and the dad-to-be was escorted to first class and given a glass of champagne. His fellow passengers in the first-class cabin held their champagne glasses aloft, and one of the passengers—a father of four—offered up a celebratory toast. The would-be dad responded by saying he was very excited and then added that he imagined this would be his last first-class flight for quite some time. While very few parents of twins are likely to have such a public revelation, the news itself packs a wallop under any circumstance.

The dad on the plane was surprised but very excited from the moment he heard the news. He and his wife were both in their early thirties, financially stable, and as the dad said, "We just kind of went with it pretty much from the beginning." But that is by no means typical of all expectant parents of twins—and understandably so.

The manner in which the news is delivered has a significant impact on the new parents. You may have heard the news from an ultrasound technician or perhaps your doctor. Sometimes parents are young and have not yet had any children; there are no twins in the family and they are taken completely by surprise. Other times the news comes to couples, often in their late thirties or forties, who have been undergoing infertility treatments. Even though they've been advised that this may result in a multiple pregnancy, the news can be overwhelming. Not only are they pregnant, but they are pregnant with twins or maybe even triplets. There is a tremendous range of feelings set in motion when you learn you are having twins. Sometimes it's disbelief, and sometimes it's an enormous level of excitement— quickly followed by a sort of general concern about *what it all means*, quickly followed by a sinking sense that the physical and financial implications may be staggering. Then, within moments you're back to being excited, and the cycle of emotions starts again.

TAKING IN THE NEWS

It may not be until you are at home that night that one or the other begins to think about the potential health implications for you and the babies. While it has never been safer for a woman to have twins, a multiple birth is usually considered a high-risk pregnancy. When an expectant mother is receiving good medical care, a multiple pregnancy is usually diagnosed fairly early and monitored carefully by an obstetrician and, where appropriate, other medical experts. The possibility of preterm labor is increased in multiple pregnancy. A mother may be found to be at high risk for preterm labor and need to be on bed rest or take other precautions throughout her pregnancy.

Expectant parents may find themselves at odds with each other before the babies are even born. It is not unusual for a husband to feel very protective of his wife's health, while his wife grows more concerned about the babies. An expectant father of twins (who are now healthy nine-year-olds) recalled being very worried about his wife's health and safety when she was placed on total bed rest:

> In her fifth month, she went into the hospital on total bed rest. She had been real sick with the flu, and then there were serious problems with low levels of amniotic fluid. She lost weight and looked more tired than I'd ever seen her. I actually cried when I left the hospital. But it was like she had no patience with my worries about her health, and all she thought about was the babies. She accused me of not caring about them, and you know what? In a way she was right. I was just afraid I was going to lose her. I felt very connected to them as soon as they were born. They are so much a part of me now that it is impossible to imagine there was ever a time without them. But for my wife, it seems like that connection and maternal instinct was there even before they were actually born.

Expectant parents of twins may find it helpful to talk about their fantasies regarding pregnancy and parenting and recognize that their twin experience will offer its own unique pleasures and trials. Some parents are hesitant to tell other people that they are having twins. Most bounce back and forth between ecstasy and anxiety. Friends and family may be saying, "Isn't this wonderful? You're having twins!" And inside you may not feel that way. Or just as many people will say, "Oh, you're having twins. I'm glad it's you and not me." And that colors your fledgling parental attitude as well.

It is not at all unusual for there to be a disparity between the reactions of expectant parents. As the pendulum of their emotions swings back and forth, one settles into a happy sort of excitement while the other remains anxious and unhappy at the prospect of twins. Sometimes a woman who has planned to return to her career and pledged a commitment to her employer is stunned to discover that she is pregnant with twins. She wants to look into child care or live-in help, but her husband expresses a desire for her to stay at home with the twins for the first three years. Or vice versa, the husband had planned to stay at home with the new baby for the first few years, but now they need the money and both of them will have to return to work. Often, both are working and anticipate returning to work and providing part-time child care for their baby. They discover they are having twins, and all of a sudden what seemed like a sound plan is up in the air. Can both of them go back to work? Can they afford child care, or with the complexities of caring for twins, do they even want it? How will their finances hold up? Not only is it more costly to have twins, but the life they imagined with their new baby has suddenly been recast with twins. The physical, emotional and financial concerns that begin at the ultrasound diagnosis of multiples has begun to settle in.

SETTING THE STAGE FOR THE ENTRANCE OF YOUR TWINS

The human gestation period of nine months allows for more than the development of the infants. It is also a preparation time for parents. If the world is indeed a stage, your pregnancy is a sort of extended rehearsal time that allows you to pre-pare for the grand entrance of your twins. If we continue the theatrical metaphor, you can be sure that no two performances (and no two families) are ever exactly alike. The psycho-social environment within your family is an enormous factor in how you respond to this very important event in your lives. Of course, this is the case when any child comes into any family, but parents of twins are immediately confronted with complex parenting questions that make their situation unique.

The family unit welcoming the twins may consist of a young childless couple; a single mom; a blended family; parents with older children; older parents having their first children; families who have a special needs child already in the home. The list goes on and on. The family may be financially comfortable; they may be having a temporary financial setback; or they may be of very modest means. The marriage that provides the emotional setting into which the babies will arrive may be warm and stable; it may be loving but volatile; it may grow stronger with the arrival of the babies or begin to fray under the strain. Is it a quiet, somber home? A joyous, noisy home? A place filled with activity? Or is it calm and meditative? The kindest and wisest thing you can do for yourselves and your unborn babies is to make sure that the lines of communication between you and your mate are open and active even before your twins are born. The following tips might be used differently by every family, yet they apply equally to all parents of multiples:

- *Start talking with each other.* Get a head start on imagining some of the par-enting scenarios that are bound to occur. What are your thoughts about having twins, naming your twins, or how they will dress? Will they share their toys or each get their own? The list goes on and on. You are both more likely to keep a cool head if you discuss things ahead of time.

- *Good fences make good neighbors, but not good partners.* Try to avoid staking out your separate parental territories. Your twins will be very effective at figuring out when there is dissension in the parental ranks. (Some people even theorize that children's ability to "divide and conquer" their parents is innate—especially to adolescents in search of spending money or the keys to

TWIN TALK

Dr. Pearlman

Susan, mother of Bradley and Taylor, 5-year-old boy/girl twins

BEING A WORKING MOTHER OF TWINS

Dr. Pearlman:

Can we talk a little about being a working mother of twins?

Susan: Yes. I went back to work out of necessity, because my husband and I are both in real estate–related jobs, and as you know, the money is there and then it's not. You have to work when it's there. There were times when I felt a certain amount of guilt about not being able to be with my kids more. I think I also enjoy being out, using my brain and doing different things each day . That challenges me. Then I come home and I'm better off because I turn off the work and I'm with my family. So I don't think that you are a bad mother if you go to work. But one of the things that made it much easier is the flexibility I have in my job. There are many times when I can take the kids to school. I make a tremendous effort to be at all the kids' activities—anything that's important; any doctor visits when they were very young; any type of school event since they've been in preschool or kindergarten. I think that those are things that are important. For a working mother who has no flexibility, it's very difficult. And I know a lot of working people have to go on a very strict schedule. They drive a long way to get to their office and can't come to their children's events. A lot of my friends don't work, and I look at those who don't work and I think in some ways I'm much more happy with myself.

Susan and John

(left to right) *Bradley and Taylor*

Dr. Pearlman:

> What kind of help did you have when Bradley and Taylor were infants?

Susan: I had a woman who came and lived with us a week before the twins were born. She was with me while I was at home for about four months. I worked from home when they were born. So she was with us then and continues to come now once a week. We were very lucky to have her.

the family car.) Of course, you should not expect to agree on everything, but try to talk to each other about your parenting styles, and support each other where it is possible. You might find, for example, that you have very different ideas about feeding or discipline or even privacy when it comes to parenting your twins. It is not unusual for the parent who spends the most time with the twins, usually the mother, to establish certain routines around play or sharing or bedtime that are in opposition to the way the dad might handle them. Many parents of twins have described a growing feeling of estrangement from each other as one grows all powerful in establishing the rules of the roost and the other begins to feel marginalized as a parent. Try using each other as a sounding board about your parenting ideas before you turn them into parenting policy.

- *Don't wait too long before you seek additional support if you think it will be helpful.* There are many resources out there for parents of twins. You just have to take some initiative to find them. Don't be shy about asking for help if you feel you're having a real breakdown in communication with each other. Sometimes counseling is useful for a couple; other times only one of you may need the support. One couple (parents of twelve-year-old twins) described a deal they made early in their marriage that if either asked the other to participate in couples therapy, they would do it without complaint for at least half a dozen sessions. (They have done this three times in their marriage, all at the wife's request, and both agree it has been very useful.) The same goes for any concerns you may have about your twins' development. Observe your children over time and if your instincts tell you that you need help—be it medical, social or psychological—the resources are out there for you.

THERE ARE NO INSTANT EXPERTS

Just as the best tool in the parental toolbox is to observe your children carefully before taking any action, the best technique available to your couple relationship is to look fearlessly at your own belief systems and talk honestly with each other about what you find there. Even before your babies are born, you will have some intuitive feelings about twins, as well as many questions. The following questions are typical of the issues you might want to talk about:

- Is there a disparity in your reactions to discovering that you are pregnant with multiples?
- What are the financial implications?
- Is one or the other of you especially thrilled while the other is secretly distraught?

In lives filled with learning, being a parent is one of the longest and most complex learning experiences any of us will ever have. While expectant mothers and fathers are at the very beginning of the parenting curve, most come to child-rearing with certain ideas in place: You have thoughts about how you're going to feed your baby; what sort of education you envision; how you'll handle discipline as your child grows up. Even though you haven't had any reason to think about it yet, you have similar ideas in place about the very notion of "twins." Some people quickly come around to believing that twins are a wonderful miracle, and they feel tremendously blessed. Others are overwhelmed, and a sense of crisis arises.

After considering some of the very fundamental issues that come to mind, you may want to dig a little deeper and discuss some of your thoughts or beliefs regarding twins. Often, each member of a couple has had some childhood interaction with twins and may have some deeply held impressions that have never had an opportunity to come to light:

- Do you believe that twins are always each other's closest friend?
- Do you think twins are always competitive, and that there is always a winner and always a loser?
- Are you concerned that twins argue more than other siblings?
- Do you believe that in twin couples, one will inevitably lead while the other follows?
- Do you think twins are kind of snobby types who don't have many friends?

Each of these questions is perfectly reasonable, and yet you may have different intuitive responses to them. One mom-to-be entered therapy early on in her twin pregnancy. She was concerned that her twins would be a source of embarrassment. She eventually traced her concerns to a set of adult fraternal male twins who lived in her Queens, New York, neighborhood when she was growing up. They dressed alike in very flamboyant outfits and were an object of derision by the local kids. Expressing this fear made it easier to understand that she would have the opportunity to dress her twins differently and to guide them through the process of individuation that the twins of her childhood had not negotiated.

Talking to each other about your beliefs is as important to your healthy twin pregnancy as sound nutrition and monthly visits to your obstetrician. Hopefully, these conversations will have begun before your babies are born and will continue as they grow up. Communication between you as partners and parents will establish a foundation for your twins' arrival into a home that is as ready as it can be for the adventure to come.

After getting a little more acclimated to the idea of having twins, the next wave of emotion for both parents may leave the fundamental questions about twins behind. You may experience very personal concerns, usually tied into wanting to know the babies are developing normally, and that you will be able to handle the added responsibility of having two babies at once. These questions, which sometimes are not even verbalized, are very much a part of preparing to become the parents of twins:

- Will I be able to nurse two infants?
- How will I bond with two babies at the same time?
- Will I be able to give each one the proper care?

If you look carefully at these questions, you see that they all focus on factors that make having twins different than having a singleton baby. As thrilling as it is to become the parents of twins, it may also be very stressful. Parents need to acknowledge that stress; discuss it with each other; and talk about the fact that along with the blessing of twins comes the loss of the fantasy of the one baby they were anticipating. Let's return for a moment to our understanding of human development. The typical fantasy for the little girl playing at becoming a mother is of one baby and one mother. Unless there are twins in the family or the girl is herself a twin, it is unusual to see a little girl playing at "Mommy and the twins." All parents of twins should know that it is not unusual for either parent to experience some ambivalence about their situation. This was the experience of one mom, now the 48-year-old mother of twin boys:

> I spent eight years trying to get pregnant. It was my complete obsession and nothing, not my husband's concerns for my health, not my age, nothing was going to stop me from getting pregnant. Then, when I finally got pregnant with the twins and made it through my first trimester, I suddenly thought, "What have I done? How will I handle this?" And even though I adore my boys and could not imagine life without them, that returns from time to time. I've learned not to be frightened by it. It does not mean for one second that I'm not a completely loving mother, because I am.

JOINING AN EXCLUSIVE CLUB—THE STATUS OF PARENTING TWINS

Although the rate of twinning has risen dramatically with advancing maternal age and the advent of fertility treatment, a multiple pregnancy is still a remarkable event in our society and in the lives of parents-to-be. Expectant parents of multiples have certain concerns that set them apart from the rest of their peers who are having babies. Most inexperienced parents look to their friends or family who are a few years ahead of them for insight into pregnancy and parenting. A now-experienced mother of twins recalls her feelings when her twins were born:

My sister is three years older than I am, and she had a two-year-old when we discovered we were having twins. We've always been close, and she was a really confident mom, and I just assumed she'd be my major source for advice about caring for my baby. After the twins were born, our doctor advised us to get them on a fairly strict feeding schedule. My sister had always just nursed on demand, and she thought the doctor was wrong, and I felt trapped in the middle, and it was like a never-ending nightmare until the nurse in my pediatrician's office suggested I call the Mother of Twins Club here. It was such a relief to talk to other mothers who had gone through the same stuff and, most important, who had very practical information about nursing and sleeping and just plain coping. I really recommend it for any new mom with multiples.

There is a definite element of exclusivity in being the parent of twins. Many veteran parents, some of whom are now grandparents, look back on the years they were raising their twins and agree that it was a sometimes difficult, often rewarding and always interesting process. When asked if she thought raising her twins was different than raising singletons, a mother of four (a son, a daughter and identical girl twins who are the youngest) said:

I'd have to say that it was probably very useful that I'd already had two kids, but my twins, who are now 22 years old, put me through parenting paces that I'd really never experienced with my two older kids. And I really never felt like anyone understood—all they saw were these two gorgeous little girls who seemed to just have it all going for them. Going out shopping or playing in the park with the girls was kind of a treat when they were little. I never dressed them alike, or I'd have them in the same shorts with different-colored tops, but they were unmistakably twins, and people really fussed over them. I'd be lying if I didn't acknowledge that I got a kick out of it. I was approached several times to have them audition for television commercials, but my husband was very firm that he did not want them to do that. I have to confess that I thought it might be fun, but we never pursued it. But by the time they were in middle school, we started some very tough years. My two older kids went through all the normal ups and downs, but I really don't recall either of them having the kind of dramatic situations that we went through with the girls. Don't misunderstand me—they are wonderful, and I think, well-adjusted girls, but there were times that trying to see to their emotional needs left me feeling in desperate need of a Club Med holiday for one! By the time they left home to go to college, I felt like I deserved a medal.

This mother's response represents both ends of the exclusivity experience: She took great pride in the public attention her daughters received simply for being themselves—beautiful, friendly twins. But later on she felt she "deserved a medal" for supporting and surviving their stormy adolescence. Being a responsible, loving parent is hard work that has its great rewards. Being that same parent of twins often leaves parents feeling they are deserving of additional accolades. When your children are young, sometimes those accolades come in the form of frequent compliments and comments from family, friends and even strangers who stop to admire your children at the mall or the park. People are naturally curious about twins, particularly if they are identical, and may compliment your children and your ability as a mother. It is not uncommon to hear a comment such as "I don't know how you do it. I can barely keep up with my one child."

No kidding! You are working really hard and deserve to be recognized for it. But sometimes the attention can be overwhelming. It is very useful for parents of twins to realize that while being a parent of multiples grants you immediate membership to an exclusive club, you do have some say over just how public that membership is. While it can be very rewarding for new parents to be out and about with their twins, it can also be downright annoying. Just as twins have many pet peeves over the questions they are asked by unwitting strangers, parents have similar complaints. The following are a sample of questions asked of parents while they were out with their infant or young elementary-age twins:

- *"Are they identical?"* Asked about your boy/girl twins.
- *"Are they twins?"* Asked about your identical twins.
- *"Why are they so tiny"*? In response when you tell the age of your premature twins.
- *"Is one smarter than the other?"* Asked about any twins.
- *"I have two who are both under five. How much harder can this be?* Spoken by a mom without a clue.

While some of these questions may seem amusing at first glance, they actually range from uninformed to foolish to intrusive. The thrill of going to the mall with your beautiful babies wears pretty thin after you've answered the same question several dozen times. On the other hand, after a morning of two cranky babies cooped up in the house, a trip to the mall may be just the thing. The mother of boy/girl twins described her idea of a pick-me-up:

We lived in Minneapolis when the kids were small. I rarely dressed them alike, but I actually had a few little sweatsuit outfits that were the same. And sometimes in the winter when they were about a year-and-a-half, I'd dress them alike and take them to the mall in their side-by-side stroller, mostly for the guilty pleasure of talking to people who admired them. With the exception of that winter, I always dressed them differently. When I think about it now, I feel a little foolish, but the winters are pretty bleak back there.

This story really illustrates the importance of asserting some control over the way you present yourself and your twins to the world. Clearly this mom was conscious that her twins were not going to dress alike on a consistent basis, but she was perfectly aware of the powerful and pleasing effect of that visual image. And more power to her for seeking a respite from being cooped up in the house with two cranky babies. She went on to talk very honestly about how, particularly in her twins' early years, she felt supported by the "strokes" that came from people's pleasure in her twins.

Some mothers report being branded as the "Mom of Twins," as though anything else they had accomplished or expected to accomplish was no longer of consequence. It is not unusual for parents, particularly mothers if they have left their work to be the primary caregiver, to experience anxiety or even resentment over this myopic view of their identity. It is important to realize very early on in your parenting experience that you have some control over how you and your twins are perceived in the world. The following tips may be useful in negotiating the public part of the balancing act of parenting twins:

- *Map out your public appearance strategy.* Going out with twins can be a little bit like a celebrity event, so plan accordingly. If you're in a rush or not in the mood to interact with people, try to avoid having both twins with you, or at least be sure to dress them differently. Or if you're out as a family doing some marketing, split up and each take one child. This has the added benefit of giving your twins some one-on-one time with each parent.
- *Plan some responses to frequently asked questions.* By the time ten people have asked you if your boy/girl twins are identical, you better have a quick but pleasant response prepared or you're likely to bite some poor soul's head off. Just say, "Actually, they have to be the same sex to be identical. My twins are fraternal." And you can be gone without a trace while

they're still pondering the facts. No need to knock yourself out trying to be a comic genius. Just respond and retreat. As your twins get older, you'll need to help them to learn how to field the same silly questions.

- *Don't be afraid to fib.* The incidence of prematurity is higher in multiples than it is in the rest of the population. If your twins were born prematurely, they may be smaller than their peers of the same age. Your 10-month-old twins who were born three months early are likely to be smaller than the average 10-month-old who was born at term. So if you get tired of hearing people remark that they are small, lie about their actual age: Tell them they are seven months old. At this stage of their development, a little white lie that protects you and your babies from irritating questions is just fine.

- *Make sure your other children share the spotlight.* It is not unusual for twins to get more than their share of attention in public. If you have other children, you can help spread the glory around. Whether it is another mom in the park or your own extended family, be sure to include your other kids. There is the tendency for twins to get a lot of positive attention *simply because they are twins.* If a stranger at the market is gushing over how beautiful they are, be sure to mention your other children who are standing at your side. Explain that they were instrumental in teaching the twins to be kind to the family dog or how they help you prepare dinner or . . . you get the idea. Be certain to work the conversation around to support all of your children who are also present.

- *Don't feel guilty for wanting a bit of the spotlight yourself.* It is perfectly natural and appropriate to relish the fact that you are the parent of twins. In fact, the whole extended family often takes pride in being related to twins. Many mothers of twins are very tough on themselves, saying they feel awful that with the family's need for extra money, they are unable to go out and work. Well, you are working, and working hard every day. We have grown used to equating work with financial compensation, and a mom who is caring for her twins every day does not take home a check at the end of the week. You should never feel guilty for accepting accolades, even from strangers who rightly intuit that caring for twins is a very complicated and special opportunity.

HOME, HEARTH AND HELP!

A lot of what we've talked about so far pertains to developing and supporting your couple relationship so that it will function well over the long-term commitment to raising your twins. But there is no getting around the daily stress and just plain exhaustion that is an inevitable part of caring for two children. As new, often first-time parents of twins, you can expect to feel overwhelmed by your two babies. And to top it all off, you're sleep deprived. So first things first: Let's look at the things you can do to get yourself a little rest, and move on to talk about support systems that will be helpful until that distant day that you look on proudly as your twins collect their high school diplomas:

- *There really is sleep after twins.* But you have to search for it as though you were looking for buried treasure. The physical toll of carrying and delivering two babies is enormous. Once your twins are born, you are instantly at odds with your own desire to be with them and see to their many needs, and your own need for sleep, rest and a little private time. Well, unless you make a conscious attempt to care for yourself, your impulse to place the babies first will win out every time. As adults, we are always seeking balance between emotion and intellect. If you think this through, you'll know that in order to best care for your children, you should first care for yourself. Watching the world through the filter of sleep deprivation will not do you or your children any good. Take whatever means are available to you to eat healthily, exercise moderately, rest and, most importantly, sleep! If you are nursing your babies, get in the habit of pumping milk so that you can sleep through alternating midnight feedings and get a nice, long uninterrupted slumber.

- *Just say yes to help.* Our daily lives are filled with the social pleasantries that help make the world go 'round. You've just heard that your car needs an expensive overhaul and you're miserable. But when you run into a casual friend who asks how you're doing, you say, "Fine, thanks. How about you?" As a new parent of twins, you need to give yourself special dispensa- tion to throw those social conventions out the window, and when someone, *anyone*, says, "Wow, twins. Do you need any help?" say "Yes!" There are any number of ways in which people can help: cooking meals that can be stored in the freezer for easy preparation; doing the shopping or laundry; bringing you some material from work so that you can do it at home; taking your older child to a movie; taking one or both babies for a stroll while you have some time with your other kid(s). As your children get older, you'll need help with carpooling to different activities or maybe even a daily ride to school if your twins are in separate schools. You can always find an opportunity to say thanks to the friends and family who help you out, whether it's an annual "Thanks for Keeping Us Sane" party, a note of thanks or some reciprocal support down the road.

- *Rethink your priorities.* Surrendering to the realities of your daily life can either make you feel like you're losing a battle or winning an almost spiri- tual release. A supermom is not the one who takes the twins to the most activities while holding a full-time job and baking fresh bread every Sunday before she collapses into an exhausted, resentful heap. The real supermom does what she can to balance her time among her kids, her husband, her work and herself and is able to let the house get messy without feeling like she has failed. The occasional frozen dinner never hurt anyone. Remember, as your twins grow up, they should participate in the household chores, eventually helping with the cooking and even doing their own laundry. While they're young, get whatever assistance you're able to afford to help out with the house, but be prepared to relax your standards as far as tidiness is concerned. One family had the clever idea of asking their extended family on both sides to pool the financial resources that would have gone to holiday and birthday gifts for the family, in order to pay for a monthly cleaning service for eighteen months. It had the added bonus of allying both sides of the family in a really meaningful gift for two very exhausted parents. Another family put aside the money they would otherwise have spent on a week-long resort holiday and used it for alternating weekly home massages for mom and dad.

- *Making time for each other.* One of the most frequent concerns of parents of twins is that they begin to feel that the cost of devotion to their children is the loss of intimacy with each other. One couple with two-year-old identical twin daughters have made a commitment to having a "date night." Even at this very young age, the girls are aware that this is Mommy and Daddy's special time, and they have become a bit of a cheering section. They help their parents get ready, maybe choosing a tie for their father or dabbing perfume behind their mother's ears. It makes departure time easier for them and for their babysitter. And most importantly, it is establishing a standard, very early on, that parents have a need for private time together. Parents lose intimacy with each other, beyond being too tired for sex. The sheer volume of work, particularly from the toddler to early elementary years, has the tendency to turn a loving, intimate connection into a cell phone relationship: "Don't forget to pick up diapers. Did you remember to get the dry cleaning? Julie has a ballet class— can you get Teddy to his game?" Not terribly romantic. Retaining or reclaiming your intimacy as a couple is vital to the healthy environment in your home. It is also an important model for your twins. It is simply not healthy for them to believe that they rule the roost, or that their every need supersedes the need for closeness between their Mommy and Daddy.

- *Be as patient with yourself as you are with your twins.* We've all heard it said that children don't come with instruction manuals, but that doesn't seem to keep mothers and fathers from thinking they should be instant parenting experts. This is sometimes particularly true of parents of twins who say things such as "I manage a staff of forty at work. Why should this be so difficult?" They tend to be very hard on themselves, not acknowledging that there is a learning curve involved in parenting any child, and that curve is even steeper when you're getting to know your twins. Think of it: Two children of the same age who are individuals with different needs, and you're on call every day as their primary resource for love, nourishment, intellectual stimulation, and the list goes on. When you become a first-time parent of twins, you start off running and may not feel as though you have a moment to reflect until their first birthday. If you remember the developmental plateaus we discussed for your children, you can apply them to your own development as parents. Remember to think of parenting as a process and not a job title. Try not to push yourself too hard. Just as you relish those plateaus in your twins' development as times for a little calm contemplation before the next developmental leap, try to slow down occasionally and reflect on your own accomplishment as a parent.

- *Don't suffer in silence.* Sometimes, a woman who is perfectly comfortable about going with her husband to speak with a counselor during a rocky marital patch would never dream of looking for parenting support. Many mothers of twins equate asking for help with weakness or a lack of competence. In fact, nothing could be further from the truth. In the constant attempt to balance our emotions with our intellect, the ability to recognize a problem is a sign of maturity.

One mom of three-year-old twins finally told her internist that she had been battling what she described as depression ever since her twins were born. This tearful confession was accompanied by her description of how ashamed she was and how she felt like a terrible mother. To the outside world, and even to her husband, she was the model of the happy, busy mom, but her escalating unhappiness was getting harder to hide. A thorough check-up, including laboratory blood work, revealed a hormonal imbalance that was easily rectified and made a very positive difference in her day-to-day outlook. Of course, not every scenario is so easily remedied. But the point is that this particular mom suffered needlessly for three years because she was ashamed of needing help and worried about her ambivalent feelings about being a mom. The exhausting emotions of parenting your twins may subside after a few nights' rest or continue for months. We know that the incidence of postpartum depression is higher in mothers of multiples. Sometimes a mother of twins seeks out a therapist and describes a very general feeling of exhaustion and anxiety, without any specific concern. Others report feeling ashamed of having ambivalence about their children and wondering why they ever imagined they could be a mother in the first place. Still other mothers enter therapy with a well-thought-out list of all their expectations and how they are falling short of them. While any of these women will benefit by being patient with themselves, sometimes the insight of a mental health professional is a useful and necessary tool for healthier, happier parenting.

- *Time is on your side.* It may sound silly to say, but remember, they are going to grow up. Just when you think that by the time they're out of diapers, you're going to need them yourself, they're potty trained! And when you're wondering if you and your husband will ever again wake up without a tangle of extra little bodies between you, they decide that big kids sleep in their own beds. And when all of a sudden it's eighteen years later and you're looking at family albums waiting for your children to come home from college so that the house won't seem so empty, you'll wonder where the time could possibly have gone. So try to keep your wits about you, laugh as much as you can, whenever you can, and know that you're doing the best you can and that is almost always more than enough.

TWIN TALK

Dr. Pearlman

Diana, mother of Amaro and Hermes, 11-year-old fraternal twins

BEING THE MOTHER OF TWINS

Dr. Pearlman:

How is it to have your first children be twins?

Diana: I think it helps that my dad was a twin. Once I got used to the fact that I was having two, which I think took about three days, I was excited. They have been a very positive experience in my life.

Dr. Pearlman:

A lot of people say they experience difficulties as their twins get older and they have to share certain things, such as a computer. How does that work for you?

Diana: I worked a lot with the Hispanic community, and in many cases the limitations on resources were extreme. I remember once the president of the Vickie Carr Foundation told me she'd had five girls in the family who shared one party dress. She said that in the most natural way, not feeling sorry for her-

(left to right) *Hermes and Amaro*

self. I think being around people like that has made it easier for me. I don't see the boys as a hardship; I see it as something I need to work on. We work around each other, and it works okay. When I have a deadline, they are incredibly supportive. They troubleshoot any problems that I have. Ever since they started using the computer, they're been extremely respectful of my work and my files.

Dr. Pearlman:

Have there been difficult times?

Diana: Obviously there are a lot of children who don't really understand the twin relationship. So they make demands of Hermes and Amaro that they are not prepared to respond to. If my sons are somehow being manipulated by other children, it's very painful, but they have to learn to be able to work through that.

Diana

Dr. Pearlman:

How about comparisons between the two boys?

Diana: I actively discourage it from other people in front of me and in front of them. I was compared throughout my childhood with my older sister and I hated it. I really thought it was unfair, because we were very different people. I always discourage comparison. I was surprised the first time they told me that people would say things like "You should be more like your brother." If I had heard someone say that to my child, I would have gone to her and talked about it. It is intrusive for an adult to interfere that way with any sibling relationships. Each of the boys have their qualities, and they have their faults.

My family has been supportive. I think my boys are lucky. People tend to like both of them. They are both very bright, and teachers like them. Teachers love having them in their class—they really do. They are very serious about their work, and they try hard. They put a lot of effort into things that they do.

One of the things that I would recommend to parents is to be sure to provide supervision in social relationships. When they're young and just learning to make friends, they need more supervision than is often provided. My kids were allowed to bring home some very difficult kids, the kinds of friends that you wouldn't want your child to have. I would tell them it may not work because of this and that and the other thing, but if you want this child to visit, I will be here. Then we would see what would happen. I allowed them the room to experiment with friendships. But they were supervised—always supervised—and not by a nanny, but by me. Social skills have to be taught. I think kids need a lot of help learning how to make friends.

Chapter 4

Myth: an imaginary or unverifiable person or thing.

Truth: the body of real events or facts; a true or accepted statement or proposition.

—*Merriam Webster's Collegiate Dictionary*

TWIN MYTHS

TWIN MYTHS SPAN CENTURIES AND SPAN THE WORLD

Myth has been an element of every society since the beginning of recorded time. Myths provide order in a chaotic universe, attempting to make the unknowable known. If we, with all our sophisticated understanding of human biology and psychology, are still struggling to comprehend the nature of twins, imagine our ancient ancestors confronted with the miracle of twin birth. Is it any wonder that the myth of twin rivalries such as Romulus and Remus from the ancient Greeks, or Jacob and Esau in the Bible, endure today?

The phenomenon of twinning has been with us since our beginning, and it crosses all ethnic, cultural, social and economic lines. Myths associated with twins can be traced across centuries and across the globe. It is important to examine these myths to see how they influence the way we see twins and how we parent them. First we'll look at some of the attitudes associated with twinning from a varied and ancient cultural perspective. Many of these myths are cited in an article by Alice Vollmar in *The Twinship Sourcebook*.

ANCIENT TWIN MYTHS

Honor and Dishonor

- In Africa twinning occurs more frequently than throughout the rest of the world. There are many tales of twins being gods or demons. In Yoruba, twins are honored now, but in the past they were killed. A vision came to the Yoruba, telling them to stop killing twins if they wanted life in their village to thrive. Twins began to hold a place of honor in the village. Suddenly their families became wealthy. Today, the birth of twins is welcomed. Also, upon the birth of twins, parents are given two wood statues. When one twin dies, the surviving twin has the destiny of caring for the statue until his own death.
- In New Guinea, twins are revered in the community and honored with extravagant gifts.
- The Iroquois Indians of America believed there was one good twin and one evil twin, and the evil twin was exiled.
- The Plains Indians of North America believed the younger twin was "attacked by monsters," taken away and never seen again.

Control Over Nature

- An Indian tribe of British Columbia believed twins brought good luck. The birth of twins was associated with nature's bountiful supply of fish and wild game.

- North American Mojave Indians thought twins controlled the natural elements. They sought their good influence by sprinkling water on twins' graves.
- In India, the Hindu people believed twins protected them from bad weather. The buttocks of twins were painted black and white to help provide this protection.
- The Balinese performed complex cleansing rituals on twins in the hope of honoring the balance sought in nature.

Moral Beliefs That Guided the Destiny of Twins

- In ancient Egyptian dynastic tradition, boy/girl twins were forced to marry in order to maintain the purity of the dynastic line.

Regression in Human Development

- Some African, Brazilian, and American Indian tribes believed twinning was a regression—similar to animals being born in a litter.

Paternity Questioned in Many Cultures

- Africans, American Indians and Japanese believed that twins were fathered by two different men.
- Brazilians believed twins to be the product of adultery, sometimes resulting in the execution of the mother.

As citizens at the dawn of the twenty-first century, we find that many of the myths described above feel unrelated to the facts of our modern lives. The ancient myths may interest or amuse us. We may also find them intriguing or even disturbing from an anthropological standpoint. But as readily as we distance ourselves from these ancient myths, we come up with our own myths to take their place. Twins have always been a rarity, and people have always been fascinated by them. You just have to say the word *twins* and you are guaranteed to have people's attention. The following are some of the many myths about twins that pervade our culture today.

MODERN TWIN MYTHS

- A *parent can not bond with two or more babies at the same time*. Perhaps the most frequently asked question of experienced twin parents and experts in twin development is, "How am I going to bond with two babies at the same time?" The answer is that you won't bond at the same time—you'll bond with each of them individually over a period of time, but you will surely be able to bond with both of them. The term *bonding* has become an emotionally loaded expression that parents believe must occur in the very earliest hours and days of their baby's life or be seen as a lost opportunity. This is simply not the case.

    Bonding is a process that is better described as an intimate connection between each parent and each baby that takes place during one-on-one activities such as feeding and nursing; through individual connections such as cuddling and uninterrupted gazing into each other's eyes; and during physical interaction such as diaper changes or dressing. It is one-on-one intimacy, and it will take longer to establish with twins than it might with a singleton. But as you begin to note each of your baby's little idiosyncrasies and see their individual temperaments developing even in the very early weeks, you will know that you are beginning to form a lifelong bond with each of your twins. Some twins who are born prematurely may need to remain in the hospital for an extended stay, but with the help of an enlightened family-centered approach on the part of the medical and nursing staff, these parents will also be able to form a strong bond with their babies.

- *All multiple births are premature*. While there is an increased risk of preterm labor and delivery with twins and higher order multiples, not every multiple birth is premature. We are used to calculating a full-term singleton pregnancy at 40 weeks, but most obstetricians will tell you that a term pregnancy for twins can be any time after the completion of 37 weeks. Some twin births occur after 37 weeks, but many early deliveries also take place. Mothers of twins who have been put on bed rest and are at risk for preterm labor should be highly motivated to work with their medical team to hold off delivery for as long as they can. Each extra day your twins have in utero is a wonderful gift you can give to them. Every expectant mother of multiples should speak with her physician about the signs of possible preterm labor.

- *Twinning always skips a generation.* There is no truth to the myth that twinning skips a generation. The genetic predisposition for dizygotic (fraternal) twinning—producing more than one ovum during a menstrual cycle—is genetically inherited and may not show itself in every generation. Since only women ovulate, it can be displayed only in the mother. There are many other factors that can cause fraternal twinning. As discussed in Chapter One, age appears to influence multiple birth. It appears that between the ages of 35 and 39, a woman is more likely to produce more than one egg at one time, therefore increasing the likelihood of having multiples. As far as monozygotic (identical) twins are concerned, the jury is still out. Research is continually trying to understand the fertility process and, therefore, investigating what actually causes the single fertilized ovum to split.

- *All twins have the same genes and chromosomes.* That's true for identical twins, but not for fraternal twins. While fraternal twins occupy their mother's uterus at the same time, they are no more genetically alike than any two singleton siblings. It is interesting to note that even identical twins do not share the same fingerprints.

- *Identical twins are always identical in every way.* Even though identical twins share the same genes and chromosomes, they are less alike than commonly thought. For any measured characteristic, such as height or weight,

FAMOUS TWINS FROM GREEK MYTHOLOGY

- **Romulus and Remus. Their father was the Roman god Mars, and they were abandoned and raised by a wolf. They became the founders of Rome, but then Romulus later killed Remus in a struggle over power.**

- **Pollux and Castor. These two sons of Zeus were inseparable. Neither felt he could survive without the other. We can see them today as two bright stars in the constellation known as Gemini.**

twins are not 100 percent identical. This indicates that environmental effects are far more influential than we realized. These environmental effects go all the way back to include differences in the intrauterine experience. For example, inside the shared space of the uterus, twins have their own place. They are in different positions, and as they grow, one may have more room than the other. Placement within the uterus may have an effect on what they hear, including different perceptions of their mother's heartbeat. They each derive their own separate nutrition as well.

The birthing experience also has its own unique impact on each twin. In a vaginal birth, the firstborn twin is pushing open the birth canal, leaving a wider opening for the second infant to pass through. If the first baby's more pressured passage through the narrow birth canal is headfirst, as is the normal birthing position, its facial/skeletal features may be slightly elongated. In some births, one baby delivers vaginally and the other is a cesarean birth, which may also result in subtle differences between the two infants. It is also possible for one twin to have a congenital medical problem that is not present in the other. And that is just the beginning of the differences between them. As identical twins grow up, their individual experiences as well as the relationships they develop with their parents,

siblings, extended family and friends will all contribute to shaping them as individuals.

- *When parents have twins, they love them both the
  same.* Parents see their twins as individuals. They
  love them each uniquely as a separate person.
  Think of it this way: Do you love your parents
  the same? Probably not, but you do love them
  both. You love them uniquely for who they are,
  and you can't quantify your love and say you love
  them the same. That's how it is with twins—you
  love them uniquely but not equally. Just because
  they're twins doesn't mean they should be
  treated the same. As a parent, you respond to
  each as an individual, just as you would with any
  siblings. As long as you are aware of the importance of treating each twin fairly, appreciating
  each for whom they are and valuing the unique
  gifts each brings to the family, then you are loving
  your twins in the best way you can.

- *Twins are clones or clones are twins.* Twins are not
  clones. While clones, like identical twins, may
  share the same genes and chromosomes, they do
  not share the same uterus. Therefore they have
  none of the concurrent uterine influences that
  twins experience. Recent scientific study is also
  looking into the fact that cells cloned to grow a
  separate organism may age differently than the
  original. On the simplest level, twins develop
  within the same uterus, at the same time, from
  the same impregnation and share a common birth.

MYTHIC TWINS OF THE BIBLE

- **Jacob and Esau.
  These two were the twin
  sons of Isaac and Rebekah.
  Esau sold his birthright to his
  younger twin, Jacob.**

A clone is an individual grown from a single body cell of its parent that is genetically identical to that parent.

- *Twins receive the same if not more of their parents affection and attention than non-twins.* This is not usually the case. Mothers of twins tend to spend more time with both their babies, but do not spend as much time alone with each twin. Simply keeping up with the tasks of caring for two babies or small children leaves limited time to engage each twin one-on-one. As a result, twins tend to develop their twin relationship by engaging each other. An interesting study indicated that some twins experience less verbal interaction and fewer expressions of affection, praise and approval from their parents. It is very important for parents to understand that this study in no way implies that parents of twins love their twins less than singleton parents. It simply points out the value of parents seeking more opportunities throughout twins' lives for individual time and attention. Once again, being the parent of twins is all about balance in the family: creating some time for each twin with their mother and father, for the family all together, for the twins with each other. As twins get older it will be equally important for them to learn to spend time apart from each other.

- *The twin relationship is like any other sibling relationship.* Of course, it is true that twins are siblings, but there is a difference between the twin and non-twin sibling relationship. With non-twin relationships, there is at least ten months between sibling ages, and more often, two to 10 or more years. Non-twin siblings have their own time, at least as infants, with their parents. They also have their own space and they occupy their own position within the family. There is a natural age-determined hierarchy among siblings, with the eldest receiving more privileges and more responsibilities. If there are other siblings within the family, the twins still take their place in the hierarchy but have additional factors influencing their relationship. They must, for example, share their place in the family hierarchy with each other. And while it can be said that fraternal twins, particularly if they are a boy and a girl, are simply siblings who happen to have been born at the same time, they are still dealing with having to share attention from birth, being the same age at the same grade level, and receiving attention from outside the family simply for being twins.

- *Twins are each other's opposites, so there's always a "good twin" and a "bad twin."* The battle between "good" and "evil" has been acted out since ancient times in countless cultures. Most people are fascinated by these opposing and dynamic forces—we examine them in a broad cultural, moral and religious context, as well as in a very personal, psychological way. Children play at being "the good guys" or "the bad guys," and personal temptation is described by the presence of "an angel on one shoulder and the devil on the other." It isn't too hard to imagine how over the centuries the idea of a good and bad twin was almost irresistible to the human mind. But as compelling as the idea may be, it is completely without merit. Twins are no more likely to be each other's opposites than are any other siblings.

The impulse to compare twins is understandable but misguided. Each twin grows up, and while they certainly influence each other, they are also individually influenced by their experiences as well as their relationships with their parents, siblings, friends and extended family. At any given point in time, the temperament, characteristics, and habits of each twin may be more compatible with one parent than they are with the other. But parents are well advised to realize that their relationships with both their twins are likely to flip flop, sometimes every few months, but some days as frequently as every few hours.

Labels are a kind of shorthand that even parents may be tempted to use from time to time, but in the long run they serve no purpose and can be harmful. The twin who is labeled "good" feels pressured to achieve and never make mistakes, and the "bad" twin is likely to act out negatively. The twin who is positively labeled knows she is not always good and may feel guilty, while at the same time feeling badly for her twin. There is likely to

MYTHIC TWINS OF LITERATURE

- **William Shakespeare, author of *Comedy of Errors* and *Twelfth Night,* in which confusion over twin identities abounds, was the father of fraternal twins.**

- **Peter Shaffer, author of *Equus,* and Anthony Shaffer, author of *Sleuth,* are twins and highly regarded playwrights.**

- **Alexandre Dumas was the author of *The Man in the Iron Mask,* a story about identical twins.**

be resentment between the two as they grow up. Parents are the first line of defense from peers, teachers or even extended family who may unwittingly burden twins with labels. Be vigilant about trying not to label your twins. You, they and their relationship will be richly rewarded.

- *All twins have a special language.* Many twins do have a unique way of communicating with each other. It is wrongly called a "special language." The scientific names for this twin-talk are idioglossia, cryptophasia or autonomous language. It is defined as an inability to articulate properly, so the sounds that are spoken are like that of an unknown language. This is not as magical an explanation as we might be tempted to believe, but it is fascinating in its own right. Twins tend to spend a lot of time together, and they model each other's early language, which is understandably inaccurate in many ways. They may, for example, leave the beginning and ending consonants off words. Yet their constant exposure to each other, coupled with their strong desire to communicate, makes for a sort of spoken code that is reinforced and understood only between each other.

This language that delights your twins but baffles everyone else contributes to the acceptance on the part of parents that their twins' language skills will be a bit delayed. Parents are sometimes so confused or charmed by their twins' speech that they don't attempt to correct them. If their "twin language" appears to be continuing through toddlerhood and into preschool and kindergarten age, you may find it helpful to expose them to other children during play dates or visits with friends. Studies have shown that twins who had difficulty in their language development showed improvement in verbal language skills after they were able to separate from their twin and also have some training to support their language skills. Playing separately with other children gives them the dual opportunity to model other children's speech as well as experience the need to communicate with peers other than their twin. Speaking as frequently as possible to even the youngest children is very important. Opportunities present themselves often during the day—for example, while bathing, diapering, feeding, and so on. One of the very best things you can do to support language skills, even in your infant twins, is to read books aloud to them—and when possible, read to them individually.

If their language skills are a little slower, it may be a temporary factor of the twin experience or premature birth or there may be a significant speech or language delay that requires professional attention. As always, patient observation is your best tool. If you have any concerns about your twins' language skills, discuss it with your pediatrician and see if any further assessment is recommended.

EARLY SCIENTIFIC INTEREST IN THE STUDY OF TWINS

In 1875, Sir Francis Galton (a cousin of Charles Darwin) investigated the nature/nurture issue using twins as study subjects.

- *Twins are supposed to be best friends.* This is a big issue for parents and for twins. If parents believe that twins may be *always* supposed to be each other's best friend, they may be setting their children up for having a hard time separating and individuating from each other. There is a natural push and pull to any close relationship, and that is no different for twins. Zygosity and gender tend to have an impact on the twin relationship. Identical twins are more likely to have similar temperaments and interests, and those factors may tend to support a closer friendship between them. But all twins are likely to experience times when they are closer and times when they look to others for close friendships. Parents can support their twins through all these circumstances by letting them know that fluctuations in their relationship are natural and healthy even though it may be tough to handle at times.

- *All twins have ESP.* So far there is no research to support evidence of ESP in twins. Twins are similar to other individuals who are close in age or who live together and spend a lot of time with one another, such as husbands and wives who have been married for many years and are familiar with each other's habits, temperaments and so on. But regardless of the lack of scientific proof, some twins themselves will swear to a sort of magical connection that they attribute to their twin relationship.

  While ESP may remain in the pages of science fiction, empathy is a far more likely explanation for the deep connection experienced by twins. Some people are empathetic by nature, which is to say they experience a deep insight into, and awareness of, others' feelings and behavior. Twins, who are already primed to respond to each other, often have a strong empathetic relationship that they and others may describe as ESP.

  Sometimes parents grow dependent on one twin to express what the other is feeling. There is danger in a parent expecting one twin to know when the other one is in distress, unfairly making him responsible for his twin: "You should have known John was out with those kids. . . ." Try to keep the lines of communication open with each of your twins, and let their empathetic connection be the deeply rewarding, private connection it was meant to be.

- *One twin is always dominant and assertive, while the other is passive.* Many twins will tell you that the balance within their relationship is very fluid, sometimes shifting back and forth quite obviously, and sometimes with great subtlety. It is also very likely that where one twin is dominant in a particular facet of the relationship, the other will assume a leadership role in some different way. Twins may also acknowledge that while one may appear to be the more passive in public, the dynamic between them may be very different in private.

  It is also important to note that social relations differ among identical twins, same sex fraternals and opposite sex fraternals. For example, in the case of boy/girl twins, the girl may appear to be more assertive in the social arena, because like most girls, her verbal skills are somewhat more advanced than her brother of the same age. Identical twin toddlers may appear to have established a leader-follower pattern when suddenly the "follower" who has been carefully observing his trailblazing brother will surge ahead, putting his months of astute observation to work. The important point is that once again, your twins are sure to defy, outgrow and confound any attempt to label them.

- *Identical twins always experience greater problems in establishing their identity.* Neither identical nor fraternal twinning are definitive factors in determining identity problems. The fact, however, that twins so closely resemble each other may complicate the process of establishing identity for some twins whether or not they are in fact identical.

  Individuality is influenced by many factors, such as parents' attitudes, cultural attitudes and what the twinship means to the twins themselves. If parents see their twins as a unit, believing that they are supposed to do everything the same, then their twins will try to please them and will tend to develop similarities that may be so extreme as to stop them from becoming whole and individuated.

Cultural influences can be equally powerful, either endowing twins with power for their sameness or encouraging them to be more individual. In some cultures they believe that twins should be the same or are the same. This tends to encourage similarities while discouraging the search for their own personal identity.

Perhaps the most powerful influence of all is what the twinship means to the twins. If they perceive themselves as being separate and unique, then their external relationships will be very important to them. If their twinship is the primary focus in both their lives, then their identity will be more fused with each other. But if there is balance among each element—the importance of the twin relationship, outside friendships and being individuals—then they are not likely to have difficulty establishing a personal identity.

- *Twins are more likely to be homosexual.* Rates of homosexuality are no more prevalent in the twin population than in the non-twin population. If homosexuality is identified in one identical twin, there is a 25 to 50 percent chance that his twin will be homosexual. This could indicate a genetic link, but it is by no means certain. There may also be environmental factors influencing sexual identity. It is important that parents realize that if one of their twins is gay, they should not jump to the conclusion that the same is true of their other twin. The fact that twins have a close relationship does not indicate that they have a greater propensity for homosexuality.

- *Twins show more signs of psychopathology that non-twins.* Scientists have long used identical twins as subjects because they have the same genes and chromosomes, thereby offering a unique controlled opportunity to study the genetic or environmental components of human psychopathology. The fact that twins are frequently used as subjects for studies of mental and emotional illness has undoubtedly contributed to the misconception that twins represent an outsize percentage of the mentally or emotionally ill in the population. This is absolutely not so. It's important for parents to be aware that twins have normal mental health on average, but if one or both twins do need some psychological counseling, their twin relationship should always be made known to the counselor.

- *Twins are more likely to divorce than non-twins.* A 1990 study suggests that divorce rates for twins and non-twins are approximately equal. But some twins may have an unrealistic expectation that their spouse should *know what they are thinking* or *should anticipate their needs.* Sometimes, a twin is used to being so familiar with another person (their twin) that they don't feel they should have to verbalize their thoughts or desires to their spouse. Also, some spouses of twins have not anticipated the power of the twin relationship, and they under-standably feel left out when their husband or wife turns first to his or her twin with good news or bad. Communication, commitment and professional counseling, when needed, provide twins and their spouses with the same opportunity for a healthy marriage as any non-twin couple.

- *When parents experience the death of one of their twins, there is less grieving because they have a surviving twin.* That's not the case at all. Every child occupies his or her own cherished space in a parent's life and heart and can neither be forgotten because there is a surviving twin nor be replaced by the birth of a new baby. When a twin of any age dies, there is a grieving process for the lost twin that must somehow coexist with the ongoing love for the surviving twin. Friends or extended family may offer well-intentioned but misguided advice to "move on" or "be thankful that one of your twins survived." There are no shortcuts to the grieving process, and though it is difficult and confusing at times, joy and appreciation for the life of one child can coexist with pain and grieving over the death of another.

- *When one twin dies, the survivor is no longer a twin.* The death of a twin at any age is a deeply significant loss. When a twin dies, the surviving twin has lost either the person who has been very close to him, or in the case of a very young child or infant, the potential for one of life's most extraordinary relationships. A child who is born a twin is always a twin.

◺

"There is really no good twin and bad twin. Each one is good some days, and each one is bad some days."

—Chloe, 11-year-old fraternal twin

THE BALANCING ACT

BEING INDIVIDUALS TOGETHER

When asked about the goals and dreams they have for their children, parents of twins respond as would the loving parents of any child: They want their twins to be happy, independent individuals; they want them to contribute to the society in which they live; and to perform to their greatest potential. Who among us would not want this for our children?

Individuation, the developmental process by which a complete and individualized personality is formed, brings with it a sense of self and the ability to function autonomously, as well as an awareness of one's own character. In Chapter Two of this book, we talked about individuation from a developmental perspective. Our focus in this chapter is on the real life experiences of twins and the ways you can provide support and encouragement for them along the way. In this chapter's Twin Talk segments, we'll hear from twins who range in age from 5 to 21. We'll begin with the youngest twins and end with a post-adolescent perspective. It is fascinating to recognize the deepening experience of twinship that emerges as twins mature. In this first Twin Talk segment, it is clear that even at their very young age, these two children are doing the important work of establishing separate identities while remaining dear companions.

TWIN TALK

Dr. Pearlman
Bradley and Taylor, 5-year-old boy/girl twins

BRADLEY AND TAYLOR TALK ABOUT BEING TWINS

Dr. Pearlman:

I heard you have a birthday coming up.

Bradley and Taylor:

August 6th—we're going to be six years old.

Dr. Pearlman:

Congratulations. What a great celebration. Will you have one or two cakes for your birthday?

Bradley: Two. One for each of us.

Dr. Pearlman:

Do you each choose what you want on your cake?

Bradley and Taylor:

Yes.

Bradley: I like chocolate. She always wants a white cake.

Dr. Pearlman:

What else do you like that's different.

Taylor: Brad likes chocolate things, and I like vanilla things, and I like jelly beans and he doesn't.

Dr. Pearlman:

What kinds of things do you like to play with?

Bradley: I like to play with trains. Taylor doesn't.

Taylor: He doesn't like to play with my little babies.

Dr. Pearlman:

What kind of things do you like that are similar?

Bradley: Baseball and basketball. But Taylor doesn't like to play basketball really. It's too rough.

Dr. Pearlman:

I know that you used to share the same room and now you have different rooms. How did that come to be?

Taylor: We used to be in my room, and we used to have bunk beds, and we had ladders to climb up to the bed. Then my dad and grandma and my mom said, "Do you want your own bed?" And we said, "Yes." A long time ago when we were only four, we used to call it the front

Bradley   Taylor

room, and it had Play-Doh and coloring books, and there was no bed there.

Dr. Pearlman: [to Bradley] Do you ever decide to stay in the same room?

Bradley: We can stay in the same room if we want. Taylor can stay there, and I can go in there. Sometime I go in my bed and Taylor goes in my bed, and then I went in Taylor's bed and she went into her bed.

Taylor: I have two beds, and I can let him be on the top bed, 'cause I like the bottom better. He never really comes there often. He usually stays in the front room.

Dr. Pearlman: You are fraternal twins. Do you know what that means?

Taylor: We're different from each other. A girl and a boy.

Dr. Pearlman: What kinds of things do you like to do that are not together?

Bradley: First Taylor goes with Mom and I go with Dad, and then she goes with Dad and I go with Mom.

Dr. Pearlman: What do you do?

Taylor: When we go on our night out, we get to have dinner. I go with my mom or dad.

KEEPING THE BALANCE

In order to become a happy, well-adjusted adult, a child must become individuated. This poses a greater challenge to twins than it does to non-twins for two reasons:

- *In addition to separating from parents, twins must find a way to separate from each other.* Individuation does not take place at a steady rate, nor does it conform to a particular standard that looks or feels the same to all sets of twins. The push/pull of the twin relationship will be with them all their lives—needing to be apart in order to become separate and whole, and then needing to come together to refuel and share the unique experiences they had on their own. This dynamic push/pull is most conspicuous when twins are very young, between ages one and three, and again during adolescence. Ironically, separation often follows an interval of particular closeness, after which one or both twins begin to feel a need to flex their muscles of individuality.

The more individuated each twin is, the more resilient their relationship is to the twists and turns of life. The healthier their relationship, the better model it is for the always changing nature of other intimate relationships to come. Parents and twins need to be reassured that individuation need not break the twin bond. If you want to better understand this, look to an intimate relationship of your own, such as your marriage. Two "whole" people who enter a marriage, seeking to compliment each other's skills and support each other's needs, are more likely to succeed than two less mature people who enter a marriage hoping to find the mate who will "complete" them.

Twins and parents need to recognize that the process of becoming an individual and the separation it implies will be challenging for all of them. Individuality can be encouraged or discouraged in subtle ways from the time your twins are very small—your choice of names, the way you dress your young twins, whether you hand both a cookie when only one has requested it, whether they are two children or "the twins." It is important to realize that your influence, and even the influence of the extended family, is central to twins becoming individuals. Identical twins seem to face the greatest challenge in finding their individuality. Opposite sex fraternal twin sets face the least challenge in this regard, and same sex fraternal twins fall somewhere in the middle.

- *Though twins need to separate from each other, they also maintain the unique relationship of their twin bond.* Twins share a unique relationship. As we discussed earlier, they share the womb and all the growing-up stages of their development with each other. When they are young their co-twin is the first person they see in the morning and the last person they see at night. It is a unique relationship bonding them in ways no other relationship can, and it needs to be understood, respected and maintained. The quality of the twin bond varies for all twin couples. Some twins have a very close bond, others do not.

The twin bond is often stronger in identical twins than it is in fraternal twins—identical twins share the same genes and chromosomes and may have similar interests and temperaments. Like all children, identical twins are very focused on their own needs, but unlike non-twins or even fraternal twins, identical twins tend to be more aware of each other. Identical twins often establish and maintain a closer social profile. It is very important to them to establish and maintain a relationship they both enjoy. It is interesting to note that studies of identical twins usually characterize them as being quite cooperative with each other.

Fraternal twins grow up with more obvious differences distinguishing them from each other. They tend to be not as close, physically or socially, as identical twins. Studies of fraternal twins do not necessarily characterize them as being particularly cooperative, and their differences make it more likely that their parents will establish unique ways of relating to them.

When one twin seems to be drawing apart to a degree that is painful to the other, you may find it helpful to speak individually with your twins about every person's need and right to have some time alone. Twins have less opportunity for solitude than other children and may be intimidated at the prospect of private time. You might point out the positive side of having time alone to find pleasure in a quiet space.

TWIN TALK

Dr. Pearlman
Eliza and Chloe, 11-year-old fraternal twins

BEING TOGETHER—BEING ALONE

Dr. Pearlman:

When did you stop sharing a room?

Eliza: I think we were four. Chloe would bother me sometimes. I wanted a little time alone, but I still liked sharing a room. But then I asked my mom if I could have my own room and now I do.

Dr. Pearlman:

Can you tell me a little bit more about alone time. A lot of twins talk about the fact that they don't have much time alone.

Eliza: I like togetherness, 'cause it's fun. But sometimes I want to play with something and after I take it Chloe says, "I want to do that, too." It gets complicated, and sometimes I want to be alone and be by myself. We play a lot together and have a lot of togetherness still, even if we don't have the same room.

Chloe

Chloe: One time I wanted to be alone and play a game in my room, and then she just came in and she wanted to play with me, and I didn't want to play. I said it nicely, but she came in and started fighting.

Dr. Pearlman:

Do you like being apart sometimes?

Chloe: Yes. Whatever we want is okay, 'cause we just go in our rooms.

Eliza: I'll do what my sister just explained. Sometimes she'll say, "You can't play here. I'm playing." So the next day I'll do something and say, "You can't play here. I'm playing."

Dr. Pearlman:

When you're in your own room, is that your private space?

Chloe: If you want to go in, you just peek in the door and say "Hello."

Eliza

THE NAME GAME

Once you've taken the opportunity to think about a few important factors in choosing names for your twins, common sense will take you the rest of the way. Rhyming names (such as Willy and Lily), names that begin with the same first letter (such as Maureen and Michelle) or names that evoke childhood rhymes (such as Jack and Jill) are all inviting others to see your two children as halves of a whole instead of as individuals. Twins face an uphill battle to be seen separately, so don't give them names that will add to their struggle.

People tend to refer to all multiples in a collective fashion. Whether they are the same sex, and regardless of their zygosity, there is the tendency to call them *the twins* or *the triplets* or *the boys* or *the girls*. From early in their lives, the idea that these children are components of a unit may be reinforced in school, on the playground, in the extended family and, to some extent, at home. Twins relish being called by their own names.

In addition to the tendency to view twins as parts of a collective, there is also the tendency to label them—the smart one, the sweet one, the feisty one, the pretty one. An adult female identical twin described her experience growing up:

> My mother called us "Sisters." She rarely used our given names. And if she wanted to identify one of us for some reason—say, she was talking to my aunt on the telephone—she'd call us "Skinny" (that was me) or "Fat" (that was my sister). I was maybe a few ounces lighter than my sister, but those labels have stuck with us all our lives in an unconscious way. I didn't even realize it until I figured out as an adult that every time I was going to see my sister, I would diet to make sure I was going to be slimmer than she, all because I was called "Skinny."

A label—the shy one or the talkative one, or the leader or the follower—can stick with a child for a lifetime, even if it is only in their mind. Your willingness to avoid labeling your twins will be well worth the effort. It is also important to make an effort to educate the extended family about clearly identifying each twin and using their names.

Try to make it easy for others to call your twins by their correct names. The use of specific features that are always in sight on their clothing or in their hair, such as a red barrette or purple sneaker laces, is a helpful clue to teachers, grandparents and new friends. Different haircuts, as long as the twins want to try it, can also go a long way in helping your twins to establish their own identities. It is also helpful to promote individuality by not calling your twins by their two names fused together as one word. For example, a set of twins named Kathy and Rose found it disturbing that they had spent their lifetime *always* being referred to as "Kathy-Rose"—always together and always in that order. Try to be aware of these issues by using your twins' names either separately or not always in the same order. Instead of "Kathy-Rose, it's dinnertime," try "Rose, time for dinner. Let's go, Kathy."

TWIN TALK

Dr. Pearlman
Katie, 13-year-old identical twin sister of Robin
Alex and Nick, 15-year-old fraternal twins

KNOWING OUR NAMES

Katie

Dr. Pearlman:

I imagine you've had experiences with people not being able to tell you apart.

Katie: Sometimes when people can't tell you apart, they'll call you by your last name, like people call us "the Vanes" or "the Vane girls," and that's really annoying to me.

Nick: Last year on our baseball team, our coach treated us like one unit, so we could never play on the team together. It was like, "One of the twins is in, so one of the twins has to be pulled out now." Was it because they couldn't tell us apart or something? I don't get it.

Alex: It's like they don't know your name, teachers especially. Like with Nick's teachers that I don't have, one of them calls me "Hey, are you the other one?" or "Hey, you're Nick's twin" or "Hey, twin." In class they'll say, "How's your twin?"

(left to right) *Nick and Alex*

CLOTHING AND APPEARANCES

It really helps if you think ahead of time about how you are going to handle things such as names and clothing. These matters are an integral part of differentiating between your children—and helping them to differentiate between themselves. This is of particular importance to same sex twins, whether they are identical or fraternal. Even when you are pregnant (and before your baby shower), if you know you are going to give birth to same sex twins, tell friends and family that you don't intend to dress them alike. Or if you want them to wear the same outfits when they are very young, purchase them in different colors. If you dress your twins in non-matching outfits when they are young, it will be more natural for them to choose their own clothes without the constraints of worrying about what their co-twin is going to wear. The same goes for hairstyles. Encourage them to have different haircuts at an early age. If they choose to have the same cut later on, let it be their choice.

Help your twins offer clues about their own identities. Even children who wear a school uniform can carry a particular color backpack or a certain piece of jewelry that is identified only with them. Teach your twins to be relaxed and friendly when people are getting to know them. A simple reminder such as "I'm the one with the red backpack" or "I always wear this friendship bracelet" may help new friends to get over the embarrassment of not knowing which twin is which.

Creating a signature style gives your twins a sense of pride and identity. *This is who I am!* Be sure to provide each twin with their own clothes and their own place to keep those clothes. Having one's own space, in a separate location, even if it is one half of a shared room, or a separate drawer, is a helpful tool in seeing one's self as a unique and separate individual. If twins share a bedroom, give them the opportunity to customize their half of the room by choosing their own bedspreads, linens and posters for their walls.

Many parents of twins have described excruciating shopping expeditions in the company of both children. One good idea is separate shopping trips. For example, both twins may have the same budget and shop at the same time but with a different parent. They then return home to check out each other's loot. Try this when your twins are young elementary age, maybe eight or nine. It is guaranteed to generate some interesting insights into each of your twins. You may be surprised at how similar or different their choices are.

Of course, sometimes twins may want to dress alike, or have the same hair-cut regardless of your efforts to the contrary. This is common in adolescence when many kids want to dress like their peers. Naturally, one's twin is also very much one's peer. Sometimes even boy/girl twins will want to dress similarly in order to highlight their twin relationship. Remember that while this process of individuating is in full swing, there is still considerable cache to being known as a twin. Keep the lines of communication open. Be available to your twins, at any age, to discuss their feelings about their clothes and appearance.

GOING SOLO WITH A TWIN

The opportunity to be alone with each twin is a gift shared by the whole family. The twin you're with will experience your full attention. The twin you're not with may spend time alone or with friends or other family members. You have a wonderful opportunity to get to know your child as an individual. You may be surprised at the things you'll discover. One mom of boy/girl twins, who are now sophomores at different colleges, described a drive she took with her

TWIN TALK

Dr. Pearlman
Eliza and Chloe, 11-year-old fraternal twins

CLOTHES—SHOPPING AND SHARING

Dr. Pearlman:

Do you share any of your clothes?

Eliza: We used to share more, but now that we're getting older and we like different things from each other, we've been sharing less. And sometimes when we're mad at each other, we just don't want to share. Sometimes it's hard, 'cause I will get frustrated at Chloe and I'll say, "I want to have it, so you're not wearing it." But lately we've been sharing better.

Dr. Pearlman:

Chloe, how has it been for you?

Chloe: We share, but we don't share a lot of things.

Dr. Pearlman:

What does your mom say about sharing?

Chloe: She just lets us work it out, but I don't want to look alike. . . . Sometimes we used to wear the same outfits but in different colors.

Dr. Pearlman:

How old were you when you decided you did not want to dress alike?

Eliza: First grade, I think. When we were younger my mom got us the same clothes in different colors. Then she started getting different clothes in different colors. Then we both got clothes the same day when we went shopping, and we'd get the same amount of clothes, but different kinds of clothes.

Dr. Pearlman:

How do you feel about that? Do you feel your mother handled it okay or would you have liked her to do something different?

Eliza: She wanted us to share more, but you can't force someone to share.

then 15-year-old son to a sporting event. In the course of conversation he revealed to her that he had been writing a story about fictionalized twins and had been working on it for over a year. She was astonished. His sister was known as the "writer of the family," and he had not felt comfortable sharing his effort with the family. The story turned out to be more like a novella that was several chapters long. The boy allowed his mother to read his work, and she was amazed at its skill and sensitivity. She encouraged him with his writing, and he enrolled in writing workshops while still in high school and has declared a creative writing major at his college. "Who knew?" said the mom, who believes this wonderful ability might not have seen the light of day had they not had that private opportunity together.

It is never too early to establish your mindset about making individual time with your twins. Even during pregnancy, you should begin to think about your twins as individuals. Just as you plan to sensitively choose their names and clothing, you can begin the strategic planning that will enable you to have one-on-one time with each twin. In addition to the side-by-side stroller, try to make sure you have one or two light, compact strollers for impromptu solo excursions. Perhaps you go to the park as a family and then separate for an hour, with each parent taking one of the twins. This can continue as they get older and you cycle separately with each child and then come together to picnic and compare notes on your rides. The same goes for outings, whether it is to the market or out on the town. Get into the habit of each parent soloing with one of the twins. Remember to alternate which child goes with which parent in these early years, thereby providing ample opportunity for the family relationships to develop in all directions. You may also want to provide each of your twins solo opportunities with siblings and members of your extended family.

MAKING IT WORK WITH ALL YOUR CHILDREN

Being the sibling of twins is very challenging. For the singleton child who is older than her twin siblings, there is the huge adjustment of making way for the entrance of two babies into the family. It is like being dethroned—parents have less time, and all eyes are on the twins. There is suddenly a spotlight on the miracle of two new arrivals, and the older sibling often feels as though she is standing at the darkened edge of that very bright spotlight. For the child who enters the family as the younger sibling of twins, there may be the feeling that it is very hard to catch up and even more difficult to compete. She has to confront a dual presence just above her in the family hierarchy.

Many families describe their great pleasure in watching the bonds of friendship develop among all their children. Singleton siblings often take pride and pleasure in the antics of their twin sibs. Relationships for all siblings are fluid. Don't be surprised when today's archenemies are tomorrow's closest friends. Non-twin siblings will develop their own lifelong relationships with each other and the twins in the family. The following are a few pointers to keep in mind while supporting the singleton children in your family:

- If an older sibling is feeling unhappy about the attention given to her twin siblings, acknowledge her feelings and talk with her about your wonderful memories about spending time alone with her. Pull out her baby album and point out that she had you all to herself, but the twins don't have that opportunity and must share her attention.
- If a singleton feels left out of the twin bond, encourage opportunities for the singleton sibling to spend one-on-one time with each twin.
- Point out to your singleton child that if it appears her twin siblings are getting twice the attention, that they are in fact two people, each in need of as much attention as she. This is not to deny that twins get a lot of "special attention" simply for being twins, but it may help your singleton child get some perspective on the issue.
- Encourage your child to express himself. Ambivalence, jealousy or isolation are all natural feelings and need to be aired and understood by you as caring parents.

TWIN TALK

Dr. Pearlman
Jill Ganon

Alex and Nick, 15-year-old fraternal twins *Carol, mother of Alex and Nick*
Katie and Robin, 13-year-old identical twins *Gregg, father of Katie and Robin*

ALONE TIME WITH PARENTS

Dr. Pearlman:

Are there times when you would like to have more one-on-one time or attention from your parents?

Katie: No.

Robin: No.

Jill: Spoken like true teens.

Alex: Getting privacy with a parent comes naturally. Say, if you go in the car with your mother or your father you have plenty of time to talk to them, so it just sort of works out.

Nick: I think it's nice if your twin isn't there sometimes, 'cause you get more attention.

Carol: I do remember when the boys were little, we used to have a thing called a "you and me day." Maybe you don't remember, 'cause you were very small *[looking at Nick and Alex]*, but we would try to engineer times when we could have one-on-one time with each of you. Maybe it felt like it was just a normal part of family life. I remember both of them asking me for a "you and me day" when they were little: One or the other would say "Let's go shopping together"

(left to right) *Alex, Carol and Nick*

or "Let's go down to the park together." I know as a parent it's important for me to have individual time with each of the boys.

Gregg: We did the same thing in our family. It's interesting that neither of the girls seem to remember that. There was a period of time when I was doing a lot of field work, and we'd have a sort of rotating schedule so that somebody got to go with me on a field trip. Robin, you went up to the desert with me once on a field project, remember that?

Robin: It was fun. It was kind of weird, 'cause before that trip I remember if one of our parents was away they'd call and say, "I really miss you." It wasn't until I was on that trip with my dad and I got to call our family that I realized I missed them a lot. I never understood it before because I'd never experienced it. But it was still nice to be with my dad alone.

(left to right) *Deb, Katie, West, Robin and Gregg*

SUPPORTING INDIVIDUAL INTERESTS

As your children mature, you may find that they have interests that naturally align them with one or the other parent. One twin may be fascinated with the job site where the father is a construction foreman, while the other twin could care less. In this situation, it makes no sense to require the disinterested child to accompany dad to work one day, when the other clamors to go at every possible opportunity.

Your twins are not the only ones participating in a balancing act. As parents, you walk a high wire as well. Should one twin not be allowed to attend ballet class because her sister has already staked out that territory? Do you try to coerce one twin into gymnastics because his brother is loving it so much? Let things happen naturally. Allowing for and encouraging various kinds of experiences for your twins is vital to helping them become confident, unique individuals. Children try on and shed interests and hobbies with astonishing speed sometimes. Your best bet is to help them find and explore their interests without forcing them to participate together or forbidding them from doing so. As with so many other elements of parenting twins, try to remain flexible and observant.

In addition to the individual time you spend with your twins, you are their social secretary in the early years of their lives. Just in case you thought you had four minutes to put your feet up, forget about it. It is up to you to encourage and facilitate extended family, social and extracurricular opportunities for your children. For example, what if the annual trip to buy school clothes was a team event with each twin accompanied by a different grandparent or aunt or uncle. Perhaps your twins' aunt alternates taking one twin on a solo Saturday excursion each month. You might also want to educate the families of your children's friends about how you desire to manage their social lives. You can suggest your children be invited to separate sleepovers and have individual play dates. As far as your children's interests and hobbies are concerned, once again it's the old standby—observe, observe, observe. While they may get tremendous pleasure from participating in some activities together, keep your eyes open for their individual interests. And these don't have to break the bank. Maybe one twin loves to bake with you, while the other would have a great time learning, with you, how to make origami figures.

Remember that establishing a commitment to individual time, when your twins are small, sets the stage for individual communication in the more complex years of their adolescence. Many parents of grown children, looking back on their lives, have commented that, contrary to the popularly held belief that their work is done by the time their kids are adolescents, their children really needed them more in those adolescent years. It was just a far more subtle form of support.

TWIN TALK

Dr. Pearlman
Eliza and Chloe, 11-year-old fraternal twins

DIFFERENT INTERESTS

Dr. Pearlman:

What kind of things do you like to do?

Chloe: I go to art class. I like art, and she hates art. Her colors are so different. I like pink and yellow on me. I like different kinds of foods.

Eliza: I can sketch and make it look nice, but I can't make it as nice as Chloe. She has a talent for it. I like sports, I love animals, I love my friends. I do basketball, tennis, sports, and we go to camp. Chloe likes swing dancing. My mom really wants us to have what she didn't have. We can swim and play tennis.

Chloe: Next year I'll probably be doing art, and she'll be doing gymnastics. We'll both maybe do basketball. Track I may want to do.

Dr. Pearlman:

How do you decide who's going to go to what class?

Eliza: We don't really decide. I do what I want to do and she does what she likes. Sometimes Mom may not have the money to do that or it's too far away or something. Sometimes I don't want to do something that much, but I do want to do it and my mom says, "I know you want to do something different, but this time you needto do this together," and that's okay.

(left to right) *Eliza, Lauren, Chloe, Todd and Julia*

TWIN TALK

Jill Ganon
Dino and Marco, 21-year-old fraternal twins

A SHARED INTEREST IN MUSIC

Dino: I play guitar and Marco is a drummer.

Marco: Actually, we both started out playing piano and we both hated it. Then we both went to guitar and I hated it and he stuck with it. Then I got a gift certificate for some free musical instruments and started playing drums.

Jill: You're both studying music in college. Are you committed to careers in music?

Marco: Yes, I think both of us have known it for a long time. There's certain things where musically we've always just connected really well. We know all the same records, that kind of thing. It has been interesting in that once we came to college some of our musical tastes really diverged. That was great in a way because Dino's record collection has built up with one thing and my

Dino

record collection has developed another way. So as we move through musical interests, we already have this person who's studied it and the world gets bigger . . . your ears get bigger. The other thing that is nice is that we're always right at the same level. When we were growing up in high school, we won all the same awards, all the same scholarships and all the same honor bands, everything. So that was good. There wasn't any competition. When we got to college our musical directions started to diverge, so things aren't quite so clear cut anymore.

Dino: There's some professional jealousy and we manage it, but it's not like it's not there. Every time he gets a call for a gig, if it's a really good gig with somebody I wanted, I may be happy for him, but I'm still jealous. But I'm really glad we share this musical connection.

Marco

COMMUNICATING IS NOT JUST A LOT OF TALK

There are studies that suggest that twins tend to have less personal one-on-one interaction with their parents due to the obvious pressure of the parents having to deal with the needs of two children. This is one of those situations where being forewarned can help you to develop the habits that will promote one-on-one communication with your twins. We've talked about the importance of using your twins' names singularly or, if together, alternating their order. You can also work at singling them out for praise and affection, while being careful to see that they both receive their fair share.

The importance of communicating goes beyond initiating conversation with your twins, or even being available for their questions. Nonverbal communication, such as touching, hugging, smiling and eye contact, plays a vital part in helping your twins to be confident and willing to engage in their own lives. This is an area where temperament plays a leading role. What if you have one child who loves to hug and kiss and be physically close, and another child who is less comfortable with those displays of affection and prefers a more reserved style of communication. Do you kiss and hug the reserved child, because that is your style as well? Or do you hold back and figure out what kind of expressive communication makes that child feel loved, cared for and respected? Of course, you try to respond to the real needs of each child as an individual. *Equal does not mean the same*, and that is particularly true in the area of communication.

One child may be sailing through a given period of her life while her twin is a little troubled. As a parent of twins you face the formidable task of tailoring your approach to meet the needs of two different children every day. Wave good-bye to the child who is happily running off to be with friends. Tell her she looks like she's feeling great and you hope she has a wonderful time. Then turn your attention to the twin who may be floundering for the moment. She may need a little extra coaxing to share her concerns with you. Or she may need a good private cry, or she might just appreciate your company to the movies or the mall. You are treating them with equal love and care, though you are certainly not treating them the same.

All parents have expectations for their children. Often these expectations are closely related to those goals and dreams we have for ourselves. The father who found a sense of self-esteem in academic achievement is likely to expect, or at least hope, his child will strive for and attain similar personal pride. The same goes for the mother whose extroverted personality has contributed to her great career and rewarding friendships. She may project her belief that a temperament like hers is the key to success. But there is no guarantee that your twins' temperaments will mirror your own. You need to accept each of your twins for whom they are and support their innate desire to be fully realized individuals.

TWIN TALK

Jill Ganon

Dino and Marco, 21-year-old fraternal twins

ADVICE TO PARENTS

Jill: Are there pointers that you would like to share with parents about supporting a healthy twin relationship?

Dino: Yes! Really basic things like not forcing your kids to dress alike. And don't compare them to each other, 'cause it will make them hate each other and you. I know we are lucky that our parents could afford to buy us separate toys when we were kids, but even if it is just a little inexpensive thing, like a ball or some crayons, it helps for twins to have their own stuff. Our parents helped us to be separate at home, like we both had our own room. Eventually as kids get out in the world more, there is going to be a lot of pressure, so you need to help them be as confident as they can be. For us, once we were out of the whole high school thing we really began individuating more, and a lot of that is because of our parents' attitudes with us in our formative years.

Marco: I'm really grateful for our parents, 'cause I think they did everything they could possibly have done to support us as twins. If you're a twin, even if you do everything right at home, you're still going to have some kinds of problems. Like competitiveness and comparison—you can't avoid it no matter what you do in the home. Most of it is not put on you by your family. But our parents made sure that we had individual attention from them. For example, when we were in elementary school, my mom used to do a thing where every once in a while she would take each of us out of school for a day and just spend time with one of us. It was sort of her way of making sure that we both knew that she loved us. Parents should really try to take a day alone with each twin once in a while.

Dino: It is also important to be understanding when your kid does have a problem. I remember being a kid and when Marco won a prize or got some special recognition I'd get upset. My mother wouldn't act disappointed in me or make me feel worse. She'd tell me that things like this would continue to happen, and that sometimes it would be in my direction. She told us we needed to learn to be happy for each other. I also think it's tough on parents, because they have to moderate their own displays of happiness sometimes to be sensitive to the other twin.

"I think maybe the boys don't remember, but when they were toddlers, they did kind of evolve toward a sort of half English language that was very intelligible for the two of them, but harder for outsiders to understand. I think I picked up on it; I could kind of interpret some of it because I was around them so much. And their dad could do it pretty well, too. But they had this little language. They invented words, and they both knew the meaning of the words. It was some version of English that had their own mark on it."

—Carol, mother of 15-year-old fraternal boys

TWIN TALK

LANGUAGE ACQUISITION

There is some research indicating language is innate and that we are born with a capacity for it. There is also much research to support the idea that language is learned. A reasonable compromise is the premise that the human brain is wired for receptive, inner and expressive language, while the process of learning language is supported by our capacity to imitate as well as respond to the language that surrounds us. Our discussions will focus primarily on acquiring expressive language.

When a baby is born, its parents' initial communication is made up of smiles, cuddling, gestures of affection and cooing at their newborn. Parents also seem to intuitively imitate their baby's vocal sounds. There have been studies that indicate that the children of parents who used a lot of "baby talk" were faster to acquire expressive language skills. These parents may also have been particularly physically affectionate with their infants, so it is not really possible to pinpoint the reason their children were ahead of the language curve. Yet knowing as we do the overall importance of early one-on-one communication between parents and young children, environmental factors give us important clues about language development in twins. Twins usually engage in three-way (triadic) conversations instead of two-way conversations. They have less language directed toward them and less opportunity to participate verbally. The more available the mother and father are to the child, the stronger the symbiotic communication between them. Parents of newborn twins typically do not have the luxury of extended periods of one-on-one time with each baby. This may account, in part, for some of the delays in twins' language acquisition that sometimes occur.

Multiple births are at a higher risk of prematurity than singletons, and researchers have long associated low birth weight (typical of premature infants) and other complications of prematurity with developmental delay. A 1986 study compared low birth weight twins with low birth weight singletons (less that 1,500 grams) ranging from one month to four years of age. They found there were intermittent differences in hearing and speech at some ages but not at others. They also found that there were no significant language differences after the age of two and that by four years, twins measured marginally ahead of non-twins on several measures.

As in our developmental discussion in Chapter Two, we'll look at the milestones in non-twins and then examine the implications for twins. The following touchstones of language development in non-twin children from birth to two years are described in the *Pediatric Clinics of North America*. Remember, these language milestones represent the average age at which they are likely to appear for singletons.

AGE	LANGUAGE MILESTONES FOR SINGLETONS
Birth	Cries
1 month	Quiets in response to noise
3 months	Cooing sounds and other vocalizations
4 months	Produces different sounds for different needs
5 months	Babbles, "razzes"; turns to voice
6 months	Imitates sounds; makes consonant sounds; differentiates friendly and angry voices
7 months	Imitates noises; responds to name
8 months	Understands "no"; nonspecific "mama"
9 months	Recognizes familiar words
10 months	Specific "dada"
11 months	Follows gesture command
12 months	2 or 3 specific words
13 months	3 or 4 words in addition to "mama" and "dada"; looks toward named object ("Where is the ball?"); responds to name
14 months	Brings coat to indicate desire to go outside; names all family members
15 months	Jargons; follows 1-step command without gestures; 4 to 6 words; 1 or 2 body parts
16 months	Enjoys explanations of pictures in book; points to simple pictures
18 months	Follows 2-step commands; points to one picture in book; 10 words; uses "no" mostly
19 months	10 to 15 words; likes being read to
20 months	Labels actions: "up" for pick me up; questions "What's that?"
21 months	Uses word combinations; echolalia; uses pronoun "I"
22 months	Listens to stories; repeats nursery rhymes
23 months	Asks for food and drink
24 months	Associates names with familiar objects; up to 50 words; distinguishes one versus many; communicates feeling using words and gestures; verbalizes toileting needs

Between the ages of two and five non-twins grow more adept at the use of inflection. They are busily filling in the gaps they perceive between their expressive language and what they hear around them. They test their power by using "no" or "I can't" just to experience the reactions they will receive. By the time they are three or four years old their expressions may be very concrete: "I want ice cream" or "I want a ball." They're starting to assert their individuality in their language. There is also increased use of pronouns, prepositions and so on.

At five years of age they quickly seem to develop correct syntax. Then between five and seven years they will request appropriate answers to many questions, such as "why" or "how" and "what." During these years children will also start answering questions and losing some of the infantile quality in their speech. You may begin to hear expressions of very vivid imaginations as children respond to questions in a way that has no factual basis.

As they start getting older, between seven and twelve, they begin to have more cognition in that their language more or less mirrors their thoughts. The issue of cognition in children is very significant because sometimes we expect our children to respond to us at an unrealistic developmental level. The three-year-old who *promises* to go to bed after one more story and instead asks for yet another story does not have a real grasp of what a promise is. It is also useful for parents to know that children between the ages of five-and-a-half and nine-and-a-half are better able to comprehend spoken language when the speaking rate is reduced and the sentences are simple. As they are able to comprehend more, you can use more complex sentences.

Children in their early elementary years are also drawn to nonverbal forms of expressive communication. A child's movements, whether as dance or simple play, can express a great deal about the way they are feeling, just as their response to music, both creating and listening to it, can be very revealing. Children also express a lot of themselves in the pictures they draw. Many parents find that their children are willing and eager to talk about their pictures in a very personal way.

THE LANGUAGE OF TWINS

There are aspects of communication, both verbal and nonverbal, that are unique to twins and other higher order multiples. We're going to discuss some of the issues that may account for language delay in twins. Let's first consider a very positive aspect of their communication: Twins learn communication early. They experience a very meaningful give and take of vocalization and gestures and may tend to complete each other's sentences. Twins learn very quickly that language brings closeness; that there is an intimacy in language; and that the expression of ideas, thoughts, and feelings is deeply rewarding.

Also unique to twins is the revealing use of pronouns to express their innermost sense of identity. It is not unusual for a twin to use the pronoun "me" to describe the collective unit of her twin and herself, just as a twin speaking as an individual may use the term "we." While this usage may become perfectly natural to twins, it does offer family and friends a glimpse into the way twins view their own identity and the character of the twin unit.

Communication between twins has long been of interest to the general population. Whether it is their ability to finish each other's sentences or to speak in a language comprehensible only to each other, twins sometimes appear to hold the rest of us at arm's length as they share their own intimate forms of communication.

Many parents talk about their young twins having a "secret language" that seems to defy logic. In fact, this idiosyncratic language is not as mysterious as it might appear. It is more accurately defined as an "autonomous language" that develops as the twins model and mimic each other's early language acquisition. About 40 percent of twin pairs have some form of autonomous language. Experts call this secret language *cryptophasia* or *idioglossia*—an inability to articulate correctly, so the sounds and words that are emitted sound like an unknown language. In some cases, this language process is limited to several words, though in other cases it goes on to include considerable idiosyncrasies in vocabulary, grammar and syntax. Obviously, this fascinating communication between twins provides a degree of intimacy that they are likely to enjoy. To a lesser degree, close family members may come to understand and even participate in the language as well. But language development is enormously important to participation in all social settings outside the home, and your twin's idiosyncratic language may not be adaptive to the world at large.

UNDERSTANDING IDIOGLOSSIA OR "AUTONOMOUS LANGUAGE"

Most children create some words of their own when they are acquiring language. Often, these are words that are heard frequently, are important to the child and are not yet within the range of sounds that the child can vocalize. For example, to the breast-feeding toddler, nursing becomes *nuh-nuh*, a treasured blanket is a *bankie*; and breakfast pancakes may be known as *pank-panks*. Often these charming words enter the family lexicon for years or even generations to come.

Since twins are acquiring language at the same time, they will tend to share their words at a greatly enhanced rate. As they model language for each other, the words often grow more and more distorted until it sounds unintelligible to everyone but each other—thus the "secret language" or idioglossia. The initial reaction of many parents is to be somewhat awed by the mysterious, wonderful intelligence that enables their twins to develop their own complex language. They may also take comfort in the apparent closeness that this language appears to foster in their twins. One mother described listening to her twins over the baby monitor when they woke from their nap, and trying without success to decipher the conversations that sent the two toddlers into gales of laughter every afternoon as they awakened from sleep. She shared the following:

> This went on for months, and they actually grew more adept at amusing each other with conversation to the point that I would wait for over half an hour before going in to get them out of their cribs. I felt like this was some kind of affirmation of how close they were. I am an only child, and it really made me feel great to listen to them babble on to each other.

This mom was touched by her twin's happy intimacy—and understandably thrilled to have a little extra time each afternoon while her identical baby boys seemed perfectly delighted with each other's company. Yet ironically, it is just such a scenario that may inadvertently contribute to slower language development in twins.

Parents may find it useful to think of the special language between their twins as a sort of temporary symbol of intimacy that is not unlike the quiet, secret murmurings of a romantic couple. Sharing a special language is a time-honored and treasured form of intimacy. The fact that your twins may have this private, at times, endearing way of speaking with each other is fine, as long as they begin to develop the language skills that will allow them to communicate effectively with others.

TWIN TALK

Dr. Pearlman

Alex and Nick, 15-year-old fraternal twins

Katie and Robin, 13-year-old identical twins

LANGUAGE

Dr. Pearlman:

Do you think being twins has provided you with a special capacity to communicate with each other?

Katie: When I'm talking with Robin, sometimes I can leave off a whole part of the sentence and she can understand what I'm saying.

Robin: If someone in our class does something we think is really stupid, we'll look at each other and we'll understand exactly what the other is thinking.

Nick: For me, it's more like I don't have to explain the whole background of a situation. Maybe that's just 'cause we're there together. But I'm sure we can . . . like I can give him a glance and he'll know exactly what I'm saying. Or our parents say something to both of us and we can just communicate about it without saying anything.

Alex: But that secret kind of language they always talk about with twins, I don't think that I experience that.

Nick: Nor have I.

POSSIBLE LANGUAGE DELAYS

It is essential to have your twins' hearing assessed at their annual checkups, in that hearing impairment can contribute significantly to language problems. It is also very important to understand that not all twins experience language delay. But in cases where some degree of delay is apparent, both environmental and biological factors may contribute.

Studies have indicated that some parents of twins may have shorter and less focused verbal exchanges with their twins than they would with singleton children. It is not at all difficult to understand that the mother who has two wet diapers to change is not likely to linger and chat with one infant while the other cries for attention. As the infant twins mature into toddlerhood, this same busy parent does not have the time of the singleton mother to reinforce correct syntax or pronunciation. All children are responding to several language models, such as caretakers, older siblings, extended family and peers as they mature. Twins, simply by the volume of time spent together, model each other more closely and are, therefore, more likely to reinforce each other's spoken idiosyncrasies. All parents of twins should be reassured that this phenomenon is not rare and will almost always fade over time.

One common occurrence in early twin language use is dropping the ends of certain words. Many have speculated that this is a sort of shorthand language that twins develop in order to make their points quickly. Competition to be heard and to be understood can be fierce in families with multiples, particularly if there are also other children in the family. There is a well-known paper by George L. Engel, who is an identical twin. He and his twin brother were unable to say the word "other" (shortened from "other one") as toddlers and began calling each other "Oth," a habit they retained until they were well into their adult years.

It is not unusual for twins, particularly those who are deeply invested in their close relationship, to experience some language delay. In a 1987 study that documented delays in language development in twins, 30-month-old twins and singletons were administered a test that measures expressive language and verbal comprehension. The findings indicated that on comprehension, twins boys were zero to four months behind singletons, and female twins were slightly above normal. On expressive language, the twin girls were again found to be normal and the boys were two to six months behind the norms at this particular age. *On average*, delay in language skill is more prevalent in twins than in non-twins, but it is by no means an absolute and should not be automatically construed to be an indicator of a learning or intellectual delay. Among twins, identicals usually share the most intimate language bond and are at greater risk of experiencing some language delay in their vocabulary or rate of speech. The next most likely twin type to need additional support in language acquisition is fraternal boys. Parents of boy/boy twins, whether identical or fraternal, should be aware that in the general population (non-twin as well as twin) males are statistically more likely than females to experience language delay. Fraternal twins, whether boy/girl or girl/girl, are the least likely to develop a complex language between them and, as with non-twins, are at the least risk for delay in spoken language skills.

SUPPORTING LANGUAGE DEVELOPMENT IN TWINS

In order to move successfully from the home and into a larger social setting, twins need to develop the language skills that are consistent with the world around them. Exposure to modeling appropriate language and correct usage is the best way to achieve that goal. Of the many insights you will provide for your children, a calm and resourceful approach to supporting their language development is one of the most important. Let's consider some very practical ways in which you can support and encourage successful language development for your twins:

- *Seek one-on-one time with each twin to better develop and assess their language skills.* In the hectic world of raising twins, time with one child individually is not easy to find. As a suggestion, make an effort to create a regular weekly or even daily opportunity to spend at least fifteen minutes of individual time focusing on communicating individually with each of your twins. This might be while playing with the family pet or cuddling one child while the other is playing with a sibling or on an excursion with your spouse. Maybe Mom and Dad can alternate bathing one child at a time in order to have the opportunity for individual verbal exchange. This is especially important if you notice a tendency between your twins for one to answer for both of them. This one-on-one time gives the less verbal child an opportunity to establish the habit of speaking out for himself.

Language delay in twins often has implications in play and group participation, so early and appropriate intervention is important. If either or both twins express any embarrassment with their ability to communicate at any age, assure them that you take their concern seriously and that there are speech therapists who will be able to help them.

- *If you are concerned about language delay, make a discreet recording of your twin (or twins) speaking.* Whether you are consulting with your pediatrician, a speech therapist or some other professional about your concerns, you will be well served by providing a tape recording of your child's speech. A child on an initial assessment visit may be shy about speaking at all. Record your twin in his natural environment, when he is unaware that you are recording him, and offer the tape to the professional you are consulting.

- *Model correct language in your verbal exchanges with each child.* Some parents are so fascinated by their twins' idioglossia that they seek to be included in it by reiterating incorrect pronunciations or grammatical errors. Your mission should be to encourage your twins' participation in your correctly modeled language.

- *Be aware that modeling, imitation and expansion are far more effective than correction when it comes to supporting language skills.* Correction, whether it is of an individual word or a more sophisticated use of syntax, should always be made through a positive response. For example, when a toddler reaches out his arms to you and says "Mama, up," you might model syntax by saying "Mama will pick you up" as you proceed to do so. Imitation is a child's very positive participation in language. When you point and tell your children "There's Daddy's car," they may imitate in two words, saying "Daddy's car." Or you may seek to expand their rudimentary exclamation "Doggy eat" by saying "That's right. The doggy is eating." Stay alert to learning opportunities, and seek to expand each of your twins' individual language skills one step at a time.

- *Read to your twins, and encourage them to make up stories with you.* Starting with the simplest picture books and sharing stories with your twins offers them rich opportunities to develop an interest in words, which leads to enhanced vocabulary and communication skills. Reading aloud to young children leads eventually to the sharing of their skills as reader and speaker when they begin to read aloud to you. Familiarity and a comfort level with books goes a long way toward creating lifelong readers. Both the spoken and written word are important creative tools for children. Encourage your twins to participate in round-robin storytelling sessions while driving to the market or even as they take their bath. Begin with a simple "Once upon a time . . . " and have each twin take a turn in continuing the story where the last person left off.

- *Encourage each twin to speak individually, and speak individually to them.* Parenting twins is always a struggle for balance. Where language support is concerned, you may need to make a special effort to balance your need for efficiency (to say nothing of sanity) against their individual needs for communication skills. While it is certainly easy to bring the cups to the table because you assume that both kids will have milk with their sandwich, but that simple assumption may be a missed opportunity. Knowing, as we do, that verbal communication between parent and child is vitally important to successful language development, seek opportunities to speak with each of your twins, and encourage each of them to respond individually to your questions. Let's go back to the cups of milk you were going to bring to the table without any discussion. By asking each child what he or she would like to drink, you also get an opportunity to teach them to ask politely, and say "Thank you." And if, as is often the case, one child responds for both, take the time to ask the other twin to answer for herself.

- *Discourage intrusive habits, such as interrupting or shouting for attention.* In any family with more than one child, there is inevitably competition for attention from Mom and Dad. When there are twins in the family, those competitive stakes are sometimes heightened before either parent realizes what has happened. In the case where the "squeaky twin wheel" is shouting or interrupting or grabbing the spotlight in an inappropriate way, be conscientious about establishing some ground rules and be consistent about enforcing those rules.

- *Create opportunities for your twins to interact separately with other children.* You may find that separate play dates for each twin with an outside friend or two provides the greatest opportunity for strong social interaction and enhanced opportunity for language development. By providing interactive opportunities when children are young, you encourage them to improve their language skills and, thus, help them in related areas, such as reading and writing. By the time most twins are eight years old, they will have been socialized enough to shed the secret language they shared with each other. The desire to make friends is a great enticement to communicate effectively, though they may retain some remnant of their special language when they are together in private. By the time your twins are in middle school, they should have ample opportunity for socializing separately. This is particularly important in the case of boy/girl twins where the female of the twin couple may be dominant in both social and language skills. Separation in school and an opportunity to develop different social groups will encourage your twins to step out socially and become more assertive in their use of language.

- *Recognize that social problems are sometimes rooted in language delay.* Sometimes, a child who is experiencing a language delay will have, what

experts call, problems in social relatedness. This means the child has difficulty relating successfully to other children. This condition may manifest
itself in "acting out" or in being a "loner." You may sense some detachment
and a feeling that such a child is not interested in others. Children experiencing this difficulty often are uncomfortable with expressing themselves
about even the simplest desires and may tend to point to an object they
want rather than using words. If you suspect your child is experiencing this
kind of problem, consult your pediatrician for an immediate referral to the
appropriate professional, and keep your child's teacher appraised of the situation.

- *Talk with other parents about their experience with language development in
  twins.* This is yet another opportunity for outreach to the twin community.
  The insight of a parent is not a substitute for consultation with a professional, but it may go a long way in helping alleviate your worries or sense of
  isolation. As an example, many parents say they would never have
  described themselves as "joiners" until they became involved with their
  local twins club. You may find that parents with older children who have
  "been there and done that" are able to provide you with personal encouragement, useful tips or even professional referrals.

- *Involve your children's teachers in a team effort to support language skills.* As
  parents of twins, you will find yourself needing to advocate for their best
  interests throughout the many years of their education. This may mean anything from bucking the system, to being receptive to a teacher's comments,
  to interpreting your twins' reactions to their individual classroom environments. If a child has difficulty in acquiring, interpreting or understanding
  either written or spoken language, he may act out in the classroom by
  behaving inappropriately, or he may retreat in an attempt to hide in plain
  sight. An experienced teacher may see this behavior as a symptom of a language delay and be instrumental in catching the problem early on. A less
  experienced teacher may say that your child doesn't seem to pay attention

or tends to daydream. If you hear comments like that from your child's teacher, you may be looking at a language processing difficulty that needs attention. If there is a problem, your child and your child's teacher will benefit from the resources of a language professional or learning specialist as well as the insight and encouragement you offer as a parent. Remember, this is a team effort.

- *Consider individual differences.* Although it is important to look at each child as an individual, it can be difficult to resist comparisons, particularly with language. This is another opportunity to test your mettle and resist the temptation. Remember, each twin develops at his own rate, particularly fraternal twins. Try not to label—he is the "quiet one," this is our "chatterbox" and so on. If there is a noticeable difference, however, particularly in identical twins, who usually develop along similar time frames, you may want to contact a professional for an evaluation,

- *Support your twins' efforts to be who they want to be.* Ours is a culture that tends to define "successful people" as those who speak well and are outgoing, social and interested in being out ahead of the pack. Clearly, not every well-balanced, contributing member of our society fits that profile. Try to support each of your twins in their own effort to become the person they are inclined to be. There are many shy and somewhat reserved children who grow up to be healthy, happy, well-balanced adults. While all children should be encouraged to express themselves and given every opportunity to maximize their expressive language skills, not every twin is temperamentally designed to be on the debate team. By knowing who your twins are, both individually and collectively, and responding to them positively, you will be able to telegraph your support of them individually.

Chapter 7

"It's weird being a twin, but it's fun."

—Eliza, 11-year-old fraternal twin

TWINS INTERACTING

LEARNING TO SHARE

Sometimes there is an unfounded expectation on the part of parents, grandparents, teachers or the world at large that sharing comes naturally to twins. The fact that twins spend approximately nine months sharing the same womb within the same mother and are born at almost the same time does not in any way predispose them to being "good sharers." They are no better equipped than a singleton child to share their mother, a favorite toy or a friend until they have taken the appropriate developmental steps. Your twin babies may take great comfort in each other's reassuring presence in a crib: They may seem to conform to each other's body language in ways that appear almost magical. But sharing, like language or feeding oneself or skipping rope, is a skill to be learned.

Many singleton parents have had the experience of watching their eighteen-month-old baby as he jealously guards against losing his mother's complete attention and affection, even protesting vocally or pushing Daddy away when he tries to give Mommy a kiss or hug. In the case of twins, by the time they reach eighteen months and Daddy swoops in for a kiss, they have already had plenty of practice at sharing Mommy's attention with each other, so sharing with Dad may come more readily.

Twins are more likely to begin sharing earlier and with greater consistency than their singleton playmates. But what are the developmental steps that help prepare your twin to share? First, before they are able to share with each other or anyone else, each twin must develop a sense of self. In early infancy, the first flickerings of identity occur as a baby identifies with his mother—viewing "mommy-baby" as a sort of merged identity that meets his needs for nourishment, love and warmth. After the baby emerges from the oneness with Mommy, he begins to experience his separateness—from his mother, his twin and others. As the baby moves toward toddlerhood, one of the first expressions of the concept of *self* is the vocal or physical demonstration of "mine." This sense of ownership of something external is a very important step toward "owning" oneself. The unmistakable pride on the face of a toddler who waddles toward you, stuffed animal in hand, saying "mine . . . mine" is the beginning of the same pride you'll see in the faces of your twins who are participating in sports or succeeding in their schoolwork or forming meaningful friendships.

Once your twins have that sense of what is *mine*, they are able to go on and progress to what is *yours* and finally to what is *ours*. By providing your very young twins with their own individual toys or stuffed animals, you are helping them to see themselves as individuals. This will, in turn, enable them to respect each other's ownership, which will finally lead to the ability to share what is jointly theirs—from the attention of their parents, to the rope swing in the yard, to the TV remote control.

Sharing is a long-term learning process: learning to interact with each other, learning to challenge each other and learning to cooperate with each other. Parents of twins need to help them learn about different ways of spending time: Now we are having time with you; now it is your twin's time; now we are together as a family; now it is time for Mommy and Daddy to have their own time. This teaching and learning extends to toys, friends, clothing and so on. It will help your twins establish respect for self, others and family.

It is important to recognize that your twins' early exposure to sharing is ultimately going to work in their favor out in the world. It will be very helpful to the twins, and to the whole family, if steps are taken early on to provide appropriate opportunities for each twin to have individual time with each parent, as well as toys, clothing and eventually skills and interests that can be individually "owned." There is a lifetime of negotiating associated with being a twin. *Listen to your children when they talk to you and when they talk to one another.* As a parent, you may find that some of the best parenting you do will involve quietly observing as your twins negotiate and renegotiate their relationship with each other. The following pointers have proven very effective:

- *Be realistic.* Sharing takes time. Twins aren't born knowing how to share. This is a process to be learned over and over in different age-appropriate scenarios. Be ready for the process of learning to share to take two steps forward and one step back for many years and under many different circumstances. Not all twins are the same. Some twins are more equally matched in such areas as being more cooperative, having similar or compatible temperaments and being more comfortable sharing with each other. Other twins are not as compatible or equally matched; they may have different temperaments and ways of expressing themselves and may have difficulty sharing.
- *Provide consistency.* As your twins grow up and you establish rules about sharing, be sure that those rules are enforced lovingly and consistently by mother, father and other caregivers as well. Remember that rules need to

be age-appropriate: Your five-year-olds cannot be expected to wait 30 minutes for a turn at anything. A kitchen timer set for five minutes may even provide its own bit of fun when it comes to trading off with a favored toy.

- *Be creative.* Try to offer other creative options to the twin who is waiting for the chance to share a toy or hear a story or lick the icing spoon. Give your young twins concrete opportunities to learn to share. Perhaps they can help you slice and serve a pie, while you praise their success at working so well together. Sitting around and waiting for a chance to have fun can turn into a recipe for obsessing on how horribly long a minute can be. Have alternatives ready in the wings. If a seat on your lap is the coveted treasure for a story, offer the waiting twin the chance to color or choose the next book or have a story with Daddy instead of counting the endless moments till it is "my turn!"

- *Keep your sense of humor intact, or at least within reach.* Try to use a very light touch when it comes to encouraging sharing. When one or both twins backslide, try a gentle, humorous response. Remember that particularly with very young twins, much of sharing centers on their need to share *you*, and a stern admonition will be deeply heartfelt. *And that goes for yourself as well!* Don't beat yourself up if you run out of patience from time to time—who wouldn't? All the parenting tips in the world just aren't going to cut it for you on some days. One mother of twins at her wits' end once defused an escalating battle over the sharing of a toy by *giving herself a time out* to the vast amusement of her seven-year-old daughters. Try to reward all positive steps toward sharing, and reassure your twins that you know how much effort it takes. With preschool-age twins, a funny story about how you struggled to learn how to share a favorite toy when you were a child may be fun and helpful.

TWIN TALK

Jill Ganon

Carol, mother of Alex and Nick, 15-year-old fraternal twins

Mary, mother of Chris and Andy, 7-year-old identical twins

Kathy, mother of Brian and Nathan, 6-year-old fraternal twins

MOMS TALK ABOUT SHARING

Jill: You've talked about your twins being pretty good at sharing. How do you account for that?

Mary: I think the reason why they share so well is because when I was nursing them I let one cry. The advice I got was to take care of one fully, and then the other child will know that when it's their turn they will be taken care of fully. I can remember when they were eight months old and I was nursing them, one would be crying, crying, crying, and I'd just keep taking care of the other. I'd let him nurse till he was full, change him, put him down and then handle the crying baby. Eventually, it reached the point where as soon as I put one twin down, the other one would come up to me, ready for their turn. I never buy two of the same things. I think it's foolish to buy two of the same toys. You can buy different toys and then they have more toys to share.

Carol: We did things a little differently. When the boys were little, when it came to small things, we would always give them each their own because we wanted them to have their own stuff. We didn't always want them to feel they were growing up in a communal room, sharing space and sharing clothes. As they got a little older, we told them we were going to give them different things. They'd have more stuff. I mean it was appealing to a three- or four-year-old. It was like they could have more toys, 'cause they didn't necessarily want the exact same things anymore. Over time, we've found the computer is something we haven't felt the need to duplicate.

They've always been very gracious about their time on the computer. It's, "I think I need to have a turn now." They have developed a style between them that I don't think I even influenced or had any part of. Maybe when they were very little it was *your thirty minutes or my thirty minutes.* Whatever they've worked out between them seems to have evolved naturally. If Alex has homework on the computer, he has learned to speak up and say, "I still have some English and I need the computer. Can you wait till I'm done?" They're both pretty gracious taking their turn. But they each have their own bike, their own tennis rackets, things like that.

Mary: I think twins know how to share better than singletons.

Kathy: When we started out, my husband was adamant: We're not going to buy two of everything, 'cause it is wasteful. But it very quickly became obvious we had to have two or there was going to be fighting all the time. Now that my boys are five, they're beginning to express I want Monopoly, or whatever the game might be. My sister-in-law took them to the store for their birthday and they wanted completely different things.

BITING

Biting may begin and end in the early toddler period, or it may continue to occur even in the preschool years. Biting often occurs accidentally, the first time. There are several common underlying reasons one or both of your twins might bite:

- teething
- frustration
- anger
- fatigue
- hunger
- overstimulation
- need for attention

A teething child may place his twin's arm or foot in his mouth and bite. When you think of the proximity in which these very young twins live, sometimes nestled together sleeping or napping, it is not hard to envision one twin grabbing a nearby body part and biting by accident, without any emotional objective and certainly with no intention of causing pain to her twin. One suggestion on how to "attack" this situation is to give your teething twins something to bite, such as a teething cookie or a cold wet teething cloth. Even though they are still preverbal, you can tell them in a nice tone of voice not to bite each other but to bite the teething toy instead.

Although biting can be inadvertent, it can also be an act of frustration or anger in the preverbal child. For example, one twin wants the other's toy but is not able to take it away or charm her twin into sharing it, and so she bites. The tired or hungry toddler may also act out by biting his twin. Any toddler may bite a parent or twin either out of frustration or in an attempt to establish separation—*I am biting you.* This can happen with twins as they go through the process of becoming individuals and separating from each other.

Knowing that biting incidents are likely to occur may help you avoid overreacting. The twin doing the biting, especially the first time, will have no understanding of the fuss that may erupt as a result of his actions. If you overreact with outsize anger or frustration, it will only serve to compound everyone's frayed nerves. Remain calm, comfort the one bitten, and don't be surprised when the child who has done the biting also begins to cry and is in need of support and consolation.

A surprising number of parents think the most effective response is to bite the biter so that he will "know how it feels." This is never a good idea. A child at this age simply does not have the cognitive skills to understand the cause and effect of such a misguided exercise. Instead he learns that the appropriate response to anger is to bite. You need to model appropriate behavior by encouraging your twins to use their words to express themselves. (It is also not a good idea to suggest that the bitee bite back.)

When any biting event occurs, address both twins. Sympathize with the child who has been bitten: "I know that it must have hurt you, and I'm sorry it did." You also need to talk to the child who did the biting: "I know you are upset, but biting hurts a lot and that's why we don't do it." In trying to get to the bottom of things, you may find that the child who bit her twin was provoked in some way.

Biting is often the result of hunger or exhaustion or just plain crankiness. Once again, observation is key. If you notice that biting is more likely to occur at a particular time, such as before dinner or just after bathtime, anticipate the problem. It may be time for a few quick words on the importance of sharing and then off for a snack or a nap or a change of scene. Try at this point to allow for some physical distance between the two children. That could mean putting them in two separate highchairs in the kitchen or sitting between them on the couch as you read a story. You might even tell them in a clear upbeat way that it is time to be separate until they are ready to be kind and enjoy each other again.

Sometimes, the child who is bitten is not hurt and does not make a fuss. If this is the case, don't exacerbate the situation by drawing attention to it. Let it go by; it may simply resolve itself. Talk to both twins about using words to express themselves. Even when their language skills are limited, you can try to give them verbal options to use instead of biting. If they are too young to say "Don't take my toy!" they may be able to state an emphatic "NO!"

If your child is biting in preschool, you and the teacher need to continue to model proper behavior. If a biting incident is severe, a little time out may be helpful. If a preschool-age twin is biting, she is likely to be conditioned out of it by peers in the classroom who will not tolerate being bitten. Biting can be a very frustrating problem, and sometimes it feels like it's going on forever. But the more language your twins acquire, the less problematic biting becomes until it does indeed go away.

FIGHTING AND ARGUING

All siblings fight, and all parents say it drives them a little crazy. Fighting (like biting) between twins is often a manifestation of the long individuation and separation process: this toy is *mine* or *I'm* stronger than *you*. Also, as is the case with biting, children fight out of frustration, anger, fatigue or hunger. Children also fight to relieve boredom. Picking a fight may not be the wisest decision, but it is never boring. Fighting is a natural outgrowth of sibling rivalry, which allows twins to maneuver for position and grapple with the always shifting balance in their relationship.

Twins can fight over everything and nothing. Fights can simmer and erupt over significant, deeply felt issues or they can be silly and insubstantive: who sits in the front seat, who gets the remote control, who takes the first bath or, for that matter, who gets to bathe last.

Many times, twins fight because fighting is fun, or at least it starts out that way. Parents of twins sometimes think that if their children fight, they will not be close. They see themselves as the facilitators of their twins' loving relationship and equate fighting between their twins with their own failure as parents. That is not the case. In fact, most fighting is not a barometer of whether twins are or will be close. Fighting is part of the way all children gain insight into what makes people tick—what happens if I say this or how far can I go before he gets really mad. Fighting is a normal part of learning how to negotiate in life. Ironically, it can actually make twins closer.

Twins are going to fight and argue. Parents can use this fact of life to help teach kids to negotiate, mediate and problem-solve. Boys in particular may need an opportunity to act out physically without anger. The simple release of energy that occurs in wrestling or roughhousing often takes place without the emotional intent of anger. If someone gets hurt, it is often accidental. Many parents have had the experience of trying to break up a "fight" between their twins, only to have the twins turn the tables on them and protest that they were handling it fine until their parents stepped in: "Just let us do this ourselves."

Of course, if fighting escalates to the point where someone is about to get hurt, you must step in immediately. The tough part is knowing how far is too far, which is a line that parents learn to recognize by knowing their own children. When you do intervene, don't try to compete with their escalating voice levels. The louder they get, the quieter and more in control of your voice and emotions you need to be. Separate the twins by placing yourself between them, and have everyone sit down at a table or on the floor. Children need to learn that feelings of anger, frustration or even aggression are parts of the human experience. Yet it is possible to work through these feelings without hurting yourself or anyone else. Pounding a pillow or punching a pop-up inflatable toy are acceptable outlets for the very human emotions that we all experience.

There are many things parents can do to place appropriate limits on their twins' fighting. As with many of the skills associated with good parenting, you need to step back and take a look at the big picture. When do your twins tend to start mixing it up with each other?

- Are they tired, hungry or frustrated?
- Are they struggling with their lack of language skills?
- Are they bored?
- Is there frequent fighting over a certain toy?
- Do they seem to be trying to connect with each other?
- Are they attempting to create distance between each other?
- Are they simply having a good time?
- Do they tend to fight before or after playing with a particular friend?
- Is there an underlying feud or misunderstanding?
- Are one or both twins especially vulnerable or cranky due to something going on at school, in sports or with peers?

For young twins, distraction is a very useful tool. A nap, a snack or a brief separation is often the answer. For twins of any age, some time apart often provides just the right cooling-off period, after which they may come together comfortably. An adult identical male twin described the mechanism he and his brother employed to signal peace.

From the time we were nine or ten and had been separated by our mother for getting into it either physically or just having a nasty argument, one or the other of us would ask some neutral question that would tell the other the fight was over. I'd ask him for a pencil or he'd ask me what time it was.

While it is unrealistic to imagine your twins will not fight, it is perfectly realistic for you to state categorically that certain kinds of fighting are off-limits in your home. This goes for both verbal and physical disputes. In order to do this effectively, it is vital for both parents to take a long hard look at the kind of behavior they themselves are modeling during their own disagreements. Physical violence between parents should always be completely out of the question. What is more discreet, yet can be equally disturbing, is verbal battering of any kind. You will never be effective in keeping name-calling or foul language out of your children's arguments and fights if you, as a couple, curse a blue streak or name-call in front of them. Parents who bicker constantly can expect to see that sort of pettiness appear in their children's exchanges. Pettiness is an unpleasant and ineffective mechanism for dealing with life's problems. It is very tough on all members of the family. You can teach your twins that there is such a thing as a fair verbal disagreement. In a fair fight, you do not name-call, insult or disparage each other; you use your powers of critical thinking to put forward your position. You exercise your mind and make use of your verbal agility.

Once you have agreed upon the behavior you intend to model for your children's disagreements, and have a sense of those conditions that seem to trigger fights between your twins, it is important for both parents to agree on limits to fighting and establish and *enforce them consistently.* Consistency is a real challenge when you are a parent of twins, because there is so much going on. You are going to slip up—every umpire makes a bad call from time to time—but if you are clear in your intention, you'll be rewarded with twins who learn to play and fight by the rules you establish as a family. The following are parameters that several twin families have established and found successful:

- No foul language or name-calling.
- No hitting in the face.
- No kicking.
- No throwing or striking with toys or other objects.
- Disengage physically when either uses a previously agreed-upon cue word, such as *STOP*.
- Establish a time limit.

Get your twins involved in problem-solving. When they are very young, start having weekly family meetings or even an end-of-the-day roundup to air grievances. Make sure that everyone listens to everyone else. It is helpful to have your twins repeat what they hear in order to make sure there are no misunderstandings. Help them to see the value in talking about their own feelings instead of hurling accusations. Also, never underestimate the power of humor. There is nothing like a groaningly bad joke from Mom or Dad to unite twins in commiseration.

When your twins are very young, you can help them to clarify their feelings by asking them to point at pictures of faces registering unmistakable emotions: a happy face, an angry face, a sad face and so on. Some parents use very simple line drawings of faces, while others cut clearly expressive pictures of faces out of magazines and use them to help clarify and problem-solve.

Think of yourself as the facilitator and encourage your twins to solve their own problems. They should be doing plenty of the talking and listening. You'll be amazed at how innovative they can be. The more involved they are in creating their own resolutions, the more invested they'll be in honoring them. Once you have established rules, write them down and keep them on display in the twins' bedroom(s) or on the refrigerator.

When you do lay down the law, make sure it can be effectively and evenly applied. Enact rules that will encourage teamwork: If there is continued arguing over computer time, the computer will remain off-limits until they can both enjoy it. Give a warning and then enact your consequence. Make sure your consequences are age-appropriate—a five-minute separation for five-year-olds, a day without their basketball for third graders.

Many times twins are not evenly matched physically or temperamentally. If your twins are not fairly matched as opponents, be careful not to make a habit of stepping in to protect one or the other. Such patronage from you is likely to encourage a victim mentality and cause a child to expect others to protect him. Certainly you need to be firm about not allowing inappropriate behavior. Help both your twins see that they have the power to walk away from a conflict if they choose to do so. Make it clear to the child who is on the losing side of the battle that he has the power to play or not to play. Remind him that he has plenty of other ways to enjoy himself, which don't require the presence of a twin who is trying to pick a fight.

TWIN TALK

Dr. Pearlman

Amaro and Hermes, 11-year-old fraternal twins

Diana, mother of Amaro and Hermes

FIGHTING

Dr. Pearlman:
Do you do much fighting?

Amaro: Yes, plenty. It's blood lust. We don't talk when we fight.

Dr. Pearlman:
I can understand that. My husband and his brother are twins and they had rules that they couldn't hit each other in the face.

Amaro: Oh no, that's the main target.

Dr. Pearlman:
How do your arguments usually end?

Hermes: Usually in the end one of us is so hurt that the last one who can stand up wins.

Dr. Pearlman:
Do your arguments go on for a long period of time?

Amaro: Oh yeah, it takes about an hour.

Hermes: Amaro is very protective of his strength. He thinks he's the strongest man who ever lived.

Amaro: Stronger than you.

Hermes: I don't know. I can beat him up. I'm quicker than he is.

Dr. Pearlman:
Does either of you lose more that the other?

Hermes: Amaro is stronger than I am.

Dr. Pearlman:
Do you fight more or less, now that you are growing up?

Hermes: Quite a lot less. We're fighting a little less. When we were nine years old we were fighting more. He kicked a hole in the wall with his bare foot.

(left to right) *Amaro and Hermes*

Dr. Pearlman:
Why do you think you're fighting less now?
Amaro: We're more mature.
Diana: When it gets really rough and they are having trouble processing the relationship, my husband and I will have one in one room and one in the other and talk to them about the incident until they reach some kind of understanding. If we have to do that once a month it's a lot. They are very physical but not violently physical. They wrestle a lot. And that's very hard for me, 'cause I wasn't raised around boys. I always think they will kill each other, but they don't. I think I can tell when it escalates to the point where somebody may get hurt, and I try to intervene before they reach that point. There are times when they need an adult to moderate. That's when I come in. But they never seriously hurt each other. You know the age when they bite? One was a biter, and that was a real problem. He got over that stage.

CONSTANT COMPARISONS

Comparison is an inevitability in the lives of identical and fraternal twins. All twins will experience it and are likely to continue to discuss it throughout their lives. They will be compared by others and will sometimes get caught up in the process of comparing themselves to each other. Comparing twins begins with the most honorable intentions: In order for parents to begin to bond with their newborn, they need to discover who their baby is. When twins are born, parents understandably look for opportunities to notice ways in which each baby is unique:

"She just loves to nurse."
"He cries the moment he wakes up."
"She settles down if I rub her back."

But as newborns mature through infancy, toddlerhood and beyond, comparison needs to be balanced with your growing ability and commitment to seeing each child as an individual. As the parent of twins, you can arm yourself with the knowledge that comparison is always going to be a part of their lives and take the necessary proactive steps to avoid saddling them with labels. The truth is, the dynamic changes in your twins as individuals, as well as their relationship with each other, will defy labeling. Today's shy twin may be tomorrow's standup comedian. Each of your twins has his own developmental schedule and will change physically, as well as emotionally, at his own pace. Remember to recognize and celebrate your twins for the qualities they possess, at the time they possess them. Labeling can result in a self-fulfilling prophecy that may only serve to impede the unique and fluid relationship your twins have with each other, the family and out in the world.

As a parent of twins you may be subjected to insensitive questions from acquaintances, coworkers or even extended family who want to know which twin is brighter; more outgoing; the better eater; even-tempered. This begins innocently enough with admiring onlookers at the market or in the park. For some parents, their early expeditions to the mall or even to a large family gathering are exciting opportunities for socialization. At first, some may dress their infants alike and welcome comments or questions from onlookers and family. Other parents are uncomfortable with the attention. Often, parents feel some combination of those two reactions. Most parents are averse to the comparison of their twins. Remember that even before your children are verbal, you can begin to model ways for them to respond to unwelcome comparisons. For those times when you are in a rush or you want to deflect attention or comparisons, many parents have found the following strategies useful:

- *Don't dress your children alike on a quick trip to the mall.* You may enjoy having your twins in the same outfits from time to time, but twin sailor suits are an invitation to comment and compare. Dress them differently, and if they are babies, put one in a stroller and one in a chest or back carrier.
- *If possible, leave one or both twins home on shopping trips or errands.* If you only have one child with you, there is no opportunity to invite comparison. If mom and dad have both kids at the market, divide the shopping list, each take one cart and one twin and meet back at the car.
- *Leave 'em laughing.* Humor can be very effective when it comes to deflecting unwelcome questions. In response to a question about which of her preschoolers was smarter, one mom responded, "Actually, I think I still am, but only just barely." Don't expect the one-liners to pop out spontaneously

when you need them. Do you think a great comedian's material is off the cuff? When you're lying in bed at night trying to figure out why you can't sleep because you're so exhausted, try to come up with a line that will at least leave you and your twins laughing.

People are understandably fascinated by twins and often ask well-meaning but uneducated questions. It is not at all unusual for parents of boy/girl twins to be asked if they are identical. When asked which twin has the *better* temperament, you might try rephrasing the question: "Do you mean what are their personalities like?" Many people will get the message. (Of course some won't, but that's just the way it goes.) You might also go on to say that they seem to change all the time and that you really can't label them. Parents can model this "non-comparison" kind of questioning for everyone from the person behind them in the checkout line, to grandparents, to teachers who may not yet be experienced with twins. If you have the time and you're in the mood, you can help educate the public about how to appreciate twins for their similarities as well as their differences, without drawing damaging comparisons in the process. There is a world of difference between looking at twins as some sort of unusual laboratory specimens and engaging you and them in conversation about their unique experience in the world.

When it comes to the twins themselves, there is no doubt that many of them establish a sort of comparison shorthand, identifying themselves and each other as the smart one or the athlete or the shy one or the stupid one. This kind of comparison usually begins with simple curiosity that is spurred on by the buzz of attention that has surrounded them since birth. It may begin with "Who is older?" and go on to:

"Who is taller?"
"Who is prettier?"
"Who is smarter?"

Remember that comparison follows twins through all stages and all ages. An adult twin shared with us that she and her identical twin even got so far as to compare who had the most freckles when they were kids. In retrospect she was struck by the fact that it was not until the comparison was made that it even occurred to her to ask her mother if having freckles was good or bad.

While self-scrutiny is a part of every person's development, constant comparison that comes from the outside world is not within your twins' control. Identical twins look similar and therefore present a challenge to others to find and announce their differences. For fraternal twins, particularly when they are the same sex, the object may be to point out ways in which they are alike. Fraternal twins are often put on the hot seat by peers who want proof of their twinship. Classmates may tell fraternals that they are not twins because they don't even look alike.

Comparison can also be a double-edged sword: The twin who is an academic achiever has pride and happiness in her accomplishment, but she often experiences pain or even guilt when her twin suffers by comparison. It can even go so far as to have one twin sabotage her own performance so as not to cause her twin pain or shame. Just as you need to develop coping strategies for handling the ways in which people compare your twins, your twins can explore the following methods for handling scrutiny or comparison:

- *Ignore the question.* Your elementary-age twins may discover that sometimes the best response to an annoying question is simply not to respond. Tell your children it is okay for them not to rise to the bait. When a classmate asks your third-grade twin if she is "the favorite twin," you might suggest that she simply say "I don't know. Let's just finish the game." If there is no enticement to continue, eventually these questions tend to fall away.

- *Tell them what it's like.* Often, friends are genuinely curious but may ask an embarrassing question or make a foolish comparison. They don't know any more about being a twin than your twins know about being a singleton. Help your twins to see the value in giving their friends a break. You might suggest that they let their friends in on the joys and hardships of being a twin. Talk to your children and help them to see that a question or comparison that hurt their feelings may have been asked quite innocently. Many parents tell their twins to be forgiving unless it is absolutely clear that someone was out to bug them.

- *Give them an attitude.* If your twins tried telling others how they felt and also tried ignoring them and those people still continue to pursue comparisons, then sometimes a slightly snotty answer will ward off inquiring minds. Unfortunately some children may want to make a target of your twins. If giving an intrusive classmate the brush off works, so be it. No adolescent wants to look foolish in front of his peers, and playground politics have a way of working out in the end. Today's pain in the neck may become tomorrow's good friend.

TWIN TALK

Dr. Pearlman

Jill Ganon

Nick, 15-year-old fraternal twin brother of Alex

Robin and Katie, 13-year-old identical twins

DO YOU COMPARE YOURSELF TO YOUR TWIN?

Dr. Pearlman:

Being a twin myself, one of the things I'm very aware of is comparison. Do you measure yourself against your twin? You know, "I'm better than him" or "She does this better than me."

Nick: For me at least, I don't have to compare myself. If I did something really well, I'm glad. Having to compete with somebody, whether it's a twin or anybody, doesn't really help me to do well. That doesn't make the win or whatever is good even better. I just feel like I did a great job and I'm happy as can be that I did a really good job.

Robin: I'm kind of pessimistic, so usually I do compare myself to others. I'm always thinking I'm worse than someone else, so that's kind of a bad aspect of being a twin, 'cause she's the closest person to me and I'm always comparing myself to her. She's my sister, and she's only two minutes younger than me, stuff like that.

Jill: What do you mean by pessimistic?

Robin: If we were to draw the same picture or

something, I would probably look at hers and at mine and then say hers was better, even if mine was actually better than hers. I guess I'm not pessimistic about every-thing—more just myself.

Katie: Most of the time I tell her she shouldn't think that way about herself, but a lot of the time she won't believe me. I never really compare myself, though. I mean I do, but most of the time I won't say it out loud.

Jill: I think some people tend to be kind of tough on themselves, regardless of whether or not they are twins. You've probably heard the expression describing a person as *his or her own harshest critic*. [to Robin] Maybe that is why you prefer to be in a separate class from your sister.

Robin: Yes, it's kind of like that, and kind of 'cause you get recognition for being your-self, not just being a twin. And also you make better friends. It's nice not to have Katie around sometimes. It's a whole dif-ferent experience. I've lived all my life with her, and yet to be without her is something really different and I enjoy doing that.

"Twins are not going to be alike always, but expect them to be like normal twins. And it's going to be a handful."

—Eliza, 11-year-old fraternal twin

GETTING DOWN TO BUSINESS

SAFETY

It is not unreasonable to start thinking about twin-proofing your home before your babies are born. Making your home safe for your twins is an ongoing process that you'll revisit several times as they grow and become increasingly mobile. The first and most vital element of home safety is adult supervision. No matter how many cabinet locks and molded table edges and childproof caps you have in your home, none of them are a substitute for the watchful eye of a responsible caregiver.

As silly as it may sound, one of the best methods of determining how to best twin-proof your home is to get down on your hands and knees and crawl around the house for an infant's or toddler's eye view. Where are the lethal corners of tables or chairs? What looks enticing to pull down on your head? How about the plant food in the container on the floor? You get the idea. Both parents should do this, as one may spot something the other has missed. A visit from a child who is six months older than your twins will also be an eye opener. Talk to other parents about their recommendations and see if they apply to your home.

Twin-proofing is really a more accurate term than the more generic *childproofing* because with twins you have two children at the same cognitive level. They will learn from each other and inspire each other to greater and greater heights of mischief. They can help each other crawl up on dressers or counters. They may use each other to reach further than you would ever imagine possible. Make sure that every piece of furniture is sturdy and well balanced. If necessary, bolt dressers, cabinets, and such to a wall so that they cannot topple over on your zealous little explorers.

Windows and doors must be latched securely. A window open even a little can be pried open further or fall shut on little fingers. Water, such as in bathtubs, wading pools, swimming pools or even a decorative koi pond, poses a safety hazard. While you are likely to be very aware of toxins that might be unsafe for your children, family friends or relatives may not be as savvy. Make sure that any gifts your twins receive, such as crayons, markers or toys are nontoxic and age-appropriate. Pay strict attention to toys with small parts, as they may pose a choking hazard. All medicines and cleaning supplies must be out of reach and behind safety-latched doors.

Every parent should know CPR, as should every caregiver to whom you entrust your twins, even if for a few hours of care. Contact your local Paramedic Center (find the number in the phone book; do not use 911 for a nonemergency question) and find out if they have the appropriate lifesaving equipment for handling an emergency involving two children of the same age. Tell all caregivers to call 911 during an emergency and to clearly state the number of children involved as well as their age or ages. Be sure caregivers have the telephone numbers where you can be reached. Keep a medical emergency kit in an accessible spot, and be sure that all caregivers know where it is. It is also wise to leave a signed *Consent to Treat*

Minors form with caregivers in your home, or with any parent who is supervising your child on a group excursion, such as a birthday party at an amusement park.

Every family needs to have a plan for the safe evacuation of the house or apartment in case of fire. Your local fire department can help you develop a plan, and you can learn how to do family fire drills in order to practice for the real thing. Earthquake, hurricane or flood precautions should be understood by the whole family as needed. If there are emergency supply kits, which include water, food, clothes, tools, blankets, pet food and first aid supplies, every member of the family, as well as caretakers, should know where they are located.

As children get older, safety measures may evolve, but they do not disappear. Your twins will need helmets if they are going to use bikes, skateboards or roller skates. They need to learn about crossing streets and obeying traffic laws. If you, as parents, respect the laws, you will be role models for your children. Remember, parents are the best role models children have, although twins will also learn to model their twin. Therein, lies your challenge.

TOILET HABITS

A young mother of boy/girl twins was despairing over whether they would ever be toilet trained. One night she was speaking on the telephone with her grandmother who raised four children of her own. After describing the day's trials of multiple "accidents" including tears and general toilet-training woes, her grandmother consoled her and said she had the perfect answer to all these troubles: "Give them back their diapers. They're not ready to be toilet trained. They'll let you know when they're ready, and it won't be such a struggle."

This story illustrates the importance of examining your own attitudes about toilet training. In telling this tale, the mother of twins acknowledged that it was *she* who was ready to get her twins out of diapers and had unquestionably pushed them into a situation that they were not prepared to handle. Some parents believe training should *begin* as early as a year. Other opinions range from 18 months up to three-and-a-half years. First time parents are easily influenced by family members, other parents and the "perceived" or "real" rules regarding toilet training at their preschool or day care center. Parents who have already raised a child may be guided by that child's readiness, instead of looking at the actual readiness of each of their children. The lure of life without diapers may entice parents to push for toilet training before their children are ready.

So when is a child ready to begin toilet training? By the time a child is 14 to 18 months old they may be prepared to *start* the process. In the beginning, you will be teaching them the vocabulary they will need to understand and make themselves understood. Every family has its own vocabulary that may include words such as *poop, pee, clean, dry, wipe, potty* and *toilet*. You might read your twins one of the books that are available in the children's section of your library or bookstore on the subject. This kind of pretraining may occur well before your child is nearing physical readiness.

When they are *physically* ready and still in diapers, they will often begin to signal their need to urinate or defecate by squatting, holding their genitals, moving off by themselves or making facial expressions. This is the time to help a child become aware by saying something like "When you have a wet diaper, can you let me know?" They also need to learn the physical control of their bladder and bowels so that they can release either.

Your twins also need to be *cognitively* aware of the toilet training process. A child needs to organize several processes: to be aware of the urge, to sit on her training toilet and to stand when she is through. The child who is toilet training also relies on imitation skills, learning to copy parents and older siblings. Eventually children will need to learn to wipe themselves, and boys will learn to pee standing up.

The vital component is *emotional* readiness. This is when a child feels invested in controlling herself and enjoys an element of order in her life. She can take pleasure and pride in caring for her body and keeping it clean.

For twins there are a couple points that are important to consider:

- *Twins may or may not be ready to begin toilet training at the same time.* Simultaneous readiness is more common in identical twins than fraternal twins, and more common in same sex fraternal twins than boy/girl twin pairs. If one is ready before the other, you may want to wait until both are ready or teach one and wait for the other to pick up the cue. Twins are very good models for each other. One parent describing a scenario of successful modeling told the following story: One of her fraternal twin daughters was just a little ahead of her twin sister learning to go on the potty. One morning, the mother woke up to find the slower twin helping the other wipe herself after going on the potty.

- *Avoid competition.* Each child should have his or her own little potty. Part of training is to get used to sitting on the potty regardless of whether it is put to use each time. Praise the child in a matter-of-fact way. If both children are present, be casual and find a good word for your other twin as well. You might say to a child who has used the potty, "Great job." To the other child, "You're really getting used to that potty." Don't make a big deal out of it.

Accidents are a perfectly natural part of the process. Often an accident occurs because the child is too happily engaged in play to pay attention to the urgency of her bladder. If a child has several accidents in a short period of time, it may be a sign that the process is being rushed. The child may be more comfortable back in diapers for awhile. As long as you, as a parent, maintain a relaxed attitude, these little steps forward and back will feel like a natural part of the process. It is also helpful to be aware that setbacks in toilet training almost always occur when a child is stressed in some way. A child who has been accident-free for weeks is likely to wet herself in the event of illness, a move to a different home or preschool or a crisis in the family. Of course, there should never be any punishment for toilet-training accidents.

The process will be much less trying if you follow the lead of each twin as to when toilet training should begin. It is also important, as with all teaching, to be consistent, patient and encouraging. If by the age of four or five, either of your twins is not well on the way to being successfully toilet trained, you should consult your pediatrician.

TRAVEL

The most important thing to know about traveling with your twins is that every minute you put into planning and preparing will come back to you doubled or even tripled in genuine enjoyment on your trip. Traveling with children is hard work, but the potential payoffs in family bonding, shared memories and tremendous growth for all family members are incomparable. Forget the trips you took as a couple BC (before children). Gone are the hours of relaxing on the beach with a good book and a pitcher of margaritas. Wave good-bye to dancing out and sleeping in. Say hello to calling ahead to make sure the two roll-away cots will be in the hotel room when you arrive.

A successful vacation might be the whole family flying across the country to see grandparents, or it may mean a long weekend just an hour or two from home, or it might be a trip by car to several national parks. As your children grow up, you may want to add to or revise your tried-and-true family vacation by offering your twins and their siblings an opportunity to take a solo holiday with one parent. Every child and parent would benefit by even a long weekend in only each other's company. In any of these scenarios, the following points are worth thinking about:

- *Don't forget their blankies.* If your twins have comfort items, such as a cuddly animal or special blanket, don't leave home without them. Many a cuddly has been sent FedEx to an inconsolable child who is just not going to be happy on his first trip to Disneyland unless his Cuddles is along for the ride.
- *Bring along temporary twin-proofing supplies.* Throw a couple of outlet covers in your suitcase and a few pipe cleaners to bind up drape or electrical cords. Also take a crawl around the room in which you are staying, as described in the discussion of safety earlier in this chapter, to see what potential hazards you might find.

- *Bring two bags of tricks.* Supply each twin with their own little surprise goody bag, filled with items such as travel checkers, cards, stickers, a travel bingo game for car or train rides, books and coloring supplies. Be sure to have a blend of activities so that they can amuse themselves and each other.

- *While you're at it, bring your own bag of tricks.* Be sure to have a small bag with a few essentials that are age-appropriate. Beyond the standard diaper bag for little ones, have a simple change of clothes handy for each young elementary-age twin. A spilled soda in the first ten minutes of a trip can make for a very cranky traveler (and we don't mean you, Mom). A fever reducer, some bottled water, a couple of bandages and antibiotic ointment should be standard on any trip. Talk with your pediatrician about whether you should take any antibiotics along. Never, ever go anywhere without a couple of large resealable plastic bags—remember the spilled soda?

- *Have food, will travel.* Be sure to have individually bagged snacks and box juice for each twin. You do not want to depend on airline food or the next restaurant stop when cranky children are hungry.

- *If traveling by car, the younger your twins, the more frequent the stops.* Be alert for potential fun stops along the way. If you're traveling in the country, have some simple nature tools: insect repellent, a magnifying glass, binoculars. Look for a little park to stop and eat lunch; check out a pond for tadpoles or minnows. Most important, these stops are wonderful times to let your twins just get out and *run*—it sure feels good for all, especially little ones, to let out some physical energy before getting back in the car.

- *Call ahead before you drag along two of everything.* Many airlines, car rental companies, hotels and resorts rent or offer complimentary gear, such as top-quality car seats, strollers, highchairs and Portacribs. Even if you're going to visit family or friends out of town, place a call to the local Mothers of Twins club to see if they can help you locate some equipment you can rent or borrow.

- *Build flexibility into your trip that supports your twins' interests.* If you're on a road trip with a couple of ten-year-old baseball fans, check out a minor league ball game in a town you're passing through. If your twins have different interests, you might want to split up for a few hours and take one white-water rafting and one to the Rock and Roll Hall of Fame. Imagine the fun they'll have telling their friends when they get home.
- *Plan an age-appropriate trip.* There is nothing more aggravating than spending a fortune to take your eight-year-old twins to Italy and having them want to spend the whole time in American-style hotels, complaining because they can't understand *The Simpsons* in Italian. This would be a trip for twins who are at least young teens, who are able to get involved in the trip's planning and maybe study the language a bit.

PLAY DATES

One of the wonderful benefits of raising twins is the joy of watching your two children becoming playmates from a very early age. Many parents of twins describe each of their twins as having "a built-in friend." Most parents also come to realize the desirability of scheduling play dates with other children for their twins.

Play dates encourage language development and communication skills as your twins practice talking with and listening to other children. Twins are usually with each other a lot throughout their infant and toddler years. Much of their language is based on mimicking and modeling each other. Playing with other children supports these early language skills, which in turn help to create a sound base for developing reading skills.

Play dates also develop social skills. It is very helpful for twins to learn at a young age that not all children play like their co-twin. Play dates broaden experience and teach twins new ways to play with each other. The importance of early play opportunities with other children is underscored by the experience of this junior high-age twin:

When we were younger we [he and his twin brother] played with each other all the time, and we had our own way of playing with our toys and figures. When we went to someone else's house, the other person didn't seem to play the same way we did and told us we were babies and stuff. So our mom didn't make a lot of play dates for us, 'cause we were happy playing with each other. Later on we realized that we didn't really know how to play with other kids. Now in junior high we're sort of learning how to make friends.

Play has been described as the work of young children. Certainly play provides tremendous opportunity for developmental growth. We've spoken at length about separation and individuation in twins. If we overlay that developmental process onto the subject of play, we learn a lot about why our children play the way they do and how to best facilitate play dates that will enrich their lives.

- *The preschool years.* Twins are usually in close proximity to each other and can participate contentedly in side-by-side play while they are also learning to interact with each other. Some may not show a great deal of interest in other children. This is a time when twins are beginning to separate from their parents and may tend to form their own "team."
- *The early elementary years (kindergarten to third grade).* Twins are becoming more independent. They are in the midst of separation and individuation. They also may vie for the same friend. This is particularly likely with same sex twins. There may be episodes of possessiveness and competition over a friend's attention.
- *The upper elementary years and beyond.* Twins of this age are often developing more interests and hobbies. They may prefer to have their own friends, or if they have similar interests, they may want to share some like-minded friends and have some exclusive friendships of their own.

The opportunity to develop social skills is vital to all children. For twins, particularly those who have always shared a room, shared toys and so many other things, the opportunity to play *as an individual* with another child is something of their own that they may not want to share. Friendship and play dates are all about process. It is not formulaic. Twins are trying to work through *what's mine and then what's yours and who are our friends?* The answer is ever changing. Once again there is that push/pull that is so much a part of the twin experience.

Play dates can be a challenge to parents, as well as their twins. Should you have one child over to play with your twins together? What about sending one twin at a time to play with a mutual friend? Then there are the times they are invited together to a friend's house. Do you have one twin at home with a friend while the other goes to another child's house? The permutations seem endless, and there are usually good and bad points to each scenario.

When your twins are preschool age, having a child over to play offers some stimulation without being too overwhelming. The same goes for having your twins play at another child's house. Their presence, together, will help them to feel more secure in a new environment as they learn to share their twin with another friend. They also are beginning to establish a sense that there are other people they can be close to in addition to their twin. Be aware, at this young age, a new friend may tend to see your children as "the twins" and treat them as a unit rather than as individuals. You can help by making sure every new playmate knows the name of each twin and learns to use it. It is also helpful for you and the other parent to realize that twins may exhaust their singleton playmate. Welcome to playing tag-team style: One twin may play while the other rests, and then the other twin will want to jump in. Meanwhile the other child is going full tilt the whole time. A teary ending to a play date is often simple fatigue at work. Of course, sometimes twins, while pleased to have a new friend, are so adept at playing together, the third child is inadvertently left out. It is very important to observe your children at play and coach them in establishing social skills.

Not every play date is going to feel successful to you or your children. You will all learn by trial and error. Having two children over to play may end up with three of them playing merrily while the fourth feels excluded. Sometimes it works well to establish, in advance, that each of your twins is inviting a particular friend and that they are going to play in separate areas of the house. You've got to monitor the situation and go with the flow of their play. If they all end up playing together after lunch, so be it, as long as everyone is having a good time. It is always a good idea to have some play idea to offer that will help the group to reorganize itself successfully if someone is being picked on or left out. Maybe you can oversee a board game, a treasure hunt or a baking project.

By the time children are in their middle to older elementary years, it is wise to facilitate some separate play dates for your twins, particularly if they are overly dependent on each other. By socializing independently, each learns to be more self-reliant, and that is very helpful in developing self-esteem.

You may find your twins being competitive over a friend. They may be equally matched in their ability to assert themselves, or one twin may be clearly dominant in the social arena. If competition is leading to damaging play, it is important for you to establish some acceptable parameters for behavior. While there are no absolutes when it comes to organizing play dates, there *are* absolutes when it comes to behavior. If play becomes physical to the point that someone is getting hurt, it must stop. Try giving your twins and their playmates a cue phrase like "stop it," which means when they hear that phrase while roughhousing, everyone must stop and untangle. This goes for play wrestling or the kinds of tests of strength in which young boys often indulge. You can also create limits for language. It is perfectly reasonable for you to tell children in your home that there simply will not be any name-calling or bad language. Physical intimidation and mean language go a long way in hurting children's feelings. By establishing some ground rules, you will stop at least some exclusionary behavior in its tracks.

Other parents will take cues from you about managing your twins' play dates. Some parents will feel obligated to invite both your twins for every reciprocal play date. Talk to your children about this. They might prefer to play separately with this mutual friend. Maybe the twin who isn't on the play date gets to go on a special outing with Mom or Dad. Use your imagination and be flexible about play. You also have to be understanding of other parent's rules or limitations. After four or five years of parenting twins, two extra friends around the house may be a walk in the park for you, but managing both your children for a play date may (quite understandably) be more than another mom is prepared to handle. That may mean you have one child at home while your other child goes off to a play date. Nobody said it was going to be easy.

TWIN TALK

Dr. Pearlman

Nick, 15-year-old fraternal twin

Carol, mother of Alex and Nick

Jill Ganon

Katie and Robin, 13-year-old identical twins

Gregg, father of Katie and Robin

FRIENDSHIPS AND SOCIALIZING

Jill: Have you ever had difficulties finding a good balance in your friendships with other kids?

Katie: I had a friend when I was six until I was about eight or nine who stopped paying attention to me and sort of went over to Robin, and that made me feel really bad.

Dr. Pearlman: How did you handle that situation?

(left to right) *Nick and Alex*

Robin: Katie got mad at me, and she said I was taking her friend away and stuff like that.

Katie: I talked to Robin, and a couple of times I talked to the friend.

Jill: What did your friend say?

Katie: Well, she said that she wasn't ignoring me. I guess either she didn't want to hurt my feelings or she didn't think that she was. But then a couple years after that we became friends again.

Jill: Robin, how did you feel while this was going on?

(left to right) *Sarah, Skylar, Molly, Robin, Katie, and Kira*

Robin: I kind of felt like it wasn't my fault that she was kind of paying attention to me, 'cause we had been friends, too. It's just that Katie had been in her class for a longer time than I had. I kind of felt like it wasn't my fault and it shouldn't be weighing on me. But later in the school year, this friend ended up accepting both of us as good friends.

Nick: I think our friendships are mostly determined by who we have our classes with.

Carol: It's interesting, when the boys were younger and people would call one or the other for an overnight—say, they wanted to invite Alex for an overnight—the moms always wanted to know if they should invite Nickie, too. They were concerned that he'd feel left out if they didn't invite him over. It took a lot of work with other parents to let them know that it was okay to invite one and not the other. They were always very concerned about parties. Many times people would call and invite them both, even though only one of the boys was really good friends with the child. I kept saying that they needed to be seen as separate people. It's okay to invite one and not the other.

Gregg: In my daughters' school, it's such a small community that you're all going to know each other—the school goes from kindergarten to eighth grade and has less than two hundred students total. There are only twelve girls of approximately the same age in the same classroom and about as many boys. The school has a very strong policy toward non-exclusion. So in this community it's much more of a natural thing if you're inviting a group, you invite everyone. I recall a few times when Katie or Robin would go off by themselves, but it didn't happen very often.

BIRTHDAY PARTIES

Turn back the clock, or better still, get out the old family photo albums and see what your birthday parties looked like when you were a kid. Were your birthdays glorious celebrations, with every kid in the neighborhood contributing to your pile of birthday loot and enjoying big slices of homemade cake? Did your parents go all out with an incredible birthday gift, such as a brand-new bike or maybe a special piece of jewelry? Did your home buzz with excitement as party preparations were under way, with siblings and extended family helping out? Or were birthdays treated as just another day, barely acknowledged? Perhaps birthdays in your home meant that your grandparents joined you for a special family dinner. Maybe you got several small gifts or some money to put in your savings account. If you grew up with lavish birthdays and your spouse did not, you both may have different expectations regarding the tone you hope to set for birthdays in your home, now that you have children. Talking about the history of your family's style of celebrating is very important.

It is also helpful to examine your inner feelings about how you felt about birthdays as you were growing up. Birthdays seem to have a powerful place in the human psyche. Even as children, some of us are uneasy about our birthdays. You may feel uncomfortable in the spotlight. You may have such a rich fantasy of what you want your birthday to be that it inevitably falls short. Many parents describe a sense of being overinvested in their children's birthdays: "I wanted them to have everything I missed."

What about your friends and community? Is there pressure to have a big blowout because, after all, you have twins? Or maybe you feel the reverse—how can you ask people to attend a party where they'll feel they have to bring two presents just because you have twins? Do your children's friends have their birthday parties at amusement parks or restaurants and do you feel pressured to do the same?

Once you've looked at your own history and the attitudes you bring to celebrating your children's birthday, one of the first things you need to consider as you fantasize about "an ideal birthday party" for your twins is how close is it to being something you have the energy and resources to actually pull off? How about your twins? One mother of twins, who are now eleven years old, described their first birthday party:

> My twins, a girl and a boy, were four weeks premature. My son spent two months in the hospital, and it was a pretty scary time. Somehow, we never got around to sending out birth announcements. When they were about six months old, I started feeling awful that we hadn't managed to do that. A friend of mine suggested that we just do a big blowout first birthday party for them, to sort of put all the really rough times of the first year behind us and celebrate the years to come. I thought that was a fantastic

idea and ended up planning a huge party for kids and adults, family and friends . . . the whole works.

I cooked and baked and had some things catered. It was exhausting. We invited about seventy people. I probably don't have to tell you that it was completely overwhelming for the babies and for me. I think our guests had a good time, and there was a real outpouring of love that my husband and I certainly felt, but it ended up with the twins totally wound up and me sort of hiding out with them in their nursery either crying or on the verge of tears.

I know my heart was in the right place, but it was just not the time to have such an elaborate party. And then, people brought them so many gifts it took me weeks to find the time to write little "thank you notes," which I felt I had to do because everyone was so generous. For their second birthday, my in-laws came over and we had Chinese takeout food and an ice-cream cake that I had my husband pick up on the way home from work. We gave each of the kids a stuffed animal in a box with a huge rainbow-colored ribbon. Of course they loved the boxes as much as the presents. It was the perfect party.

What this story illustrates so well is the need to discern why and for whom you are throwing your twins' first birthday party. The impulse to celebrate the huge milestone of surviving the first year is shared by many twin families. But think long and hard before you take on an extravaganza. The most meaningful birthday celebration of your twins' first birthday might be both parents sharing a bottle of champagne and toasting each other's survival and the exciting prospect of the years to come.

As your children get older, their birthdays become very meaningful to them. Two-year-olds are able to get into the spirit of celebration. They can have some input into how they might like to celebrate this special day. But you should probably plan to celebrate their birthday on the same day. Young children, at least through the early elementary years, find it very hard to tolerate waiting to have their birthday party "the next day." It is completely unreasonable to expect them to handle watching their twin open presents while they are not opening any themselves. As children get older they are able to say what they want, and to live with their own decisions.

Certainly by the time they are preteens (at 11 or 12) they have the communication skills to let you know how they feel. They also have more sense of self and may want theme parties that represent their different interests and hobbies. Boy/girl twins may have very different friends and interests—one may want to take some friends to a basketball game, and the other might want to have friends to a movie and lunch. If your twins do want to have separate parties, they can draw straws to see whose party comes fist, or they can alternate years. You can really help your twins set a cooperative tone by setting some limits and making their reasonable requests the bottom line for any discussions about birthday parties.

Sometimes, if twins have been having their birthday parties together and decide one year they want separate parties, it can feel threatening to parents—"But they've always been so close. What's wrong?" Nothing is wrong. If they've been close, they are probably still close; they just want to have separate birthday parties. Sometimes, the reverse happens. A parent who always had to share a birthday party with a cousin or a sibling may feel strongly that his or her twins are going to have individual birthday parties. In actuality, the twins might prefer to have their party together.

It is really up to parents and twins to use their imaginations to make it fun and comfortable. Look to your children to tell you how they want to handle their birthdays. Their reasoning may surprise you. You may think they'd enjoy having the opportunity to be in the spotlight at their own party, when in fact they find that scrutiny a bit uncomfortable. Perhaps your twins will want to alternate years: one year a big party together and the next year two smaller parties. When a "special" birthday comes along, such as entering double digits at ten or a Sweet Sixteen, talk to your twins about how they want to celebrate. This is very much a personal family decision and should not be unduly influenced by others.

Birthdays are a wonderful time to establish tradition, even if the tradition is an annual pre-birthday meeting to decide what this year's celebration will be. It is also a wonderful opportunity to take a little private time with each child. Perhaps from the time they are kindergartners, parents might alternate taking a special outing with each twin around birthday time. Keep a little book that is a diary of these excursions, one year with Mom and the next with Dad.

When it comes to a birthday cake, you can't really go wrong by having a cake and candles for each twin. Yet even this can get tricky. Some twins are very invested in comparison and may even compare their birthday cakes to see which is more elaborate or which has a better theme. Hopefully each can have the type of cake they like best. Some parents find it safest to avoid "theme" cakes altogether and decorate them with each child's name and candles. When it comes to singing "Happy Birthday" and blowing out candles, consult your twins as to how they'd like this to happen. If they want to be celebrated individually, they can take turns going first. (Remember to make a note of whose turn it is, or it is sure to be in question next year.)

PRESENTS

As the parent of twins, you will find yourself answering certain questions many times throughout the years your children are growing up. Whether it is about birthday presents or holiday gifts, you are bound to hear, "Should we give them both the same gift?" There is no perfect answer to this question when your children are very little. You cannot know what little toy will strike both their fancies. Some parents try to have similar toys (two different books or two different-colored trucks) available for their toddlers and very young twins. It is important that you give each child a gift of their own, individually wrapped with their own birthday card—even though each gift may be less expensive than one big gift. As they begin to mature, your options really open up. You can recommend that grandparents or family friends talk to each twin individually about their interests, hobbies and what they desire. Let that guide them in their gift-giving. That strategy has the added benefit of helping the larger community to see your children as individuals.

Your personal gift-giving policy should be very much guided by your children's individual desires. This usually means some degree of equality—a tennis racket for one and a baseball mitt for the other, or different clothes but in similar amounts. If you're considering a special big-ticket gift, such as a computer, you might give your twins the computer to share but add a few individual extras, such as separate mouse pads or their own boxes of disks.

When it comes to second-guessing your twins, forget trying to beat the odds—you win some and you lose plenty. When parents of twins get together, they almost all have an example to share of how they labored intensely over finding two different birthday presents for their twins—absolutely sure that their choices were perfect, only to find that both kids *really wanted* the same set of blocks or the same cassette player, *but they each wanted their very own.* When that happens, it is not the time to attempt to cajole one twin into settling for the less desirable gift. It is probably much wiser, and ultimately much kinder to all involved, to return the less favored gift and bring home the bacon so to speak. Naturally, once we're talking about teenagers and cars or other high-ticket items, you'll be very glad your twins have become acclimated to the sharing that is a very necessary part of all your lives.

A final thought about birthday gifts: Don't forget to talk with your twins ahead of time about how they want to open their gifts, especially if they are having a shared party. It can be quite difficult for a young child to wait to open her presents until her twin is done. Maybe you want to alternate, or if there are two sets of friends at a shared party, you might open gifts simultaneously in different rooms and then come together for birthday cake. The more thought you put into these details ahead of time, the more comfortable and the better it will be for everyone involved.

TWIN TALK

Dr. Pearlman

Katie, 13-year-old identical twin sister of Robin

Mary, mother of Chris and Andy

Alex and Nick, 15-year-old fraternal twins

Chris and Andy, 7-year-old identical twins

Kathy, mother of 6-year-old fraternal twins, Nathan and Brian

PRESENTS

Dr. Pearlman:

Does anyone have any thoughts about giving or receiving gifts?

Kathy: Christmas this year was the first time I struggled with deciding whether to get them the same presents, which we'd always done before, or do I get them different things? Now, they are really showing their individual personalities and interests, so I'm more confident they are not going to fight over toys. When they were little, we got them the exact same thing, because if there was a red truck and a yellow truck, they inevitably both wanted the same one. They almost always locked onto one thing, so they got exactly the same thing. But that really doesn't seem

(left to right) *Chris and Andy*

to be such an issue anymore, though they still like to dress alike.

Mary: Just a few weeks ago we bought new bikes. Chris wanted a black bike. Andy wanted a black bike, too, but he felt that he couldn't get the same color his brother had. We ended up leaving the store without a bike for Andy. Two days later we went back to the store and he was ready to get the black bike. I guess he was so used to their getting different things that it took him awhile to figure out that it was okay if he wanted the same color bike as his brother.

Chris: I didn't mind if Andy had the same bike as I did.

Andy: And mine has something in the front and his doesn't.

(left to right) *Nathan and Brian*

Katie: I don't really remember getting the same presents. For Christmas we always get different things.

Nick: For us, there might be two packages wrapped exactly the same, and so we'll have to ask if we open them at the same time. Because it's not like we each get a red shirt. But maybe both boxes are from Nordstrom's, so the likelihood is, if I see Alex open up a box that looks like mine and it happens to be a Nordstrom's shirt and tie or it happens to be a set of baseball cards, I don't even have to open my box to know there's going to be a set of baseball cards or shirt and tie in there. And they won't be exactly the same, but they'll be in the same area, like different-color shirts. I don't say, "How come you got that and I didn't get it?" I don't really mind. What he gets is what he gets and what I get is what I get and I will play with what I get or I will wear what I get or I will listen to what I get.

Alex: I remember for most Christmases we've gotten maybe two of our bigger presents. Sometimes our mom or dad or aunt or uncle or whatever will say, "You have to open this one at the same time." Right off the bat I know it must be the same thing. What you could do in that situation instead, as long as the packages are wrapped differently, they can open them at different times and they don't know that it's the same thing unless you say this package and this package are the same thing. Say Nick opens one up and it's new golf clubs, and I open my package up and it's a baseball bat. They're shaped the same, so how would we know?

Nick: Our gifts coincide with our interests. He gets a lot of baseball stuff and I get things having to do with music and stuff to wear.

MONEY AND ALLOWANCE

Money is a powerful tool. As adults we are well aware of the opportunities that money fosters as well as the traps it sometimes conceals. So ubiquitous is our use of money that it is central to many of our interactions with our children.

"Mommy, I like *those* sneakers."

"*I'm sorry, honey, but they are just too expensive.*"

"Why can't we have separate rooms?"

"*We're saving our money so that we'll be able to buy a bigger house.*"

Children are fascinated with coins and love the idea of having their own money. Its universality and dramatic purchasing power makes money an excellent learning tool for curious young minds. Individual piggy banks for your preschool- or kindergarten-age child are a great place to start. Start out by giving both twins the same amount of weekly money, perhaps attached to a simple chore, such as placing their dirty clothes in the hamper.

As they get a little older, in the early elementary years, you may want to offer a baseline allowance in order to teach your children about money. Then attach additional allowance to chores they agree to do throughout the week. A visual aid, such as a gold star for each day the chore is done, can be very helpful in encouraging young children to reach for a goal. At the end of the week, each twin might collect a quarter for each day her chore was accomplished successfully. Of course, success is in the eye of the parent. Your rules for success might include not having to be reminded or doing the chore thoroughly. Before too long, your twins will have collected enough quarters to represent some serious buying (or saving) power.

Although you start out offering your twins separate piggy banks for storing their money, don't be surprised if at some point they decide to pool their earnings. By the time they are in third or fourth grade, you might discuss the idea of saving their money in the bank. Discuss the fundamentals of savings, and describe their options for having separate accounts or a joint account to be shared. Some twins may want to begin with a joint account and separate their finances somewhere down the road. Others may choose to start off separately and pool their money years later for a high-ticket purchase or trip. Realize that like so many facets of the twin relationship, their attitudes about money at any given moment are going to reflect their individuation and separation process. What may seem wildly unfair to you, may feel perfectly reasonable to them. If their decisions do not trouble them, try not to impose your vision over their money policies. If you perceive an inequity in the way they pool and spend their money, make an effort to support their healthy relationship, and appropriate decisions about shared money will follow.

Many parents report wonderful experiences with teaching their children about fiscal matters by having them learn about the stock market. Young adolescents have the cognitive ability to study the market and can follow a stock's progress in the newspaper every day. You might want to start out by choosing one or two stocks and investing "monopoly money" that is held by Mom and Dad. Eventually, your twins may want to buy one or two shares of stock for real.

You should strive to teach your twins that money is a tool, not a weapon. Help them understand that the family tries to spend its money in the best interests of the family. Just as your twins are a team, they are both members of the larger team of the family. Be careful not to set a precedent that sends a message that love equals money, or that equal money is necessary to demonstrate equal love. As your twins grow up, one may very well become passionate about a sport or a hobby that is costly to maintain, while the other plays a donated instrument or competes on a team that requires only modest financial support. It is through your encouragement and attendance at both of their events that you demonstrate a measure of your love. Money is just money.

SPORTS AND HOBBIES

When it comes to skills and interests such as sports or dancing or artistic ability, twins (whether they are identical or fraternal) may share common interests. For some boy/girl twins, gear up for a diversity of interests that may confound even the most seasoned and organized parent. When Kevin has soccer practice and Jessie has a drama class on the other side of town, it is time to call out the troops (otherwise known as an understanding army of carpooling parents) to help keep you sane.

It is wise to allow your twins' interests to develop naturally. Some twins may share the same interests and hobbies for a lifetime. Don't get involved prematurely in an attempt to have each twin find her own niche and do not try to force one to follow the other into a particular sport or hobby. After six months, you may find that one twin is ready to stop ballet while the other goes on to dance for many years. Or after playing Little League baseball on the same team for years, your twins may ask to play on competing teams, or one may give up baseball and decide to go out for basketball in school.

Twins, like all children, are likely to have fickle passions, and each family must develop its own way of handling the rules of participation in extracurricular activities. Financing varied interests can get very costly. Many parents of twins have found instructors, coaches or even tutoring facilities to be willing to offer a discount for twins. If one or both twins want music lessons, you might want to look into renting instruments until they demonstrate more than a passing interest. And in the case of lessons, you may want to make it clear that once a commitment is made, it needs to be honored for a specific period of time. Having your twins in and out of a mind-boggling schedule of activities is no favor to them or to you—or to the family as a whole.

TWIN TALK

Dr. Pearlman

Alex and Nick, 15-year-old fraternal twins

Christopher and Andy, 7-year-old identical twins

Jill Ganon

Robin and Katie, 13-year-old identical twins

PLAYING SPORTS

Jill: Do you like to play sports?

Chris: I play soccer.

Andy: I played soccer, too, and I liked it. We played on the same team.

Alex: I played baseball for seven or eight years, but I'm not playing now, 'cause I can't find a league. But I played baseball and tennis, and I liked them both.

Nick: We played baseball with each other for six years, but I pretty much dropped baseball after that. But baseball was pretty much Alex's thing. Little League ended at about sixth grade, and it was kind of a big jump up to Pony/Colt, and I wasn't really interested, but Alex was and I think he still is. But I do keep up with tennis.

Dr. Pearlman:

[to Nick] Did you confer with Alex first when you decided to drop baseball?

Nick: It was my decision, not his.

Alex: I wasn't that surprised by his decision, and it didn't matter too much to me one way or another. But I think the interesting thing with twins and team sports is whether you're on the same team or different teams. I remember, on our team one year, we had this guy who had an older brother at the same level in our league, and so they got to play against each other. I've always thought it would be interesting to play each other on two different teams, but we've always been on the same team. What would it be like to play each other? I don't think I've experienced much sibling rivalry in sports. Maybe we've played tennis against each other, but it's not that much of a competition. Probably the most interesting thing is who the parents would root for. I think it would be harder on the parents than on the kids.

Robin: We play tennis, but we kind of stopped because to be good you have to practice a lot and we didn't have the time.

Dr. Pearlman:

Did you feel competitive with your twin?

Katie: No, I don't think I ever felt that.

Robin: I think it's sort of fun in a way just playing against my sister.

Jill: Does one of you ever give in before the other?

Katie: I don't think so.

Dr. Pearlman:

Do you think you push each other to a higher level of play?

Nick: I can really relate to that, because when we played tennis, it seemed like if I beat him one week, he'd probably beat me the next week.

Robin: I'm not sure we had an effect on each other, because generally when we played opposite each other, it was playing doubles.

"I personally think I would love to have her in the same school but not in the same class. Sometimes you have competition. You have enough time with each other, every day, every hour sometimes."

—Eliza, 11-year-old fraternal twin

SCHOOLDAYS

READY OR NOT, HERE THEY COME

Those years of being up to your elbows in diapers and baby talk seem like a distant memory on that fateful morning you wave good-bye to your children on their first day without you at preschool. Suddenly you are wondering how time could possibly have flown by so quickly. Preschool is that first step down your twins' education highway, and all parents want their children to start off with the best possible experience.

PRESCHOOL

Starting preschool is an enormous step for young children. Even if your children have been in day care, this first experience with "school" will make increased demands upon their abilities to participate in organized play and learn with other children. The life of your three- or four-year-old twins has probably been very much about being at home with the family, visiting a friend's house, having play dates at the park, maybe visiting grandparents or other extended family, and going on excursions to the zoo or the grocery store or the neighborhood pool. In other words, they have been supported and guided through an ever-expanding world that has included more and more new environments and new people, but for the most part, a parent or a trusted family member or caregiver has always been close at hand.

Choosing the Right Preschool

As you gather information about preschools in your community, you'll want to keep the following fundamental questions in mind:

- Are the administration and teaching staff knowledgeable about the early twin relationship and the impact of the preschool environment on that relationship?
- Are the administration and teaching staff prepared to treat twins as separate individuals with their own needs and learning styles?
- Does the school have a policy on twin placement?
- Are they receptive to your ideas regarding placement of your children?

The preschool experience means separation from parents, coupled with exposure to a large group of peers, sometimes for the first time. Just as your twins are meeting new children, this may be the first time those children are getting to know a set of twins. If your children look very much alike, regardless of their zygosity, they will be the object of natural curiosity from their peers. You can help teachers and new friends to tell your twins apart through the use of visual clues, such as name tags or a particular color identified with each twin, and distinguishing features, such as hairstyles, backpacks or shoes.

Separate or Together

Since this is your twins' first school experience of being away from their parents or caregiver, it is advisable that they start preschool together, in the same classroom. They have many adjustments to make: separating from parents, adjusting to a new setting and so on. It is too much to ask your twins to also separate from each other at this time. At this age and stage of development, they provide and receive much comfort and support from each other. There is no need to deprive them of that "built-in" security. Studies have shown that singletons starting school with a friend tend to adjust better than those without the comforting presence of a pal. Use your twins' relationship to its best advantage. When they are comfortable in the setting and it seems they are both ready to separate, then you can go for it.

Preschool is the time that children are acquiring and rapidly expanding their language skills. We know that some twins may be slightly behind their same age peers in their vocabulary as well as their ability to express themselves clearly. (See Chapter Six for a comprehensive discussion of language development.) It is important for parents and teachers to understand that this is not a predictor of intelligence and in almost all cases does not indicate cognitive delay. But delayed language skills can have implications in social skills and play. A child whose language skills are very obviously eclipsed by his twin's may be better off starting in a slightly younger program than his more garrulous twin. This may give him the perfect opportunity to refine his skills and gain confidence so that both children can begin kindergarten together.

It is useful to remember when your twins are this young that six months can represent a complete turn-around in language skills and social maturity. Parents and teachers considering placement of twins in a preschool need to reflect on each child's language and social skills as very significant predictors of the appropriateness of the placement. The preschool experience can be very useful in helping identify possible developmental problems, whether they are behavioral, cognitive, physical or emotional.

TWIN TALK

Dr. Pearlman

Susan, mother of Bradley and Taylor, 5-year-old boy/girl twins

(left to right) *Bradley and Taylor*

TWINS IN PRESCHOOL

Dr. Pearlman:

Let's talk about your children's preschool experience.

Susan: They started preschool when they were three years old, though we noticed a lot of people sent their kids earlier. But we had twins, and even when they were with other children, they preferred to play with each other. By the time they were about three years old we noticed they seemed to irritate each other a little bit more and seemed to be socializing with other children. So at that point we enrolled them in preschool. It was a really good experience for them. They always seemed comforted by the fact that the other one was there.

They would greet each other and play with each other during break time, but then they quickly gravitated towards other kids to play. I just think they needed that socialization.

At their preschool they were separated for a short period of time. It was interesting. One of the kids was speaking for the other, answering all the questions that might be asked of them, really assuming a dominant position. So we divided them for about a month-and-a-half and then brought them back together. They actually wanted to be back together in the same room again at that age. Once they were back together, they had a chance to develop their own peer group. Basically they became much more independent of each other.

Dr. Pearlman:

It sounds like your situation was handled well.

Susan: Luckily the director of the school approached us and suggested the separation for awhile. We wanted to do whatever was good for the kids, and so we tried that and it worked very well. As far as the length of the separation, we played it by ear, and it all worked out.

KINDERGARTEN AND LOWER SCHOOL

School Readiness

Readiness for kindergarten is a relative thing. In a group of a dozen children all of whom are "ready" to begin school, there will be a range of skills. The following indicators of school readiness are among the most significant:

- A child's ability to listen.
- The ability and willingness to follow directions.
- The focus needed to stay on task.
- The social readiness to interact with peers.

The only absolute rule about the best way to educate your twins is that there are no absolute rules. Yet it can be said that twins are generally best off if they are at the same grade level throughout their elementary and secondary school years. In cases where one twin is severely less able—say, in the case of a significant developmental or learning delay—school placement in different grades may be appropriate. Consultation and a formal assessment by an expert is a necessity in such cases.

It is very important to keep in mind that, for the majority of twins, going through school in different grades will have an enormous impact on their relationship. It may seem reasonable to hold one child back while allowing the other child to move ahead, particularly if one is raring to go into kindergarten while the other would clearly benefit from another year in preschool. But the child who appears less ready in September may have made enormous cognitive and emotional leaps by January, and the child who seemed so advanced in comparison to her twin may appear less capable in a class of new peers in kindergarten.

As parents in collaboration with educators, you have two comfortable windows of opportunity to look very carefully at your twins' school readiness: starting preschool and starting kindergarten. You may find it helpful to speak with parents of older twins who have already started school. While every twin relationship is unique, learning about the experiences of twins other than your own may provide you with useful insight. Many parents are making the decision to postpone kindergarten in order to give one or both of their twins some additional time to mature. One mother of boy/girl twins described the dilemma of whether to let her daughter go on to kindergarten while her son spent another year in preschool.

> We really felt our children's preschool was wonderful. The teachers worked well with both our kids, and we felt the socialization was very important, since until that time the twins had played mostly with each other. There seemed to be just the right balance of structured activity and free play time for our son, but by the end of the year, our daughter was growing restless with the program. It did not help matters that our daughter had a friendship going with a little girl who was moving on to kindergarten in the fall.
>
> It was actually our pediatrician who suggested that we think very carefully about whether or not to move our daughter ahead of her brother at this juncture. He said it was not the issue of separating them that concerned him, but the fact that we were setting our son up to be a year behind his sister for the rest of their school career. We ended up keeping them in preschool for an additional year but arranged play dates with our daughter's new friend even after she had entered kindergarten. I think we were very fortunate in that the preschool was sensitive to our dilemma and worked with my daughter to help her find new challenges in her familiar environment. They entered kindergarten as six-year-olds. They are now in third grade and have been doing very well in separate classes since kindergarten.

TWIN TALK

Dr. Pearlman

Brian and Nathan, 6-year-old fraternal twins

Chris, 7-year-old identical twin brother of Andy

(left to right) *Andy and Chris*

SCHOOLDAYS

Dr. Pearlman:

[to Chris] I heard you have another set of boy twins in your class. Do they look like each other or different from each other?

Chris: Different. One has a tooth missing and one doesn't.

Nathan: I have twins in my class, and the way I tell them apart is their voices and their hair. But once I switched them. I called Katherine from my class Alice, and I called Alice, the one in Brian's class, Katherine. But Alice didn't get mad. She just said, "I'm Alice."

Dr. Pearlman:

That was nice of her to be so understanding. Now let's talk about how you guys feel about being in separate classrooms.

Brian: I like it, because sometimes Nathan talked to me in class when I didn't want to talk to him, so that's why I wanted to be in a different class.

Nathan: At the start I wasn't so happy with my brother in a different class, because I only had one friend named Kelsey from preschool. I can tell you one very good thing about my brother's class is that they have lots of different kinds of pets.

Chris: We're in first, and we're in different classes, and it's good. In kindergarten we were in different classes, and in preschool we were the same.

(left to right) *Nathan and Brian*

Class Placement

The responsibility for deciding whether twins enter school in the same or in separate classrooms should be made by parents in collaboration with the school. Teachers may or may not yet have had experience with twins in their class. Even if they have had experience with multiples, they haven't met your twins. Talk with them about your children and listen to what they have to say. *Remember that there is no absolute rule that should determine whether your twins should be together or apart in school. This is a decision that is best approached at the beginning of every year on a case-by-case basis.*

As your twins grow up and you become more familiar with their learning styles, you may have the opportunity to match the learning style of each child with the learning style of the teacher and school. We'll talk more about how creating the feeling of a team effort with teachers and school administrators will help you advocate for your twins' school life. It is useful to begin your approach to the question of class placement in a very general way, considering what either option has to offer your children.

When they are very young, twins' personal agendas regarding class placement may not work in their own best interest. It is important to listen to your children's thoughts and feelings on class placement—but don't leave them with the mistaken impression that the final decision about placement will be theirs. Sometimes one or the other may be overly dependent, or they may try to use each other to filter out the need for developing additional friendships. This could have the effect of inhibiting the growth of their social skills. The fraternal male of a set of adult twins described his unwillingness to learn to tie his shoes or memorize his own address as a kindergartner because these skills had already been mastered by his sister. By learning them, he risked being separated from her.

Once you've made a general assessment of your twins and the options that may be available to them, you may want to consider other specific factors identified by the *LaTrobe Twin Study: Twins in School.* Some of these factors may apply to your twins and be useful in helping you to assess their individual needs.

- What are your twins' zygosity and gender? Girls are generally more attached to each other than boys, and monozygotic twins tend to be closer than dizygotic twins.
- Do they have independent or dependent personalities?
- How adept are their social skills, and how would you gauge their dependence upon adults?

- Do they have previous experience being apart from each other?
- How would you assess their language skills and abilities relative to each other and their peer group?
- Are they significantly smaller or larger than their classmates?
- What are your feelings, as well as the feelings of your twins and the school personnel about class placement?
- What are the views of professionals who have assessed your twins?

TWO PARENTS TALK ABOUT CLASSROOM PLACEMENT FOR THEIR TWINS

Tim and Kathy live in a rural area of New York state. They have four children, and the two youngest are fraternal girl twins, Morgan and Margo. They have had a very successful experience advocating for their twins' classroom placements and shared some insights that parents of twins may find useful.

(left to right) *Morgan and Margo*

Kathy: I think we're probably very lucky because while our elementary school recommends separate placement, parents have the final say. Margo and Morgan were together in preschool. That decision was made for us because there was only one class at each age level. At the end of that year we asked their teachers for their opinions about kindergarten placement and their reasoning was that since the girls were not competitive in their social relationships with friends they did not see any need for them to be in separate kindergarten classes.

Tim: So far, the opportunity for Morgan and Margo to be together has had no downside. They've each made their own friends, and having each other in the same classroom has only helped to make them stronger. Our question at the end of this year will be whether they should be together or apart, as the more academic phase of elementary school begins in second grade. As we get closer to the end of this school year we'll do another assessment regarding next year's classroom placement. We'll talk to the teacher, to each other, to the kids, and figure out what seems like the best plan. I think we all need to be flexible and open to the possibility that separate classes may work well at some point.

Kathy: It is very important to be a real presence at the school if you want to be heard. Not to say that you make a pest of yourself, but make sure that the people in charge know who you are. We have two older children, our daughter Sydney and our son Ben, so the school knows us very well.

Tim: I think the administrators also respond to knowing that there is unity on the home-front, because then they know there will be a consistency of response from the family.

Kathy: It is also very important to really listen to what your school has to say. I went in to advocate for our older daughter, Sydney, last year and ended up deferring to the school's recommendation. Now, looking back, I think their recommendation was the correct one and I'm glad we went along with it.

Twins in the Same Classroom

This may be the most satisfactory arrangement for twins who are entering preschool, kindergarten, or the early elementary grades. This is particularly true for twins who have not yet spent much time apart from each other or had a great deal of exposure to other playmates. Why deny them the comfort and support they have come to find in each other? Each day will be filled with new challenges, and your twins are likely to draw courage from each other's presence in this new environment.

The degree of dependence your twins show on each other is an important factor in deciding how to best place them as they start school. Twins who tend to be fairly comfortable learning and socializing, regardless of the presence of their twin, are likely to thrive whether they are together or apart in their early elementary years. If there is a mutual or a one-sided pronounced dependence between your twins, it may be very important for them to start school together, with the understanding on the part of teachers, parents and to some degree the twins themselves, that the goal is for both of them to establish an independent presence in the classroom.

Some teachers believe they will have difficulty keeping track of each twin and are averse to having them in the same class. If teachers are having difficulty telling your twins apart while in the same classroom, offer to help the teacher differentiate the twins with visual clues, such as name tags or a defining color or piece of jewelry. Talk to teachers about the importance of observing your twins together. They can learn much about their relationship and help in the evalua-tion process for the future. The willing and informed support of the teacher is very important, and you need to be prepared to be an enthusiastic supporter of a teacher who is making the extra effort to get to know your twins as individuals in her classroom.

Suggest ways to help your children learn independently, such as putting them in separate work groups or seating them in different parts of the room. Sometimes it is important for twins to know where the other is. If they are constantly worried where their twin is, it may interfere with their ability to concentrate and learn. When they feel comfortable with the situation, then they will begin to separate on their own more and more. This is a process. Parents should also try to provide some separate activities for their twins.

Twins in Separate Classrooms

If your twins have already demonstrated very different needs and skills, they may require separate classes, even separate schools as they grow older. A twin relationship in which one child is completely overshadowed by the personality, academic, physical, or social accomplishments of the other may make separate classes an appropriate option. Sometimes, twins placed together in their early elementary years can be distracted by each other to a degree that inhibits their ability to stay on task in the classroom. Distraction can also lead to disruptive behavior from one or both twins. It is not unusual for a child who is not enjoying the same rate of achievement as his twin to act out to the detriment of himself, his twin and the class in general. It is also not unusual for one twin to gradually cease performing his work in one or several class activities if he feels eclipsed by the greater skill level of his twin. And finally, different classes may provide each twin with a much needed break from the other's constant presence. In rare cases, your twins may even be in different schools.

If you believe that your young twins will find it difficult to be separated in their first classroom experience, and it is still your judgment, and that of the school's, that separation is the best way to go, you may want to consider the following suggestions:

- Make an effort to prepare them for spending time apart. You might begin with separate outings with one parent and eventually go for an overnight at a cousin's or grandparent's house.
- Reassure each of them, individually and together, that school is only a part of each day, and they will always return home to each other and the family.
- Show them where their twin's class is located and even take them inside the other's classroom, so they can see it. Most of the time their imagination fills in the wrong information of what is real and what is not.
- Show them the playground and the lunch area, and let them know they can see each other then. If the children eat with their class, perhaps you can talk to the teachers about making an exception and they can alternate days. But keep encouraging them to make friends in their own class so that they can eventually stay with their class.
- For younger children (kindergarten or first grade) they may need to check on each other to make sure their twin is okay and that they are okay.

TWIN TALK

Dr. Pearlman

Eliza and Chloe, 11-year-old fraternal twins

Lauren, mother of Eliza, Chloe and their 16-year-old sister, Julia

BEING IN SEPARATE CLASSROOMS

Dr. Pearlman:

When you attended the same school were you in separate classrooms?

Chloe: We've always been in separate classrooms. I like it better without my sister, 'cause otherwise we'd fight a little bit more. And I don't like being in the same classes. If you're in the same school, then you're competing against each other. If we were in the same class and she had this other grade, then maybe I would feel bad or she would feel bad. We're not the same level.

Eliza: I think it's fine that we're in different schools. Sometimes maybe you might have competition with your sister. That can get threatening and it's not good. But we may be together in middle school and I think it's going to be better.

Dr. Pearlman:

Do you feel some competition between the two of you?

Eliza: No, not right now.

Dr. Pearlman:

[to Lauren] Was it a hard decision to place Eliza and Chloe in separate schools?

Lauren: It was a harder decision for me than it was for my husband. But based on different things that Eliza's teacher was saying, we felt that a different school would have more to offer her. Chloe was doing fine, and she was happy with her peer group, so we investigated this other school for Eliza. Now we are at a point where we don't feel public education in middle school is what we want for Chloe. Since Eliza is in this other private school and we've been happy there, we're going to give it a try and see if Eliza's school can meet the different needs of both children. They learn very differently and have different strengths. The school they are going to is large enough that they should not be together other than lunch and maybe a few classes.

(left to right) *Chloe and Eliza*

Remaining Flexible About Your Decision

Parenting is a process with a built-in learning curve. The mother of twins who are going through the college application process now says that she looks back on the intensity with which she and her husband approached early educational decisions for their twins and says:

If I knew then what I know now, I'd have been a whole lot more relaxed about my kids' kindergarten placement. As it happens, we were in a public school with many class options and a general policy about placing kids separately to start. I was so convinced that this would be awful for my kids that I went to everyone but the Surgeon General of the United States to get written support for my position that the kids had to be together. Ultimately, they indulged us and placed the kids together, and by first grade, it was clear to us that both girls—they are fraternal twins—actually would benefit by being in separate classes, and that they liked the idea of having an opportunity for time apart. We laugh about it now—how I was threatening to run for a seat on the Board of Education—and my protective zeal was well meaning, but talk about a mountain out of a mole hill. My girls are now applying to several of the same colleges, and I wouldn't be surprised if they end up at the same place. Go figure.

It's a Fluid Process.

If your twins started kindergarten together but end the year with the suggestion from their teacher that they be separated, don't push the panic button. Children in school often behave differently than they do at home. Your twins' teacher may have valuable insights into why such a change might have little impact on one twin while offering a great benefit to the other. Talk to your children about their experience and gather their thoughts about being separated. Let them know that their feelings and ideas will help you make the decision that is the best for both of them.

Remember that school is your children's childhood career, and in the span of a twelve-year career, changes in class placement are not unusual or inappropriate. The majority of twins have been in separate classes for a few years by the time they leave elementary school. By middle and high school, there is likely to be a well-established flow of time together and time apart. Once they reach adolescence, most twins will want to be more active participants in decisions surrounding their schooling and are likely to be well equipped to do so. Your high school–age twins are likely to have many, even most, of their classes separately from each other, and some twins will be old hands at "playing the system" by the time they reach the ninth or tenth grade. There are legendary tales of twins doing each other's homework and even taking each other's exams in high school.

TWIN TALK

Nick, 15-year-old fraternal twin

APRIL FOOLS

Nick: One of the funniest things that's happened to me since being in high school is being able to play with this twin thing. It is kind of fun because I've never had a chance like this before. On April Fools' Day, everybody told me to switch classes with Alex. And this is probably the funniest thing to have happened. There's a teacher at our school, who's kind of a landmark around the school; he's been around there so long, and he had Alex in his class. He doesn't have me, but he knows I exist. Alex had interviewed him the day before, asking him some questions and trying to stir up some stuff for an article in the paper. And so he caught me and said, "Oh, Alex, I thought about some things for the article." And he started opening up and telling me all this stuff about what they had talked about, and I never had a chance to say, "Sorry, but you want to be talking to Alex." I didn't want to make him feel stupid and break his heart, so I stood there. I said, "Oh yes, thank you." It was the first time I ever played Alex.

Helping Teachers to Teach Your Twins

As parents of twins, you are already highly adept at debunking myths and stereotypes about your children: Yes, you can tell them apart. No, they do not have ESP. The teachers and school administrators you encounter throughout your twins' education are not likely to have your degree of experience with multiples. They will also have varying capacity and desire to learn about what will best suit your children's educational needs. You may encounter some "old school" thinking that insists twins should never be placed in the same classroom. Some schools will be resistant to assessing twins on a case-by-case and year-by-year basis. If this is the situation, try the following approach:

- *Try for a team effort and avoid creating an adversarial situation.* State your ideas in a manner that suggests a common goal: the best possible educational environment for your children. Taking into account the individual needs and the twin relationship, the most fundamental issue regarding twins in school is their classroom placement—will they be together or apart? If you believe your twins should be in separate classes, you're not likely to meet with any objection. But if you feel your children should be placed together, even if only for a year, you may be in for some strenuous objection from the school's administrators and the teacher involved. Approach this issue as a collaborative effort between experts: You are offering your insights into your twins' needs, relationship, temperaments and their participation in their home environment. The school provides a thorough understanding of the classroom dynamic and how it might best support your twins' educational needs.

- *Support your position with assessment from experts in the field.* If your twins have been seen by an expert in psychology, family counseling or child development whose opinion differs from the policy set forth by the school, be sure to make the school aware of this fact. Supply the school administration with a letter or arrange for a phone conference with the expert to advocate for your twins' classroom placement or to address any other pertinent school policy.

- *Provide appropriate material on the subject of twins and education.* Most teachers are not aware of the issues surrounding twin school placement. It would be advisable to provide a packet of educational materials that might support your classroom experience with your twins. Many teachers will be surprised to discover that while separating twins in school may seem to be a reasonable policy, the highly respected *LaTrobe Twin Study* states the following: "There is absolutely *no* evidence from any large-scale studies of twins that separation helps intellectual or emotional development in the majority of twins."

- *Always schedule individual parent/teacher conferences.* Your twins need and deserve the same individualized evaluation time that every student in the class receives. If your children have the same teacher, let him or her know ahead of time that you intend to schedule *separate* conferences for your children. If your schedule permits, make your appointments on different days to encourage you and the teacher to evaluate your twins on an individual basis.

TWIN TALK

Dr. Pearlman

Jill Ganon
Carol, the mother of Alex and Nick

Nick and Alex, 15-year-old fraternal twins
Katie and Robin, 13-year-old identical twins

STUDENT LIFE

Dr. Pearlman:

Let's talk a little bit about what you experience in school.

Nick: We started high school this year in a new school, and it's hard sometimes for teachers to know who we are.

Alex: Sometimes one of Nick's teachers that I don't have will say something like "Hey, are you the other one?" or "You're Nick's twin," instead of just saying, "Hi, Alex."

Nick: I think it's hard for the teachers, because in our old school it seems like people always knew who we were and we never had a problem. Now all of a sudden we have different teachers and different friends, and especially in the beginning of the year they'd come up to me and start talking about something, and I'd have to say, "Hey, wait a minute. I think you want to talk to my brother."

Carol: This was when they had the same haircut, so I think it was harder.

Nick: We're not identical, but I think we look identical when we have the same haircut.

Jill: Nick, is that why you cut your hair?

Nick: It just worked out that way. One day I wanted to shorten my hair, so I did it.

Jill: Did it help?

Alex: I think it probably does.

Nick: It's not like we said from here on out we will always have different haircuts and different clothes. It happened like it would with any brothers or sisters.

Carol: As their mother, I think it is important to say that they decide about haircuts or the way they want to present themselves as any of us would attempt to distinguish ourselves as an individual. I don't think it was a collaborative decision. There might be a subconscious motivation, but I think Alex likes his hair the way it is and Nick's happy doing the short thing right now.

Dr. Pearlman:

[to Katie and Robin] Are you in separate classes or are you in the same class?

Katie: We're together in class right now in seventh grade, but two years ago we weren't and I didn't like that very much. I think my sister did, though. I felt like Robin had a better class, and I missed being with her.

Robin: I kind of enjoy it when we're not in the same class, because we're together so much of the time that I kind of get sick of her. We see each other always at the beginning of the day and the end of the day, plus we share a room.

Katie: When we were in different classes Robin got invited to parties that I didn't get to go to. That was hard. I felt like I was being excluded on purpose. But they'd say, you're in a different class, and if we invite you, then the rest of your class might want to go. I tried to tell them it was different because I had a twin sister and it wasn't like just inviting someone at random from another class.

Jill: Have you thought about high school?

Robin: I'm not sure that we especially want to go to high school together, but we both are interested in the same school, so I don't know how it will end up.

Nick: I wanted to go to the same high school, 'cause it's easier that way. I thought we could compare notes on different classes and what happened at school every day.

Alex: I don't mind being in the same school. It's not good, and it's not bad. I'm kind of neutral about it. We're in a big high school, so we kind of separated anyway. We only have three classes together.

Nick: And that's the most we've ever had. Seventh grade was the first year we had a class together since preschool. The classes we have together are honors classes, and there is only one class for each, so we have to be in the same class.

MIDDLE SCHOOL AND HIGH SCHOOL

By the time your twins reach early adolescence, they are likely to have spent at least some time in different classes. With middle and high school come increased academic demands and heightened social stakes. The friends your twins have made may join them in their new schools, but inevitably there will be new friends and new social encounters. High school is also a time when many families reconsider their educational options. Will both twins simply go on to the local public school? Has one child shown a talent in music or science or sports that makes him a candidate for a specialty school? Do you want to consider all-boys or all-girls schools for your boy/girl twins? These are options that any family might face, but as you probably know very well by the time your kids are this age, you have a few important twin-specific issues to consider:

- *Your twins are mature enough to have a significant voice in educational decisions.* This is particularly true of high school–age twins. By the time your children are ready to begin high school, they may have some very definite ideas about school. Supporting their individual needs could include the strategic problems of dealing with two schools, but the inconvenience might be well worth it. If, for example, one of your twins is a particularly gifted violinist and has the opportunity to attend a specialized performing arts high school, you will want to think long and hard about how to support that option. If the idea of separation causes some anxiety for your twins, encourage them to remember that school is only part of the day and that this is really an opportunity for both of them to get some individual attention. Your adolescent kids are very capable of discussing their thoughts about their education and should be encouraged to do so. A visit with a school guidance counselor or therapist might be very helpful at this time.

- *Are they stepping into the shadow of their twin or older siblings?* Twins who have been sharing the spotlight with each other throughout their elementary education may be very eager to avoid stepping directly into another environment that invites comparison to siblings who have gone before. Even if your twins are to move on to the same school, they may very much want to stake out their own territory if that is possible.

TWIN TALK

Jill Ganon

Dino, 21-year-old fraternal twin

GRADES

Jill: Were you very aware of each other's grades in school?

Dino: We actually had a couple of teachers who really kidded us. We had a history class together, and we got on very well with the teacher. She would always tell us what the other guy got. She would say, "You got an eighty-nine, and your brother got a ninety-one." It was fine. The strangest thing was in that class we had different scores on every test. We had an American Studies class where we would end up with the exact same score or a half a point from each other score-wise.

Homework, Tests and Grades

Your children have a life outside school. They have their home, sports, hobbies and other extended family and friends. The mandate should be to make school as positive an experience as possible for each as an individual. Whether your children are in the same or separate classes, comparison will be inevitable. It is part of the baggage of every child's taking their place out in the world: Just how do I stack up? Where do I fit in the larger scheme of things? For twins, the process is more ubiquitous than it is for other children. Even with your best efforts to avoid it, they will compare themselves to each other. If they are in the same class, they'll compare test scores and who went further in the class spelling bee and who has the preferable status in the classroom seating arrangement. If they are in separate classes, they may compare their teachers and who has the more exciting class pets and whose homework assignments are better or worse or more sophisticated. Now is the time to remember that parental learning curve. Develop mechanisms within the family for handling the urge to compare. The following thoughts may be helpful:

- *Don't participate in the comparison game.* Try ignoring it instead. Even if you are trapped in the car with two kids who are debating the relative merits of bunnies over iguanas as classroom pets, stay out of the fray. Your involvement heightens the stakes by adding the element of competition for your attention and approval. Try to stay out of it or offer a benign response about all animals being fun to learn about.

- *Create opportunities for each child to share their concerns and achievements with you privately.* There are going to be times when one of your twins is bursting with pride over some success, while his twin has not attained that same heady degree of accomplishment. It may be receiving a perfect grade on a math test or winning an essay contest. When both twins jump into the car after school, it is just not fair or realistic to expect an excited child to delay sharing good news until you have a private moment. It is important to be able to acknowledge your pride in one's accomplishment in the presence of the other. This kind of happiness for someone you love is important for twins to see so that they can model it themselves. But at the same time, you may want to single out each child privately—to further acknowledge your pride in the accomplishment of one, and to take the emotional temperature of the twin who may be feeling jealous or insecure at the same time. These situations are going to occur throughout your twins' whole lives, and the twin who is feeling a little blue now may need to be reminded of past accomplishments and future opportunities. Interestingly, it is also important to tell the twin who has had some special recognition that it is okay to enjoy it. It is not unusual for one twin to feel guilty about his twin not sharing in the glory at this particular moment. Both twins need to know that they can be jealous of their twin and pleased for him at the same time.

- *Create an environment that is conducive to schoolwork.* Peer learning and teaching has long been established as a helpful technique. Many educators recognize the value in children assisting each other to understand concepts from arithmetic operations or grammar to chemistry or algebra as their studies grow more advanced. The student with the stronger grasp on the subject learns the valuable lesson of verbalizing his knowledge in a way that makes it understandable to another. The student receiving the friendly assistance experiences a comfort level that may not be present in the standard classroom scenario. Twins doing homework together as young elementary-age students have the opportunity to experience a kind of mini study group of the sort many high

SAVING MONEY FOR YOUR TWINS' EDUCATION

Words of Wisdom from Phil Holthouse, CPA partner of the certified public accounting firm of Holthouse, Carlin and Van Trigt in Los Angeles

There's no doubt that having twins is a financial shock, and that's in addition to any other strain it might put on the family. A couple might have planned to start a family with the expectation that the mother would return to work in a few months, a year or two, or even three. But suddenly your family goes from two of you to four. All of a sudden it might not be possible for the mother to return to work, and yet the financial need is greater than expected.

The first thing you have to realize is that it is very important for parents of twins to start saving as soon as possible. As a couple with twins, you're not going to have the opportunity to stagger your children's tuition needs like most families would. In the typical family with a few kids, there is usually at least two years, and often more, between children.

(continued)

So how do you go about planning for your kids' education? The sooner you get some money working for you, the sooner those funds will begin to earn and compound. That extra time is what is going to help get you over the bulge when your twins are in college—or in private school for that matter.

For the family that really wants to get serious about saving money, you need to know where your money is going. I'd recommend that you set aside a period of three months to write down, in excruciating detail, the ways in which you spend your money. This means from the couple of dollars you pay for coffee and a danish every morning, to your rent or mortgage check, to a new pair of shoes. Most people find out that they are spending a lot more than they realized in one of the following four categories: eating out, clothes, vacations or entertainment. How is this for some eye opening math: $3.00 for coffee and danish five days a week for forty-eight weeks each year equals $720.00 annually. The point is to see where the money is going and make a serious effort to curtail that spending and turn it into savings. Once you can identify the areas of cost, you can begin controlling them.

school students use to their benefit. The give and take of such an experience can make homework a less tedious task.

Many parents find that homework done at the kitchen table while dinner is being prepared offers insight into how their twins are relating to each other and to their schoolwork. If one twin is doing all the work while the other is just copying, neither twin is benefiting. However, an opportunity to be a bit invested in each other's learning by helping each other may serve to defuse competition. The twin who has helped her sister to get a better grasp on multiplication and division is likely to take pride in her sister's excellent grade on a math quiz.

For many twins, doing homework together does not work, particularly if one twin is easily distracted or simply prefers to work privately. While peer learning and teaching has its place, it may not be the right arrangement for your twins. Sometimes the student who is excelling or more competent in a subject feels burdened and responsible for his twin's academic struggles. If your twins work together comfortably, that's great, but don't force the issue.

Tests and grades are the bane of many a student's school life. For twins, the impulse to quantify their standing with each other by comparing test scores may go beyond the peer comparisons their classmates will experience. Again, this is a time when parents will not be able to stop their twins from seeing how they measure up against each other, but parents can try to keep from raising the stakes by staying out of the minutiae of the point-by-point analysis—who got one point higher on the final exam or who spelled one more word correctly on the spelling test. Philosophical discussions about learning and testing may be helpful once your twins get a little older: The truth is that we all have individual strengths and weaknesses. One child may excel in math while his twin gets A's in creative writing. Some students "test well" and some do not. Test grades are not necessarily a measure of intelligence, but they are a measure of one's skill at taking tests. Of course, the twin who studies and is a responsible student has the greater likelihood of doing well in school.

COLLEGE

Getting Ready for College

Even as early as their freshman year of high school, some students are thinking about college. Their sensitive social antennae pick up on the chatter of Juniors and Seniors who are deeply immersed in the process of thinking about preparing for, applying to, and finally being accepted into college. The prospect of a college education means different things to different students and their families. For some, it represents the first time a member of the family goes on to higher education. Others have been groomed for the process for many years and will seek admittance to the college or univer-

Parents of twins have to get resourceful when it comes to saving money. You don't have the "hand me down" line that is built in to most families with more than one child. You're looking at buying two sets of everything for every age. Look for opportunities in the community to share and exchange clothes and especially, high ticket items like cribs. The Mothers of Twins Clubs might be a good resource for you. Why buy something out of pocket when there are people who would be thrilled to get their toys or baby clothes out of the house. Many times these things are in near perfect condition. Then when your kids outgrow something, you can pass it along to someone who can use it. I've had the thought that a clearing house for hand-me-downs on the Web might be a great idea for some enterprising person to look into. Maybe there's one already out there. Take the time to use supermarket club cards and coupons. Be a savvy shopper and wait for things to go on sale. These are not new ideas, but they're sound ideas and they work.

You may find it necessary for one wage earner in the family to take on a second job or take on some overtime hours. Of course,

(continued)

that is completely counter to what they want to be doing, which is spending time with the family, but it might help as a temporary measure. Then perhaps when the twins are in school, the stay-at-home parent can go back to work. Of course, even for the mom or dad who is staying home, it may be possible to find some part-time work that can be done at home.

For families who are looking into buying a home or those who already own their own home, one of the very best things I can recommend is to put a fifteen-year mortgage on your house. You'd be amazed at the savings that can represent. Say you have a thirty-year mortgage with a monthly payment of $1,500. If you refinance and get a fifteen-year mortgage when your twins are babies, your payments may go up to about $1,800, but by the time your twins are ready for college, you own your house free and clear. If need be, you will be able to borrow against your house and finance a real big piece, if not all, of their college education. This is actually a strategy I'd recommend to anyone planning on having children.

Parents can establish two "gift to minor" accounts. These accounts allow each parent to put up to

sity that their parents and even their grandparents attended. For some lucky, hard-working students, college is the place to pursue a career goal of which they are certain, such as medicine or teaching or law. For most students, college will be a time of self-discovery and growing independence.

For twins, college may mean a continuation of their lives together, or a long term separation for the very first time. In order to help your twins make college decisions that will be good for both of them, it is important to start talking about the process well before they are juniors or seniors in high school. Talking about college is not unlike talking to very young children about where babies come from: It is easy to give them too much information too quickly. Before you offer a lot of information, try asking them some questions. Get them thinking about what a college experience might be like. Before you even talk about the issue of their twin relationship, you need to address each twin's individual interests. You might start with some general questions:

- What kind of school interests you? Do you see yourself in a large university with many thousands of students or a small college? Do you want to be in a small college town or a big city? What part of the country would you like to live in?
- Do you have any ideas about what kind of career you hope to pursue? If not, what kinds of classes do you imagine would be of interest to you?

While it is important to consider what kind of education will help them to achieve their adult goals, for most students, college is about becoming independent and broadening their world view by meeting a diverse group of peers and teachers. It is not useful to pressure a high school student to define a career objective if they have yet to discover one. It is far more useful to ask them about what interests them. If they could have three wishes for classes that they'd love to take, what might they be. These discussions will go a long way toward revealing what kind of college education will most benefit your twins.

The questions about college choices that relate to the twin relationship have been examined and reexamined since they began preschool. As they begin thinking about, and eventually applying to colleges, take the separation question out once again and examine it under a new, bright light. Do you or your twins see any new facets that need attention? Talk together, and make sure each twin has ample opportunity to speak with you privately about their college ambitions. Many parents of college-age twins have said that both their children seemed to find a comfort zone in applying to at least one or two of the same schools.

Once your twins have established individualized wish lists about college, eventually the time comes when you need to see where those lists intersect (if they do) and where they differ (again, if they do). In the years between beginning these talks and sending your twins off to college, reality, in the form of college admissions

$10,000 a year in each child's account under the federal estate-gift tax rules. Some parents might choose instead to put money aside in their own name and just know that the funds are being set aside for the purpose of paying for their children's education. Those who have been with a company for a long time and have built up a 401(k) account may want to consider borrowing against that account to pay for their kids' education without triggering all the taxes.

Ultimately, the question each family needs to answer is: How much can you pay out of current earnings versus how much do you have to save ahead of time to pay for your kids' education? If you could have your wish come true, you'd want to save up enough to have a "pot" to draw on to pay for school. But with twins, that is going to be a tough goal to achieve, so you may have to depend upon drawing upon a blend of savings and current earnings. Remember that some careful budgeting and planning today will pay off tomorrow.

tests, scholarships and family finances, will play its very important role. Establish and maintain a good relationship with the college counselor in your twins' school (or schools). It is also helpful to remember that college, as with the rest of your twins' education, is an ongoing process, and if one or both has made a decision they are unhappy with, it can and should be remedied.

◰

*"Even back in high school, Dino and I didn't have to say things out loud. We had
completely inside jokes or maybe just a look, and we'd say everything we needed
to. That has to be hard on the girlfriend of a twin."*

—Dino, 21-year-old fraternal twin

TEENAGE TWINS

SURVIVING AND THRIVING

Adolescence is the swaying footbridge that spans the distance between childhood
and adulthood. It is a bridge worn smooth by frequent trips back and forth—this is
not a journey accomplished in one attempt. The push/pull that is emblematic of the
separation and individuation experienced by twins is also a distinctive characteristic of adolescence. All adolescents, twin or non-twin, are working hard to establish
an identity that is very much their own—therein lies the *push* from childhood pleasures to adult lessons. In order to establish their independence, your teenage twins
respond to the *pull* away from family, and that often includes each other.
Adolescents are venturing beyond the familiar comforts of home and setting their

sights on conquering new worlds. But world exploration cannot be accomplished without intermittent returns to base camp for love, encouragement, conversation and an endless supply of food for one's self and one's fellow explorers—and therein lies the *pull* back across the footbridge to the familiar surroundings of youth.

PARENTING THROUGH THE THREE STAGES OF ADOLESCENCE

Adolescence, which begins at age 12 and extends through age 19, is a developmental process best viewed in three stages:

- early—12 to 14 years old
- middle—14 to 17 years old
- late—17 to 19 years old

Adolescence is a time when your twins are doing the hard, rewarding work of developing the personal values, beliefs and behaviors that will carry them into adulthood. As your twins advance through each stage of adolescence, they should be developing an increasingly sophisticated understanding of their role in society. They will learn and relearn throughout their lives that their actions have consequences—and it is by anticipating and being responsible for their actions that they become responsible adults. The following four areas of focus are vital to your teenage twins' development.

Early Adolescence

- *Autonomy*
  There is increased moodiness as young adolescents struggle to develop a sense of identity. You will notice the tendency to use actions instead of words. Peer relationships gain importance in daily living as young adolescent twins begin to separate from parents and each other. They may begin to develop new and separate friendships outside the twin circle.

- *Sexuality*

  Girls tend to develop physically ahead of boys. They also show more inter-est in "boy/girl" relationships than same age boys. For same sex twins, par-ticularly fraternal ones, physical development may not occur concurrently, leaving one twin ahead of the other, at least until the co-twin catches up. This is also a time when your teens may insist on more privacy from parents and their co-twin.

- *Ethical Behavior*

  They are able to think more abstractly than was possible in their elemen-tary years and are now testing limits and rules. Some adolescents may experiment with smoking, drugs and/or alcohol. In a Finnish study, it was found that twins smoked and used alcohol less than non-twins. This may be interpreted as being due to the "intertwin relationship" and the sup-port each gives to the other.

- *Work Goals*

  They are still more interested in the here and now but are growing inter-ested in looking to the future.

Middle Adolescence

- *Autonomy*

  They are more self-involved—concerned with their body and appearance. There is a need to make new friends and identify with a peer group. Teenage twins are continuing to separate from their parents and co-twin and often feel a sadness regarding the loss.

- *Sexuality*

  Girls and boys are likely to be dating and will easily change from one rela-tionship to another. It is not unusual to "break up" on Friday and date someone else on Saturday.

- *Ethical Behavior*
  The setting of future goals is becoming more complicated for some. They are beginning to look to others for role models.

- *Work Goals*
  There may be diverging interests in particular academic areas, school clubs or intellectual pursuits. One or both twins may seek opportunities for summer employment or internships in work environments that interest them, such as clerical work in a law firm or kitchen work in a restaurant.

Late Adolescence

- *Autonomy*
  Twins are establishing a greater sense of personal identity. Adolescent twins in this stage are more self-reliant. More thought goes into making decisions. As a consequence, there is less impulsive behavior. There is an increased ability to compromise with parents, co-twins, siblings and peers without fear of "losing face."

- *Sexuality*
  Boys and girls pursue and participate in longer, more intense relationships. Sexual identity is examined in a personal and meaningful way.

- *Ethical Behavior*
  There is increased insight into the consequences of behavior as well as heightened interest in setting and achieving goals.

- *Work Goals*
  Increasing concern about the future—"What am I doing with my life?" College or other training takes on real-life implications as teenage twins approach their twenties. There is increased insight into the long-term benefits and liabilities of specific career goals.

The push/pull that characterizes each individual teen experience is also fundamental to the twin/twin and parent/child relationships. Parents struggle daily with finding a healthy balance between protecting their children and encouraging them to step out into the world. It is very important to set limits by making your rules and standards of behavior clear to your adolescent twins. Yet those rules cannot be so rigorous as to prevent your teens from venturing into the world and developing the coping skills and maturity to put those rules to the test.

Each twin is an individual, and you may find that the guidelines for homework, phone calls or parties set out for both twins may be appropriate for one but not the other. If a twin ignores the "house rules" on alcohol and automobiles and is driven home by a friend who has been drinking, parental intervention is needed *for that twin*. The areas of greatest conflict for parents and adolescents are schoolwork, friends, dating, curfews and chores. Your twin's level of maturity is a much better indicator than age when it comes to setting reasonable limits in any of these areas. Each twin should be held accountable as an individual, whether it is for an accomplishment or an error in judgment. One twin should not be held back from socializing because of a co-twin's poor behavior.

CLIMBING MANY MOUNTAINS

For twins, the adolescent years offer great challenges. Not only are they imposing a degree of distance between themselves and their families, but they may (some for the first time) be needing and creating distance from each other. Identical twins may continue to be more similar in their development and interests than fraternal twins, yet all adolescent twins are becoming more individuated throughout the years of their adolescence. Twins who have always been close may recognize that they are beginning to differentiate from each other for the first time. Sometimes this process happens unequally—in a matter of a few short weeks, one twin may have a new "best friend." Perhaps a hobby or an activity will engage one twin and not the other—one twin gets involved in the drama club and is swept off into play rehearsals and a new social life. It is not at all unusual for twins to be both eager and ambivalent about separating from their co-twin at this time. They may experience great excitement at the prospect of independence, whether that means a separate school, an independent interest or a boyfriend or girlfriend.

At the same time they are differentiating, they may experience fear of being on their own and/or guilt over leaving their co-twin for new, exciting activities and relationships. The twin left behind may feel hurt and abandoned. This is the time for parents to talk to their twins about the ebb and flow of relationships. Just as one may be leaving the nest for a while, the other may not be ready. When the twin is ready to come back for refueling, his co-twin may be ready to take flight. Eventually, all will even out.

Naturally, this time of upheaval also affects parents. There is no template for the perfect relationship between teenage twins—and there is no perfect parental response to these volatile times. Suddenly, a mother and father who have been deeply invested in their twins' close relationship may feel there is "something wrong." The tales they have heard over the years of twins who are estranged from each other begin to haunt them: "Our twins have always been so close. What is wrong?" In most cases, *nothing is wrong*. There may indeed be increased friction— twins arguing a little more as they try to work out who they are and establish their separate identities. There may also be more division in their social lives as peer groups defined by new interests enter the picture. For example, one twin may be trying out for the cheerleading squad while the other is going to art films with the high school's independent film club.

It is not unusual, particularly in the early adolescent years, for twins to be embarrassed by each other's presence. As teens, they look to their peers and model their behavior. They do not see all their other non-twin friends constantly in the presence of another family member. The frequent presence of a co-twin may begin to feel "babyish," and they may attempt to separate, not wishing to appear to be each other's social appendage. A 13-year-old described being mean to his twin brother so that he would not seek him out in the hallway at school between classes. Teenage twins may appear somewhat indifferent to each other, causing hurt feelings.

This is when parents may need to step in and talk to each twin about ground rules for behavior throughout their adolescence. The following points may be useful:

- *All teenagers feel an increased need to "be on their own."* This is not a license for twins to be cruel to each other. If one twin does not want to be around the other, it needs to be accomplished without intentional cruelty. That is not to say one child's feelings may not be hurt, but exclusion with intent to hurt is not in the best interest of anyone. Pass along the good advice of imagining one's self in the other guy's shoes.

- *Everybody needs some privacy.* Adolescents need time to think, be by themselves, talk on the telephone, listen to music or simply daydream outside the presence of their co-twin or anyone else. If your same sex twins are still sharing a room when they reach their teens, don't be surprised or concerned if either or both voice an interest in having a separate bedroom. If that arrangement is not feasible in your home, establish some guidelines for each twin's private space and time. Have a family meeting and establish "house rules" to cover everyone's right to privacy. For example, if phone privacy is a priority (as it is to most teens), a cordless phone can be helpful in turning almost any room into a private phone space. If your twins share a bedroom, neither of them should be displaced when their twin wants to entertain friends privately. You may find it worthwhile for the family to make a guest room, TV room, living room or even the kitchen a teen-friendly place to hang out. Set up a schedule that allows equal time for each twin's solo entertaining.

- *Don't push the panic button.* You cannot force your twins to stay close. Pressuring them will inevitably have undesirable consequences. Parental pressure may cause twins to be resentful of each other as well as you, resulting in estrangement on all fronts. Many parents who have made it through their twin's teenage years acknowledge that they cherished an unrealistic fantasy of what the teen years would be like for their twins. As is the case with most fantasies, real life has a way of intruding and offering its own unimagined challenges and rewards.

Twins who are made to feel guilty about their separate interests may play down those interests in order to satisfy a parental need or desire for them to stay the same. The sad result of this kind of pressure is to stop an otherwise age-appropriate and necessary process of individuation in its tracks.

On the other hand, twins with similar interests, hobbies and friends should not be forced to separate due to parental concern that their twins' individuation will be impeded by their continued closeness. If twins want to explore similar hobbies or interests, parents can encourage them to broaden their social circle to include other friends with the same interest or even participate in the same activity at different times.

- *Look, listen and learn.* Make a habit of "taking the temperature" of your twins' relationship periodically, such as every three months or so. Keep a little journal in which you jot down your insights and concerns regarding their individual behaviors as well as their relationship. Look for trends, rather than addressing every flare up. Your twins' development throughout adolescence is sometimes more discreet than their early childhood milestones. It is easy to see the crawling child become the walking child. It is less obvious when the child who has depended on her twin to make friends for them both begins to reach out a bit more independently. Offer support—not solutions. If you think they seem to be a little overly interdependent, and neither has many other friends, encourage them to opt for some separate activities. If their interests have carried them far apart, rekindle some mutual connection time with an outing or activity they both love. It might be as simple as watching a movie together. A little gentle guidance can go a long way.

- *Reassure your twins that this process is normal and does not signify the end of their close friendship.* If your twins' adolescence is shaking you up, imagine what it is doing to them. Encourage your twins to talk to you and each other *at their own pace*. Whether or not they are prepared to acknowledge it, either or both twins may feel deeply conflicted about the current state of their twin relationship. You might even use your own sibling to provide a familiar context for your discussions: "Aunt Liz and I were only two years apart, and we barely spoke with each other through high school. We just didn't seem to have much in common, and now she is my very close friend as well as my sister."

- *Make your home a haven to your twins and their friends.* As any parent of a teenager knows, a well-stocked refrigerator goes a long way when it comes to keeping teens and their friends around the house long enough to gain some insight into the daily challenges of their lives. Whether it is an entire sports team, a best friend or a romantic interest, the more welcoming your home, the greater your opportunity to observe your twins "among their own kind" in these important years.

- *Seek professional help if you are concerned about the mental, emotional or physical health of your twin(s).* Part of growing up is learning to cope with anxiety and responsibility. Occasionally, a child or teen becomes overwhelmed and needs professional support from a therapist or other health care specialist. If your parental instincts tell you something is "wrong" with your child, take immediate steps to seek help. Speak with your twins, together and separately, about your family rules regarding "at risk" behavior. By the time they are teens, your twins are likely to have well-established protocols for keeping each other's secrets. You need to make it clear that when it comes to behaviors that put them at risk, the rules about keeping secrets fly out the window. The twin who knows her twin is drinking and driving or routinely disregarding seat belt laws or taking drugs or having unprotected sex needs to tell a responsible adult.

DATING AND SOCIAL LIFE

Dating. The very word conjures images of awkward first kisses, long phone calls and social complexities that have been a part of teenage life for generations. You are likely to have memories to share with your teens about your first date, pledges of lifelong love with "oh, what was his name?" and arguments with your parents over curfews and car keys. For twins, dating is all that, compounded by the complexities of their twin relationship.

One of the first complications twins may experience as part of dating is competition. It is very rare for two friends, let alone a set of twins, to have their first date or their first boyfriend or girlfriend at the same time. One twin is going to be the first to go out on a date. Dating is a dramatic expression of worldliness that will be matched only when the other twin begins to date as well. This is not to say that there will always be a mad rush to be the first to date. Ironically, the twin who has a boyfriend or girlfriend may be trading the time she used to have with her co-twin and friends for the often more demanding needs of a new romantic relationship with one person. It is not at all unusual for the twin who has rushed into dating to find that it isn't necessarily all it's cracked up to be. Today's teens have many activities competing for their attention—schoolwork, sports, school clubs, friends, family and now a steady date. Some teens find they are not really ready for a romantic involvement and return to having fun with a group of friends.

Where does all this new activity leave the twin relationship? Often, the relationship is stronger for the experience. Some twins will find opportunities to share their insights with each other, and both are better prepared when they feel ready to try dating again. The relationship can also be strengthened by conflict. As a parent, you may want to help your twins understand that as angry or hurt as they become with each other, their relationship may emerge more resilient for having survived such deeply felt emotions.

The introduction of a steady date into the life of one twin inevitably has an impact on the life of the other. This may be obvious in the case of same sex twins, but it also holds true for boy/girl twins. If, as is often the case, the girl is developing at a faster rate than her twin, she may be attracted to a boy who is slightly older than her brother. Sometimes, that makes the boy of the twin pair feel uncomfortable—his sister's boyfriend may treat him like a kid brother. For other boy/girl twins, the introduction of a boyfriend or girlfriend represents an infusion of fun and friendship that strengthens the twin bond. Same sex twins also experience complications around the ages of their dates. When one of two female twins dates an "older man," perhaps an upperclassman or a college freshman, it may inspire feelings of jealousy in her twin sister, who then grows unhappy with the boyfriend who is her age and grade peer.

What is the role of a parent who is observing these complicated scenarios take place? First of all, realize it may take patience and careful observation to figure out exactly what is going on. The days when a young man stood quaking in front of his date's father to be read the riot act is gone in many households. It may not be until several weeks of name-dropping or giggling asides from siblings that you figure out there is a romantic interest on the scene. At that point, just as you want and need to know who your teens' friends are, you will want to learn more about this boyfriend or girlfriend. But unless a dating relationship is actually damaging to your child—if there are drugs, physical or verbal abuse or other at-risk behaviors—your level of involvement should be one of the interested observer.

Every family has its own protocol regarding appropriate behavior for their dating teens, and parents must make their rules and expectations absolutely clear. Encourage your twins to establish some ground rules for dating. As they begin to encounter dating situations, they should talk about hypotheticals: Do we date the same guy or girl? If one of us stops seeing someone, how long, *if ever*, before the other might date that person? How do you feel about double dating? Finally, you come to the toughest part of parenting—the realization that regardless of your hard-earned wisdom and your deeply held belief that *you know what is best for them*, your twins need to make their own mistakes and learn their own sometimes painful lessons.

TWIN TALK

Jill Ganon

Dino and Marco, 21-year-old fraternal twins

DATING

Jill: What can you tell me about dating?

Dino: When Marco was fourteen or fifteen, he met a girl, and he got real sweet on her all through high school and up to the first two years of college. So the first girl he ever dated, he just kept dating forever.

Marco: I think part of it has to do with my need for stability, and I had a really comfortable situation. Part of it also had to do with the fact that I do have a heart condition and nobody can tell me what my life expectancy is. I've always had my cardiologist talking about a transplant and all this kind of stuff. There was always that fear that I was going to die very young, and it still is in the back of my mind. I think I really wanted some kind of relationship. It was a great relationship. She was very loving, very sweet, smart, very kind and caring, but now I'm a much different person.

Jill: Did Marco's relationship have an impact on you, Dino?

Dino: Yeah! I was supposed to be the cool guy. We were really young, and I had never kissed a girl, and Marco had his first kiss and his first girlfriend before I did. So that's probably why, later on, I tried to make up for it. *[Both brothers laugh.]*

Jill: Were you jealous of Marco's girlfriend?

Dino: Maybe at times. I think maybe one or two times. But overall it was never a real threat. It was funny, 'cause we have one other friend—he's really like a third brother to us—and the three of us were almost inseparable, 'cause we all grew up together. So among all of us—our girlfriends and our friends and their girlfriends—they all would say, "I could never compete with what you two guys have."

Marco: That was a big problem with my girlfriend. She always felt a little outside. You know, being a twin, you grow up and I've heard of other twins developing their own language and to a certain extent that was what we found. We could communicate almost effortlessly.

Dino: It's interesting, 'cause most girls who like Marco don't like me as much.

Marco: We each have very different taste in girls, very different.

Dino: The girls who like me don't tend to like Marco as much. But one of my barometers of a relationship is, if I bring a girl to meet Marco and she's rude to him, or if they just don't get along at all, I don't want to be with her. I know it just can't work. There's no ifs, ands or buts about it.

Marco: There has never been a question between the two of us of what was important. And even when I was in this really long-term relationship, there were a couple of times when she was rude to him or whatever, and I kind of got angry with her, because to me no one is more important than Dino. No one in this world is more important than him. We're lucky in that way, 'cause I know a lot of twins aren't like that.

Jill: Have you thought about whether you want to marry and have families?

Marco: I'd like to marry, but I'm not sure if I want children.

Jill: Do you think your twin relationship has in any way prepared you for another long-term relationship?

Marco: I think we know better than other people our age that you can make things work. Dino and I cannot get a divorce. We've got to make it work, and we always have.

Jill: How important do you think it will be for your wife to be comfortable with your brother?

Dino: If my wife was not comfortable with my brother, it would be like her not being comfortable with a part of myself. There was one girlfriend I dated for a while and she and Marco never really got along. And the relationship just kind of ended early. But I learned that's clearly a barometer for me. Marco is a part of me. As trite as that sounds, it's really true, so when somebody comes into my life, it is fundamental that they have to be okay with Marco. For me an ideal situation would be if a girl got along as well with Marco—but not quite as well—as she did with me. That would be wonderful.

Marco: It's funny, being a twin has really helped me and will help me in the future, especially in a long-term relationship. I know the relationship I had with my girlfriend was very deep, especially for people as young as us. Part of the reason it worked was that I already had a really good grasp of how to work in a relationship. It came naturally to me to work things out and to really work on a relationship and not just forget about it.

"*Sometimes I've resented the fact that I was born with this heart problem and Dino wasn't. I think it really made me push harder to kind of be more normal. And so that's always been kind of a thing between us.*"

—Marco, 21-year-old fraternal twin

DIFFERENT TWINS—DIFFERENT NEEDS

SPECIAL NEEDS

Multiples are at greater risk than singleton infants of being born prematurely, and the incidence of developmental disability in premature infants is higher than it is in infants born at term. The more premature the birth, and the lower the birth weight, the greater the likelihood of significant health problems. Some premature infants will have only mild complications without lingering developmental effects, and some will have more serious complications. In addition to complications of prematurity, infants may experience problems during delivery or as a result of intrauterine conditions, such as one twin getting more nutrition than the other. These complications not withstanding, it is important to recognize that the majority of preterm infants are born without major disabilities.

Until now, our discussions about twins have referred to those who function without any particular deficit that would distinguish them as being differently abled in our society. This does not mean they are without problems, because every child and every adult has special needs at some time in their lives. In this chapter we are going to talk about children and teens whose special need—whether it is physical, cognitive, psychological or social—defines them as being differently abled than their peers, and of course that may include their twin. This distinguishing condition may range from mild to severe. It may affect one child, both, or more in the case of higher order multiples. Some parents find out during pregnancy that their child or children will be born with a disability. Others make the discovery at birth, and still others as their children get older. A developmental or health problem may impede a child's ability to lead a completely independent life, or it may be so discreet as to be indiscernible to most people. Either one or both twins may be affected. A disability that is overwhelming to one family may be perceived as a bump in the road to another. What is common to every family with a child who has special needs is the importance of attending to the needs and feelings not only of the child but of the other family members as well.

TAKING THE TIME TO ADJUST

When a child is born with a serious developmental disability, parents are faced with the loss of the fantasy of parenting a healthy child. If the problem is lifethreatening or very severe, they must attend to the immediate needs of their infant before even acknowledging their own sense of losing the fantasy of raising a healthy child. As the parents of twins, they may have one healthy child and one seriously ill child. Months of preparing for "the babies" rarely include preparations for a seriously disabled child or children. The following story from a mother of three-year-old fraternal twins illustrates one family's journey from denial and uncertainty to a hopeful, realistic understanding of life with very differently abled twins:

At first I noticed that one of my sons was not responding like his brother. His language was not as developed, and he seemed withdrawn. At first I thought that he would catch up, but he didn't seem to. My husband and my parents all said "not to worry." I wanted so much to believe everything was okay, but I didn't really think it was. I took both kids for a hearing test when they were about two years old, and the doctor said his hearing was fine. But by then I knew there was a problem. I started trusting my instincts and ignored what the rest of my family was telling me. I took my son for comprehensive testing, and I was told he showed a capacity to learn, but he also had some autistic tendencies. The doctor didn't want to label him right away.

I went numb and was overwhelmed and shocked. I had very little understanding of autism. I wanted to say it was a bad diagnosis. I went through it all—denial, rage, grief, all that kind of stuff. Suddenly my life was filled with specialists. There was a speech specialist, occupational and physical therapists, a psychologist. You name it, we were there. After awhile I realized my life was completely out of whack. I had another child at home. I started to get angry. What about my other son? What about time for me? I had started to take some classes, and, of course, I had to drop them all. I saw a therapist who suggested keeping a journal on our son and all our experiences with him. That actually helped me to slow down, step back and observe, and get in touch with my feelings about the impact of my child's condition on me and the rest of the family.

I can't tell you how much it helped me to get some therapy, some support, a place where I could express all the thoughts and fears I was so ashamed of or afraid of. I was overwhelmed for quite awhile. How was I going to be there for my other child? How would I learn how to handle a special-needs child? What about my life and my marriage? I felt ashamed and embarrassed that I had a child with autism. I felt like it was my fault, like I had defective genes or had done something to make this happen. I know I didn't, but it was still a part of my guilt and shame. I finally started to search for things that would help us in the here and now. I began to think about my spirituality. My extended family was asking all kinds of questions, but I withdrew. I needed time to digest the diagnosis. Finally I decided to join a support group—other families with autistic children. My son was having temper tantrums in public, and I could bring this to the group and get good caring support from people who had gone through the same thing.

I went to a conference given by a well-known doctor who specializes in autistic children. It was a real roller coaster. I'd start feeling hopeful and then something would happen and I'd think, I can't take this anymore. After a good cry, I'd feel more accepting for awhile, but I was still all over the map—angry, sad, depressed, accepting, then angry again. I hated taking my son to occupational therapy. There were all kinds of children there with different disabilities, and it just reinforced the realization that my child had disabilities also. But we hung in there with different therapies, and my parents helped out a lot. I tried to have time with both children every day.

Between six and nine months later, my son was reevaluated and had made tremendous progress. Actually, I was aware of that before it was confirmed with his therapist. He was more connected to people, and his language was greatly improved. I think he will always have problems, but I am more hopeful and less frightened than I would have believed possible a year ago.

Before parents are able to see the ways in which both their children are going to enrich, complicate and forever change their lives, before they can help their differently abled twins to support, love and understand each other, they need to examine and process the feelings attendant to being the mother or father of a disabled child. The following three suggestions apply to every family faced with the unexpected challenge of caring for a differently abled infant or child:

- *Acknowledge the full range of your feelings.* There are many complex feel-ings that surround the birth of a sick child. Shock, denial, anger, disap-pointment, sadness, helplessness, anxiety are painful but normal responses to this situation.

  All your feelings need to be examined and addressed. If only one of your twins is ill there is sadness for one and joy for the other. Take the time to recognize and process all these feelings.

- *Make every effort to restore and maintain some balance in your life.* No matter how dedicated, selfless and determined you are to provide quality of life to your differently abled twin(s), it must not happen at the expense of your own balanced life. You have at least one other child, and maybe more, who need your attention, affection and good humor. You have a marriage partner who is also struggling. You have friends, extended family and work that need your attention. Try not to burden your differently abled child with the weight of your singular attention. Build opportunities into your family life for some alone time with your non-disabled child or children. Everyone in the family deserves the best quality of life that is possible for them.

- *Jump onto the Internet, the phone—talk to everyone.* Find out what sort of support services are available to your family. Cultivate relationships with your pediatrician, organizations, agencies, support groups and other families that share a common interest in your child's specific disorder. It is especially helpful to meet and speak with families whose children are older than yours and can offer you the "been there, done that, and we're making it" perspec-tive. Look into what options will be available for your twin once he or she is of school age. Become an advocate for your child. You will feel empow-ered when you address the issues, and learn the facts about your child's dis-ability.

BEING A FAMILY

In many cases, a differently abled twin's special needs are more subtle but still significant. There may be language delay, developmental or motor delay, or some social difficulty. When one twin is significantly delayed in one or more areas, developmental milestones may be bittersweet. An achievement for one twin such as walking, speaking or throwing a ball may evoke many different feelings in parents and eventually in both twins as they grow older and are able to comprehend the disparity between their very different abilities. Each twin will have unique milestones and achievements and need to learn by your example that they are both worthy of appreciation. Make sure both twins know you see them as individuals with their own strengths and weaknesses, dreams, and desires.

A twin family with one or two disabled children may feel isolated and "different" from other families with twins. Even close family friends may not know how to talk about it. That is why it is so important to reach out to support groups. Be sure to reach out into the community for social diversion as well. You need all the support you can get.

As your twins grow up, you will have many discussions with them, privately and together, about their feelings. Your non-disabled twin will need age-appropriate reassurance throughout her childhood and teen years: She did nothing to cause her co-twin's disability; she will not catch the disability, it is not contagious; she is not "bad" for sometimes being angry or resentful of her co-twin for the extra attention she receives; she doesn't have to be "perfect" in an attempt to compensate for her sibling; it is natural for her to experience embarrassment over her twin's condition and just as natural to grow beyond that embarrassment in time. The co-twin of a disabled twin has her own special needs, and you must recognize that fact and support her.

The differently abled twin is also in need of support and understanding. As she begins to ask questions about her disability you will need to explain that neither she nor you nor anyone is to blame for her condition. Reassure her that her disability is not the result of her having been bad—it is a part of her life that she will learn to handle and understand. Your love, support, and empathy will be vital throughout her childhood and teen years. But be careful not to indulge yourselves or your differently abled child in viewing her as "less than," because she certainly is not.

They may both express anger and frustration at times. For example, if only one twin is affected, "Why me?" from one twin, and "Why not me?" from the other. Your enormous challenge is to listen, explain what you can and try to remain even-keeled. The child who has a disability may undergo episodes of rage, as your other twin endures feelings of guilt made more complicated by relief that she is unencumbered by her twin's disability. Both twins may experience jealousy—one child may be jealous of her sister's freedom relative to her own confinement, while the other is jealous of the time and attention given her differently abled sister. Your children will benefit from your presence as a sounding board, but you need to know from the outset that you cannot take away either twin's pain.

It is very important to acknowledge that they will not have the "perfect twin relationship" that either they or you may have fantasized about. As parents of differently abled twins, you are in the unusual position of de-emphasizing their twinship. This is not to say that you devalue the relationship—instead you emphasize their individuality as a means of freeing both from the burden of comparison. Help both twins see their responsibilities are to do what they are best suited to do. Each has strengths, and each has limitations. If one twin is unable to participate in a fully physical lifestyle, what is she doing to cultivate and challenge her mind so as to participate in the world around her? If your other twin is without physical disabilities, how is she taking advantage of her mobility to be a vital and useful member of the community?

When a family member has a disability, everyone in the family needs help in developing successful coping skills. The differently abled twin will need to learn how to express her anger and frustration without hurting herself or anyone else. If she is demanding, help her learn that there need to be appropriate limits to her behavior. Allowing her to run the show by catering to unrealistic needs does her a tremendous disservice. She, like all members of the family, is responsible for her actions. You can help her to understand her limitations and strengths. See her as an individual, and help her to do the same. A balanced, loving approach to raising both your twins is the goal. The twin who is not disabled is also faced with considerable challenges. She will have to learn how to enjoy her life without a shadow of guilt clouding her relationship with her sister.

Parents need to learn how to care for themselves and each other, and seek the support that allows for a balanced lifelong approach to raising their differently abled child or children. Everyone in the family will benefit from finding at least one way to express their feelings. Children should be encouraged to find a vehicle for expression in drawings, stories, acting out skits, or even journal-keeping or photography as they grow a little older. Try giving your elementary-age twin the beginning of a sentence to complete, such as "Sometimes I feel different because . . ." or "These are things I like about myself . . ." or "Some things I am good at are . . ." Everyone in the family has lots of feelings, and those feelings may change from moment to moment. Reassure yourself, your spouse, and your children that all their feelings are okay, and they should not try to mask feelings of anger or frustration. It is much healthier to give those feelings voice in order to acknowledge and get through them. One way mothers and fathers can express their feelings is to write them down in a notebook kept at the bedside or in a briefcase or purse.

The father of two developmentally disabled twins began to dictate his thoughts into a little palm-size tape recorder that he used in his business. For the first three years of his twins' lives, he had these tapes transcribed every few months. At the end of three years, he gave the complete transcriptions to his wife, and they read through them together. The range of emotion from fear to despair to astonishment and hope became a chronicle of the richness of their complicated lives. They donated a copy of this incredible document to the NICU (Neonatal Intensive Care Unit) that cared for their twins for the first few months of their lives. It has since offered great inspiration to families who have followed a similar path with their children.

TWIN TALK

Dino and Marco, 21-year-old fraternal twins

HEALTH

Authors' Note: Marco has a heart condition, which he brought up in the course of our conversation. He and Dino generously offered to share their thoughts about this sensitive subject. We have used other segments of their very rich twin conversation throughout this book.

Dino: I think about Marco and his heart every day. It's like not knowing if the person is coming home at night. That's how I feel a lot of times. We don't really know what's going to happen. So in that respect, the older I've gotten, the more cognizant I've become of it. As a little kid I didn't really realize it, and then it got to a certain point where I think after Marco became very aware of the problems with his heart, I did, too. I think about it a lot. We all know what the situation is. The family has pretty good communication. It's not that we won't talk about it, but often there is no reason for me to talk about it. We go through periods where we'll talk about it more.

Marco: I used to be pretty dark when I was growing up. I don't know if it was because of my health or what. But I always had a tendency to be really depressed. Last July, I started having a lot of health problems. I was passing out a lot. What I found out is that—and nobody told me ahead of time—as the condition

(left to right) *Marco and Dino*

progresses, your heart rate starts slowing down gradually. And so I would start passing out when I was climbing or just passing out everywhere. I ended up having a pacemaker, and it's changed my life.

I've kind of known about the possibility of a pacemaker since I was eighteen. I remember I went to my annual cardiac checkup with the cardiologist who has known me since I was born. And he said I would probably have to put a pacemaker in in the next couple of years to keep from burning out. And I said, "So what exactly does burning out entail?" And he said, "You'll probably die or need a transplant." I know it sounds cold, but he is great and he's known me all my life. Getting a pacemaker has been fantastic. Once I got it, they had me test it out by going for a run. I went for a run, and for the first time in my life I was able to go for a run and not get tired. It really changed my life and removed all kinds of mental obstacles in all areas of my life. I can go for a run, I can do anything, and I think it also helped my relationship with Dino.

As far as life expectancy and all that, I think about it sometimes, but it's something I live with. I try not to think about it a lot. Now, with the pacemaker I workout six days a week, so I can lead a really normal life. The only thing is, sometimes I get really tired because I try to push myself too hard.

About a month after I got the pacemaker, I ended up doing a cruise ship job, playing music out in the Caribbean. I spent a good month out there away from Dino. And during that time as I was getting adjusted to it, I sort of developed this new attitude about life. Just that brief time away helped me individualize away from Dino. So when we came back together, there was more of a feeling that we were two individuals who really understood each other a lot better. *[To Dino]* I don't know exactly how to put it. . . .

Dino: *[Addressing his brother]* I think for a long time it was kind of an unequal relationship, because of the fact that for a lot of reasons you have always kind of been a little bit in my shadow. And I knew it and you knew it, and we talked about it, and I would have to sort of ease back what I was doing. *[Addressing Jill]* But then when he kind of got back to town with this new attitude, suddenly I was telling him "What happened? I'm the star." We'd go out and he'd be dressed better than me and looking better than me, and I'd feel like I'm tired, I'm going home. It used to be so easy. So it's taken me awhile to adjust. But the thing about his health is that it has finally made me think. It's one of those things I've always taken for granted. One of the reasons I started to try to be healthy is not only because of the fact that I didn't want to look like a goof, but it's also the realization that Marco kind of had this bum deal with his heart, and he's over there working out, and I'm eating a cheeseburger and having a cigarette, and I'm perfectly healthy. So maybe I should try to make the most of what I have.

"*I was having a hard time, and suddenly it occurred to me, there must be some-body else somewhere who was experiencing this. There had to be others who had lost a baby at the same time they had a baby.*"

—Jean Kollantai, founder of the Center for Loss in Multiple Birth, Inc. (CLIMB)

WHEN A TWIN DIES

GRIEVING PARENTS

The cycle of life and death is something we begin to learn about when we are young children. A beloved grandmother dies, our parents tell us she was very old, and she lived a long, rich life. Even though the family is very sad, it was her time to die. Your parents may even have spoken about the "cycle of life and death." Some of us may have experienced the death of the treasured family dog or cat when we were young. Our parents helped us to understand that our human lives are generally longer than the lives of the pets we cherish throughout our lifetimes. Though no pet is a replacement for another, we learned that there would be many pets to love throughout our lives. Depending on your family's belief system and religious practice, you may have been told about heaven or an afterlife or the reincarnation of the soul or that after life, there is death and nothing more.

When an infant twin dies, parents are faced with an enormous challenge. Just as they are supposed to be rejoicing at the birth of their two babies, they are confronted with mourning the death of one. How are they to balance their joy and their sorrow? Well-meaning friends and family may make terribly insensitive remarks, such as "Be thankful you have another one," as though your child is an object that can be replaced with another similar model. You have spent many months preparing yourselves and others for the arrival of the twins. Now while you are and will forever be the parents of both children, only one has survived. There is sometimes guilt over fears that the pregnancy was poorly managed. There may be accusations made toward the doctors, or between the parents. But finally, a couple is left with profound, understandable and natural sadness over the death of a baby, and the immediate necessity to love and care for the emotional and physical needs of another baby. In some multiple births, a family may experience the death of two or more babies. Sadly, the possibility of a twin's death is not confined to infancy. The untimely tragedy of a fatal illness or accident may also rob a family of their beloved child. In this chapter we will talk about understanding your own grief as well as your mate's. We'll also talk about the challenges that face the surviving twin and your role in helping your child to process his or her own deep sense of loss.

MOTHERS AND FATHERS GRIEVE DIFFERENTLY

The death of a child is an aberration of the life cycle—parents are not supposed to outlive their children. The baby or child who dies has not lived a rich, long life of seven or eight or nine decades; there has been no opportunity to accumulate joys and sorrows and experience. A child's death is potential stopped in its tracks. It is incalculably sad for the surviving family, both as a family unit and as individuals. Grief is powerful and inevitable, and it is a very personal *process* that happens at its own rate and manifests in its own way for every individual. Elisabeth Kübler-Ross points out the following stages of grieving:

- Denial
  There is a feeling of disbelief: "This isn't really happening."

- Anger
  Feeling angry with everyone and everything.

- Bargaining
  The point at which the gradual realization of the situation begins to set in: "If I do [fill in the blank], the situation will change."

- Depression
  The period during which feelings reach their lowest point.

- Acceptance
  After feeling the loss, there is an upward movement away from depression; the desire to begin to make contact with others. This marks the start of accepting the good with the bad and beginning to move on.

These stages do not necessarily occur in the above order, and they do not occur within any fixed time frame. It is also recurring, just when you feel you have done all the grieving you can do, something will trigger an emotional response in you and grief reappears in one of its stages. For parents who lost one or both twins even several years ago, the sight of an intact pair of twins playing in the park may be enough to set off a profound sense of loss. The ocean's waves are an apt metaphor for grief—they come and go, and you never know when you will be hit by one. The first one is the biggest shock, and as they continue, they become smaller and smaller. Yet they remain waves of emotions; you never know when one will come along and knock you off your feet.

As we've described above, a mother and father grieving over the death of a child will experience different emotions and will process their grief within different time frames. Mothers may grieve actively over a longer time and be more likely than fathers to cry and to share their grief with others. They are also more inclined to join support groups and seek out other parents with this shared experience. Fathers may tend to be more private in their grieving process. At the same time, they are more likely to give voice to anger at the tragic loss. Many wives express astonishment at their husband's ability to keep themselves busy with work. It is far more rare for a father to seek out support or even compassion among friends, coworkers or professional grief counselors than it is for a mother to do the same.

These different manifestations of the grieving process may be confusing to couples whose first impulse is the expectation that they will see each other's grief reflected between them. The hurt they feel may be so deep that it impedes their ability to care for and nurture each other. This occurs at a time when they most need caring and nurturing. Some couples may be so overwhelmed that they need professional counseling to support their relationship. At the same time they must continue in their role as parents to their surviving children. Other couples may tend to draw closer together during this time of grief. Clearly, there is no recovery from this loss. The death of a child forever alters the life of a family, yet the survival, and eventual thriving, of the family is the greatest possible tribute to the child who has died. Parents may find it helpful to consider the following points:

- *Accept each other's differences.* Realize that everyone grieves separately and in their own way. Try not to judge each other. The fact that a father is able to laugh at a joke does not mean he did not love his child, just as a mother's daily tears do not mean she is overindulging in grief. There is no *right way* to grieve. Grieve the way you need to, and accept the same from your mate.
- *Seek support from others.* Support means different things to different people. Some may find it helpful to seek religious counsel, while others may find the greatest solace in speaking with those who have experienced the death of their own loved one. Some parents report that friends and acquaintances withdraw after the death of a child, or that they themselves find certain

friends insensitive to their grief and withdraw from those friendships. Look to those who respect your right to grieve in your own way.

- *Speak with each other about your different ways of grieving.* The fact that each of you grieves as an individual should not deter you from communicating with each other. Emotional expression is a powerful bonding force, and avoiding it may leave you or your mate feeling isolated. Just remember that communication is as much about listening as it is about talking. The husband who holds and comforts his wife as she talks about her feelings is providing loving support. Don't assume that because you need to express your feelings at a given time, that your mate has the same need, *or the same ability to verbalize his or her feelings.* If conversation about your grief seems too daunting, you may want to keep a journal of your thoughts throughout this difficult time and consider sharing it with your mate at some point.

WHEN A TWIN DIES AT, OR NEAR, BIRTH

When confronted with the death of one of their infant twins, parents experience a complex fusion of the greatest possible pain and joy. They are thrilled by the new arrival and at the same time devastated by the loss. The grieving process is difficult and complex. There are some elements of grief that are universal, and others that are deeply private and unique to each person. Parents express initial feelings of shock: "This can't be happening to me. This must be a bad dream." They are grieving the loss of their baby and the twin relationship. They will miss watching their twins grow up together and they will not have the opportunity to be the parents of intact twins. They are also confused as to their role as the parents of twins, because one of their twins is deceased. Grief, raw and still unprocessed, is often put aside as parents take up the work of caring for their new baby. A mountain of stress, adjustments and decisions must be confronted in a short period of time.

The following are thoughts and suggestions that come from parents who have experienced the death of a twin baby:

- Take your time. Don't be rushed into any of the important decisions you'll need to make throughout these challenging early hours or days.
- Remember that you have the right to ask any question, now or later. Every parent wants to understand why their baby has died. Ask to have a written report on the cause of death or make a tape recording of the information. Knowing the cause of death may help in caring for your survivor, particularly if the cause was related to genetics or the intrauterine experience.
- Name both your babies. The child who died is a person, and that person has a real identity. If no hospital staff asks you the name of your deceased child, tell them the baby's name. Use it throughout the grieving process and thereafter. You, the surviving twin and your family will benefit from a "named" memory.
- Consider holding your baby or babies after death. Parents who did not take the opportunity for this physical connection with their deceased child sometimes report that they regretted it later.
- Take private time to look at your deceased child's unclothed body. This is part of the grieving process, and it can provide identity to the child.
- Take pictures of both twins—together and apart. Also take pictures of the whole family. Parents report that their surviving twins sometimes find emotional strength and affirmation of twinship by seeing themselves photographed with their deceased twin.
- Keep some mementos, such as your baby's name tag, blanket or nursery cap, footprints, hand prints, or lock of hair.
- Plan a service, funeral or memorial.
- Don't think of yourself as foolish or a "baby" as you continue to grieve. Try not to be too hard on yourself if preoccupation with caring for your surviving baby keeps you from fully experiencing your grief.
- Healing takes time. The loss is never gone. Eventually it just doesn't hurt as much. Don't hesitate to seek help from a support group such as CLIMB (see Resource Guide).

YOUR SURVIVING TWIN

Parents, dealing within their own grief, may tend to project it upon their surviving twin: "I wonder if she misses her twin?" "Does she sense that she is alone now?" The truth is that we know very little about the psychological impact on the surviving twin in infancy or early childhood. By doing the difficult but vital work of processing your own grief, you are preparing yourself to be a sound, loving support for whatever physical or psychological needs arise in your surviving twin.

The childhood stages of grieving are similar to those of adults, but with the following important stipulations:

- A child's cognitive abilities are not yet fully developed.
- Children depend on adults to take care of them.

When a twin dies, the surviving twin has lost the opportunity to have a unique and irreplaceable relationship. This may also be the first time a surviving twin has any meaningful experience with aloneness. Depending on the age of the surviving twin, there will be many significant questions and issues to discuss at the time of death or later.

- Why did I survive when my twin died?
- Am I still a twin?
- Did I cause my twin to die?
- I'll always miss knowing what we might have shared.
- I won't know what my twin would have been like as a grown up.

Each child will have her own questions and process this loss in a very personal way. A parent's greatest challenge at this time is to help their twin, and any other children in the home, to go through the process of grieving as they themselves cope with the loss of their child. Some parents state that the twin who has died has been "taken to heaven." There is a tendency to use euphemisms for death: "She has passed away"; "he is with the angels"; "your sister has gone to sleep"; "we've lost him." While it is perfectly natural to struggle with the finality of even saying the word *death*, it is vitally important that the surviving twin be given clear explanations. The confusion resulting from unclear explanations has the potential to be damaging. It is not difficult to imagine a child's reasoning: If my twin who has died has "gone to sleep," what will happen to me when I go to sleep. If "we've lost Johnny," why can't we find him again?

Children—and some adults—experience a cognitive phenomenon described as "magical thinking." It is the feeling that their thoughts or actions have the ability to cause things to take place that defy the normal laws of cause and effect. This is what allows children to believe the unbelievable—just as Peter Pan told the Darling children when he was teaching them to fly: "Just think lovely thoughts and up you'll go!" For adults the thoughts might be self recriminating such as, "It must have been my anxiety about having twins that caused one to die."

Magical thinking can also be responsible for powerful distortions of reality at times of trauma or loss. Magical thinking, in response to trauma, often leads to regressive behavior: The child who has been potty trained for a year may begin having accidents. The outgoing six-year-old may want to stay with Mommy and cuddle all the time. After the death of her twin, not knowing what death is like, the surviving twin may fantasize about dying. The surviving twin may create a fantasy friend or a wish—"If I caused her to die, I can bring her back by wishing hard enough or by being really good"—to help her cope with her loss. By understanding the power of magical thinking, we can see how the child, who is told that her twin is in heaven with the angels now, may want to join her there.

Parents need to observe their twin's behavior and listen carefully to the questions she asks and the explanations of death that she herself makes to others. Acknowledge your child's deep feelings of loss and sadness. By answering questions honestly and making clear explanations, you help your child distinguish between what cannot be altered (the death of her twin) and what can take place (while she will always miss and love her twin, the passage of time will allow for life to resume with a sense of normalcy).

The following developmental stages, organized by age, will help you understand your child's reactions to loss from a cognitive developmental standpoint. Some suggested ways you can help your surviving twin cope with, and better express and understand, this profound loss follow each developmental segment.

Birth to Three Years of Age

Infants do not have any emotional defenses at this time. They simply absorb the emotions of the people who surround them. It is very important for a parent to recognize their *own* emotional state and to understand the ways in which they understandably project their own psychological pain. During times of acute grief, parents may want to insulate their infant by allowing close friends or family to help with their baby's care. Babies and toddlers will model their parent's emotions and need lots of love and attention.

How You Can Help

- It is never too early to talk to your surviving twin about his twinship and his deceased twin. When diapering your surviving twin, you might say, "You are a twin. Your twin died when he was born. But you and he spent many hours in the womb together. It was nothing you or I did to cause him to die. I love you very much, and I am glad you are my child."
- Listen to your child. When your child asks a question, answer in a very simple and caring manner, taking into account his cognitive ability.
- Be open and honest with your twin. When your child shows an interest in his birth and his twin, you may show him any mementos you have from his twin, such as those collected at the hospital. If your child requests, you may want to give him a memento from his twin. This may include such items as a stuffed animal or a blanket that he can look at or hold onto when he desires.
- Visit the cemetery with your child, if it feels comfortable to you. Show her where her twin's burial site is. If she wants to, she can bring a flower or balloon to honor her twin. Don't expect her to be sad.

HONORING THE MEMORY OF YOUR CHILD ON BIRTHDAYS AND HOLIDAYS

As anyone who has lost a loved one knows, birthdays, holidays and anniversaries can be one of the biggest challenges of the grieving process. "Firsts" loom terribly large—the first anniversary of your twin's death, the first birthday, the first day of school and on and on.

There is a beautiful Egyptian parable titled "The Monster That Grew Small," which is about a young boy who is terrified of the tales he hears of a huge monster lurking in the dark distance, bent on the destruction of his village. He goes out to seek and slay the monster only to discover that the closer he gets to the creature, the smaller it becomes, until finally he discovers that the monster is a beautiful little mouse. The fearsome power of impending anniversaries can be tamed by your willingness to use them as natural opportunities to honor the memory of your deceased child. Don't feel you must choose a day that coin-

- Don't idealize the deceased twin or the twin relationship.
- Assemble a memory book with your child. Include photos and items collected during your pregnancy and such. It may be an ultrasound picture of them in the womb.

Three to Five Years of Age

Children between these ages are still deeply affected by their parents emotional state. But they are also deeply involved with establishing their own identity. Magical thinking is still a powerful force in their lives. They are not yet able to think in the abstract, so everything is either "black or white" or "here and now." Children at this age may think they caused someone to die, just by thinking of it. If their twin died at this age, they have developed a relationship with their twin and have their own bank of memories and mental images that will affect their understanding of this loss. Children at this age often hold the following assumptions about death:

- Death is reversible.
- Death is not inevitable.
- "I will never die."
- They can't imagine what it is like to die.
- Parents are all powerful: "Why can't you bring my brother back?"
- One of the reasons for death is bad behavior, such as "not listening to your parents."

How You Can Help

- Observe and listen to your child.
- Answer your child's questions in a kind, caring manner.
- Encourage your child to express his feelings in any way he is able. This may be:

  Drawing a picture.

  Using toys, puppets or objects to act out his feelings.

  Talking about and illustrating the life cycles in plants, insects and other animals. Use picture books from your local library if you find them useful.

  Carrying out a burial and memorial for a pet.

Five to Nine Years of Age

Children at this age have a little more understanding of death, although they still have magical thinking. They do not want to believe that death will happen to them or anyone they know or love. At times, they have fears that other members of their family will eventually die. Children at this age ask you questions about death: "Mommy, why are you going to the doctor? Are you going to die?"

At around eight years of age, children are beginning to develop more abstract reasoning. They have greater resources for comprehending more complex emotional states. They may begin, for example, to understand that even though Mommy is very sad that her child has died, she still is very happy to be a mother. A parent may also

cides with your surviving twin's birthday celebration to honor the twin who has died.

The following are several of the activities that parents have described as being meaningful for their families:

- Designate a special place in your garden, or create and name a garden area to honor your child. You may want to place a comfortable bench there for reading or quiet contemplation. Plant a tree, a flowering shrub or some beautiful perennial flowers each year to remember your deceased twin as well as your survivor child.

- Each year on their birthday, donate a children's book to your school library in memory of your deceased twin, as well as a book chosen by your surviving twin.

- Write a message you might have wished to convey on a helium balloon and set it free in an open space clear of tall tree branches, buildings or power lines.

- Arrange a candle-lighting ceremony at dusk where

anyone in the family who wants to speak can feel free to say a few words about their feelings or about the things they would have wished to say to the child who has died.

A SUMMARY OF SUPPORT FOR THE FAMILY

- Model the grieving process for your children. They will learn by your example.
- Create a safe environment for communication.
- See each child as an individual.
- Support your children and accept support from your children.
- As time passes, evoke the name and happy memories of your deceased twin in a natural way.
- Help your survivor twin to establish a new sense of identity that reflects who she is now.

explain that there will be some sad times and some happy times. An eight-year-old may show through her questions that she is able to empathize with the feelings of her parents and that she appreciates their empathetic reaction to her feelings.

How You Can Help

- Answer your child's questions in a simple and straightforward manner.
- Listen to your child's thoughts and beliefs of death and how her twin died.
- Correct any magical thinking your child may have in an accepting way.
- Reassure her that you, or other members of the family, will be there to take care of her.
- Encourage her to express her thoughts and fears.
- Initiate opportunities for expression in art projects, stories and poems.
- Inform teachers about the situation.
- Let your child know how much you love her.
- Find books written for children about death.

Nine to Twelve Years of Age

This is the cusp of adolescence, and these preteens will tend to imitate the adults around them. Nevertheless, your child's thoughts and feelings may be very difficult for her to verbalize. Preadolescents are concerned with themselves and how they look to the world around them when they show their emotions—"I bet I looked really stupid when I burst out crying." Some are able to express their anger and rage, while others repress their feelings and refuse to talk about them. Preadolescents may work very hard to bring their understanding of death into hard focus, but they need your patience, support and insight to help them through this process.

How You Can Help

- *Try to clarify magical thinking.* The preadolescent years still carry vestiges of magical thinking, but you may never know it unless you are able to solicit an explanation of your child's thoughts at this critical time. Respond rationally to questions, and don't shield a surviving twin from the practical matters associated with her twin's death. As difficult as it might be, visiting the funeral home and understanding the finality of death may be the first step in acceptance for a surviving twin of this age.

- *Encourage expression.* Children at this age are increasingly invested in their own competence at everything from writing stories and drawing to dancing and making up songs. Encourage your surviving twin to write down her thoughts in a journal or draw a picture of her twin doing something she loved.

- **Don't try to take the pain away by overindulging or overprotecting your surviving twin—or by taking the pain on yourself. Talk about the process of grieving, and explain to your twin that the degree of pain she is now experiencing will subside.**

- **Expect to have feelings of helplessness and anger at times.**

Twelve to Seventeen Years of Age

This is a time when teens have an understanding of the inevitability of death, and they may think about their own death or the death of loved ones. They fully comprehend death as an irreversible condition and are likely to concentrate on the biological and physical aspects of dying. Adolescents view death as an enemy, and they are both fearful and fascinated by it. This is a time of dramatic growth for them, both physically and emotionally, and death is a dramatic contrast to the otherwise flourishing life force within them.

How You Can Help

- *Offer teens permission to grieve.* Adolescence is a time for seeking independence from parents. Your teens may feel that showing emotion will "blow their cover" by making them appear vulnerable. Make sure they know that crying or showing their grief in any way will not make you assume that they are "little kids." Assure them that tears or other demonstrations of grief will have no impact on the privileges they are beginning to earn as young adults within the family. Encourage them, by your example, to recognize that going through the grieving process is necessary at any age.

- *Try to offer some sense of the stability of the family.* Your stability during this time of crisis is the best support you can offer. You cannot and should not hide your grief from your teenager, but they will be deeply relieved to see that even as you grieve, the family will continue. Children at this age are sophisticated enough in their thinking to recognize that the passage of time will be their ally.

- *Encourage their involvement in decisions.* The surviving twin has probably been deeply invested in her twin's life and needs to participate at her own pace in decisions surrounding the rituals of death. There may be a favorite book or poem or item of clothing that the surviving teen would like her twin to have in death. If there is to be any sort of service or recognition taking place at school, encourage your teen to participate and to accept the support of friends and teachers.

RECOGNIZING THE SIGNS: WHEN YOUR CHILD NEEDS PROFESSIONAL HELP

When parents, the family and the surviving twin are grieving, it can be difficult, if not impossible, to meet everyone's needs. Seeking out a professional at this time can help your child accept the death. It can also help your family through the grieving process. The following symptoms indicate that professional help may be needed:

- Your child is withdrawing from friends or loses interest in school and there is a sharp decline in his school performance.
- Your child is having a difficult time sleeping and/or has lost his appetite.
- Your child is exhibiting regressive behavior for an excessive amount of time.

TWIN TALK

Dr. Pearlman

Jean Kollantai, founder of the Center for Loss in Multiple Birth Inc. (CLIMB)

Dr. Pearlman:

Your son Berney is thirteen years old now, and I know that he lost his twin brother, Andrew, at birth. Would you talk a little about how your family has coped with the death of your son throughout these years?

Jean Kollantai:

When he was really pretty little, like a month or six weeks or so, occasionally I would say to him, "Gee, you had a little brother, Andrew, and he was your twin." I'd say a few things and always end up saying "We're so sad that he died, but we're so glad that you're here," and I'd give him a big hug. I figured it was a way of breaking the ice and just even getting used to saying Andrew's name or

Berney hearing Andrew's name. Babies may be nonverbal, but they are still absorbing and responding to you. It was my way of saying "Yes, I'm going through a lot right now, and there is this grief going on, and at the same time we're really so happy that you are here

(left to right) Alexander, Jean and Berney

with us now." It was kind of a way of letting him know that the grief he was sensing, in a sense, had nothing to do with him. We tried to be emotionally honest with him on a simple level. I didn't want to do that sort of "be happy for your surviving child" thing and not acknowledge the whole reality.

That Andrew was born and died is just a part of our family. Berney was the kind of kid who could pretty much relate to anything by the time he was two. He has turned out to be a highly gifted child who has blown everybody away by understanding so much, from the time he was very tiny. Somehow I feel that this all is a part of that. He was challenged at a very early age by things that kids aren't usually asked to understand. But by the time he was two, I almost felt like there was really nothing I needed to say. I mean I did, but I had this sense that he understood it all.

As he got a little bit older, we would talk about how babies are born and what twins are. Berney has always liked to talk about how he and Andrew played in my tummy. By the time he was five, I remember we were riding along in heavy freeway traffic in San Francisco trying to get to the airport. By then, I had another child, and Berney and his little brother were in the backseat, and out of nowhere, Berney just started asking me detailed, searching questions about Andrew. He said, "When I grow up I'm going to be a scientist and I'm going to find out exactly

why those babies died." He had this whole theory. It's something that he has processed in his mind, as well as his heart, as he continues to mature. He's grown up with the knowledge that it really is fortunate that he's here. He's very aware of CLIMB, and I don't think he's really ever felt guilt because he's always known that it could have been him or it could have been both of them. We have always told him that we really don't know why Andrew died. We could speculate, but we don't know.

There are a number of interesting things that he mentioned around the time of his tenth birthday, which was kind of a landmark. He wondered what it would be like if Andrew were here: Would he be in the gifted program? Would there be enough toys for everyone? We've also tried not to idealize Andrew. The idea "Oh, if only he was here, you wouldn't be bored today" or "If he were here, you'd be best friends." I know kids like to have more certainties, more absolute answers, but what they have is the truth, which is that there are many things we just don't know, and both really handle it well. That is why the key is to support parents, because if parents are not comfortable with the uncertainties that are a part of dealing with the death of a child, their kids won't be either.

Dr. Pearlman:

What do you say to parents about when to start talking about the deceased twin?

Jean Kollantai:

I'd say just always acknowledge that child as a part of the family. No matter how long you wait, it's not as if a day will come along when it is going to be the right time to deal with it. Based on my own experience, I really feel it works best if you make that child's birth and death a part of the family right from the beginning. And I also suggest that parents get support for themselves. Your kids are not your support group. Almost invariably, parents have a lot of issues that they need to deal with before they can really begin to address their child. First, you have to get involved in your own needs, and then you can focus more on theirs.

I hear from so many people who are struggling. I get letters all the time from people saying "My child is five now—what do I do?" Most times the parents themselves have not received the support they need to be able to help their children. One thing I say to parents is to be very careful about separating their needs from their children's needs. You have to be so conscious of trying not to superimpose your needs onto your children, which I'm sure I still do to some degree. You just have to struggle through your own issues, and try to be very gentle and loving with your children.

Some of the twin issues are really tough, and you have to be very aware that you might be sending a message to your twin that he or she has to sort of be both children. There's just a million things to work through. I feel strongly that you don't do your children any favor by trying to hand them all the answers. Let this be part of their lives. People aren't real good at dealing with ambiguity. Just keep loving your children and let them see what they can see at different points in their life about this experience. The pat answers really don't work in the long run.

MORE TALK

The twins and parents who agreed to speak to us about their lives had no shortage of opinions on a broad range of subjects, most of which we included in the twelve chapters of *Raising Twins*. Yet when the smoke cleared and the main text of the book was complete, we found our twins still had a few more words of wisdom to share. In addition, we had several wonderful short interviews with twins who had not made multiple appearances in the book. There could be no better way to close than with a few more words from the twins themselves: We give you *More Talk*.

TWIN TALK

Jill Ganon
Alex and Nick, 15-year-old fraternal twins
Katie and Robin, 13-year-old identical twins

"THINGS THAT PEOPLE SHOULDN'T SAY OR ASK US"

Jill: Katie, you had an idea for how to introduce this topic.

Katie: Something like "Things That People Shouldn't Say or Ask Us." I'd start with not asking if we're sisters after they've asked if we're twins.

[Laughter and agreement from all.]

Alex: We get that a lot: "Are you twins? Well, are you brothers?" Like we could be twins but not brothers?

Katie: Sometimes people think we're just friends, and then they'll ask if we're twins. I find it really annoying when people ask us if we're twins.

Alex: One of the worst questions is, "Do you guys have ESP?" Or "Where's your brother?" Like I have a psychic connection. Or sometimes I'll loan someone a book for the next class and they'll give it to my brother saying, "Here's your brother's book." Why can't they just return it to me? A lot of people think we're one person, one unit. That's kind of annoying.

Katie: People will ask me if I have a stomachache does my sister get it too? I don't like being sarcastic, and I'll just tell them that doesn't happen.

Nick: I think the one I get most is, "Do you like being a twin?" That's just such a bad question. It's like asking somebody "Do you like having a mother?" It's just your life. Of course, you like it. There are disadvantages and advantages to everything and being a twin is no different. There are some really stupid questions, like the stomachache thing Katie said, like "If you break a leg, will your brother feel it?"

Katie: I've had people come up to us when we were with my dad and his friend and they asked us if my dad and his friend were our fathers. I thought that was pretty stupid. I didn't say anything.

Robin: I usually wait to talk about it later unless I don't like the person. Then I start talking to my sister in front of them to make the point. I'll pretend while I'm talking that they're not there. I'll say, "Hey, Katie, that's probably the dumbest question I've ever heard. What do you think?" That's if I really don't like the person.

Katie: People ask me, "How can I tell you apart?" I don't really like it when people ask that. I have a thousand things that you could use to tell me apart from my sister. But a lot of them are personality, and sometimes I don't see why people can't tell us apart. It just really annoys me. Like I have more piercing in my ear than Robin. I wear different shoes, and I wear a watch.

Nick: The things that are the most annoying have to be the comparison thing: "Are you smarter?" or "Are you faster?" "Who's better at this?" Those are truly annoying. Being in high school now is the first time that I've really known other twins besides us at school. There are two in particular who I have a hard time telling apart. Now I want to ask them all the questions that people have asked me. This is the first time I've known what it's like to be in the other person's shoes. I'll start to say something and then I think, maybe I should say it this way. One of them had their arm broken for a while, so that's how I got to distinguish them.

Katie: I'm pretty used to it, so if someone asks me a stupid question, I'll just answer with a fact: "No, I'm Katie."

Nick: I'd rather have them ask me "How can I tell you apart?" than have them call me the wrong name. It's pretty simple to tell us apart. I have short hair, and he has long hair.

Katie: Sometimes people will come up to me and say, "Wait a second, let me guess." They're just sort of looking at me, and it makes me uncomfortable. So I'll say, "I'm Katie," and then they get mad at me for telling them right away.

Nick: The other thing is the phone. When you talk to people on the phone, they can't see you.

Our voices are pretty much the same. There are a few people who call and don't even say hello. They just say, "Wait, wait, let me guess." I'll wait and let him guess and then go on with the conversation. I remember when we were pretty little, Grandma could never tell us apart on the phone. She'd call me Alex, and he'd get called Nickie. And I think probably the most annoying thing because she does it all the time is that we have been nicknamed around the house Alex-Nickie or Nickie-Alex.

Robin: Some people have asked "How do your parents tell you apart" or "How do you tell each other apart." Your parents have lived with you all your life. It just doesn't make sense to ask that question.

Katie: Once I called myself Robin by mistake. Just the kind of accident anyone could make. I wasn't actually thinking I was Robin! I didn't somehow get us mixed up.

Alex: It is frustrating when someone you know real well calls you by your brother's name. Like if it happens with one of your best friends at school. I think it's more ignorant than insulting. I think I might do the same thing if I weren't a twin.

Nick: Mistakes are going to happen, but you should know people's names.

Alex: I think the most annoying thing has to be the comparisons. People say things like "Who's smarter?" How can you measure that? What do you want us to say? Stuff like who's faster or who's more athletic really gets annoying.

Nick: I think people want to label you right away because it makes it easier. So they'll say "John is faster, more athletic, better on the soccer field, and Bob is smarter and quiet and good in the classroom." Then they can remember: John the fast one, and Bob the smart one.

TWIN TALK

Dr. Pearlman

Eyi, 20-year-old identical twin sister of Yetsa

BEING THE "OLDER TWIN"

Dr. Pearlman:
You said that you were older than Yetsa. Has that had an influence on you?

Eyi: Yes, we were raised as if one of us was the older sibling and the other was the younger sibling. So my experience was being the oldest child of the family. That way of thinking resulted in the different responsibility each of us was given.

Dr. Pearlman:
Can you talk a little more about that? What kind of responsibilities were you given?

Eyi: If my mom went out of town, she would give me the key. I would do the grocery shopping . . . things like that. I often wonder how my mom made that kind of decision. I don't know if one of us appeared more responsible . . . My mother was also a little bit more strict with me. She was more indulgent with my sister.

Dr. Pearlman:
Were you aware of this as a young child?

Eyi

Eyi: Yes, in fact that led to a little bit of tension between me and my sister. I thought she was being spoiled and she thought I was being bossy some of the time. Much like you find between older and younger siblings. We got over it. We had to. But when we were younger, in second or third grade, we didn't get along as well as we do now.

Dr. Pearlman:
When did this change and you started becoming better friends with each other?

Eyi: When we went to high school our own attempts at being adolescents and our attempts to rebel against our mother were similar. We conspired with each other. You know . . . we would sneak out and cover for each other.

Dr. Pearlman:

Do you still feel like you are the more responsible one?

Eyi: I don't feel like I am more responsible than my sister, Yetsa. But I believe she feels less need to be responsible. She is a very responsible person and I don't want to give the impression she is not. But we do handle things differently. If you were to ask most people who know us, which of us is the eldest, I believe they would say it was me.

Dr. Pearlman:

Do you feel that you were required to treat your sister as the younger child or did you just do this yourself?

Eyi: I think because of the way we were raised it was just natural. My mom always said you had to look after your sister. I think that the way we were raised is probably more like the manner in which a mother would raise daughters who were born nine or ten months apart. In fact, we are six minutes apart in age.

TWIN TALK

Dr. Pearlman

Yetsa, 20-year-old identical twin sister of Eyi

BEING THE "YOUNGER TWIN"

Dr. Pearlman:

When I spoke with your sister, Eyi, she told me you were the younger twin. Has that had an impact on your twinship?

Yetsa: In our family there has been a difference. I am treated like the younger sister. That might be a cultural thing because I am Nigerian. In Nigeria the second-born twin is actually thought of as younger. We were treated differently, and as a result I acted differently . . . more spoiled and more dependent on everybody. My sister was a little more independent. She had a little more responsibility because she had the responsibility for me.

Yetsa

Dr. Pearlman:

Can you tell me a little more about this?

Yetsa: My twin sister Eyi was more accountable to my mom. When we were younger if we both did something, my sister would get in trouble for it. I was treated as though I was younger and less responsible.

Dr. Pearlman:

How did this affect the relationship between you and Eyi. Did it cause any conflict between the two of you?

Yetsa: Yes, it did. Eyi would get offended by being held responsible for me. When we were younger, about eight, she complained that I was spoiled and I was favored. I felt bad because I didn't want my sister to feel that way. I didn't want her to feel like I was favored. I felt a little guilty, but I didn't bring it up to my mom.

Dr. Pearlman:

What is the situation like now?

Yetsa: Now that we are older. I feel like we are equals.

Dr. Pearlman:

When did the change occur?

Yetsa: When we were in high school. Eyi and I wanted the same things; we were away from home more and we were treated as equals outside the house. I guess at home we had been treated differently so it made us act differently. We went to a private high school and we stayed there almost all day because we had a lot of after-school activities. I think high school was pivotal because it was when we started acting as though we were the same age.

Dr. Pearlman:

If you could give advice to parents raising twins, what would you tell them?

Yetsa: My mom said the hardest thing for her was to recognize that my relationship with Eyi was so close. It is hard for mothers of twins. Eyi and I see each other first and then we see our relationship with our mother. It's not that I don't love my mother, because of course I do. Yet I see my relationship with my sister as paramount in my life because we have been together since the womb. My mom said it was really hard for her when she was raising us. We were always content just to be with each other. We always felt we had love between us. It wasn't necessary to have that third party. Naturally we needed someone to raise us. It is a little hard to understand if you are not a twin. I would say to mothers, "Don't take it personally." My mom learned to understand.

TWIN TALK

Dr. Pearlman

Yetsa, 20-year-old identical twin sister of Eyi

CULTURAL INFLUENCES ON THE TWIN RELATIONSHIP

Dr. Pearlman:

Can you talk about how your family's culture may have influenced your twinship?

Yetsa: In the Yoruba culture there is a spiritual belief that is associated with the birth of twins. The Yorubans believe twins have a lot of power in the world that singletons don't. Twins have twin names that mean "the first that comes into the world" and "the second that comes into the world." They have a belief that the younger twin is the more wise because he or she apparently pushed the other one out to see if it was a good place. It is as though the second born twin is saying, if you don't come back then I will come out too.

The twin connection is more understood in the Yoruba culture. Twins are understood as two halves of one whole. The two are connected as one. When they find out you are a twin they will ask you how your twin is out of respect for the twin relationship. It is accepted that twins have more of a bond.

In the Yoruba culture each person is an individual and they are respected as that. It is not necessary to compare twins because it is simply accepted that all people are different. But in American culture twins are like one in the same, so people always feel the need to compare. Even in my family they do not compare us at all. They see us as individuals. It never crossed my mother's mind to compare us. But in school everyone compared us, and we never understood it. Why try to fit us into little molds that are in opposition to each other?

Dr. Pearlman:

How do you think the twin experience differs in the United States, Ghana, and Nigeria?

Yetsa: When my family comes to visit us in the United States from either Ghana or Nigeria, we get an infusion of their culture. My African relatives tell Eyi and me to look out for each other's best interest. Your twin's wish is very important. They understand more about our relationship. In this culture, in the house we get that with my mom. But when we go and interact with our American friends, we often get the complete opposite. It was interesting growing up. We had one culture in the house and one culture outside of the house. We had to mediate between the two.

Dr. Pearlman:

Was it hard for you?

Yetsa: No, because my mom is Nigerian and hers is a strong culture. As twins, I believe my sister and I relate to the Nigerian culture more than we do to the American culture. The Yorubans look at twins as their own category. You have regular people and you have twins. Twins are by themselves. In American culture I think twins are just regular siblings, all grouped together.

TWIN TALK

Jill Ganon
Dave and Alex, 8-year-old fraternal twins
Nazario, father of Dave and Alex

SOMETIMES PEOPLE DON'T BELIEVE WE ARE TWINS

Jill: Can you tell me anything about being twins?

Dave: Sometimes kids will say they don't believe we are twins even though we are. We don't look so much alike.

Jill: So what do you tell those kids?

Dave: I tell them we really are twins.

Jill: Of course you are. You can tell your friends there are more twins in the world who don't look alike than twins who do look alike. You guys are not identical twins, you're fraternal twins.

Dave

Alex: But Dave's best friend says people have to look alike if they are twins. So we have to always tell him twins don't always look exactly like each other and they are still twins.

Jill: It sounds like you are both good teachers. Are there any other twins in your school?

Alex: There are girls in our same grade who are twins and they look really alike. But we don't play with them because we mostly play with boys. I feel pretty mad sometimes because people say those girls are twins but we are not twins.

Jill: Maybe your teachers could help you by telling other kids you are twins.

Alex

Nazario:

> They are twins. I promise you that. I can tell the kids that when they were little babies, there was one night that their own mother could not tell them apart. She fed Alex, and then a little later she went back to feed Dave. A little later she heard Dave crying like crazy and she could not figure out why he should be so upset when he had just eaten and fallen asleep. Then she looked over at Alex and saw that his belly was sticking out like a big ball. She never had fed Dave. She fed Alex twice.

TWIN TALK

Jill Ganon

Lanaii and Laticia, 16-year-old identical twins

WHAT DOES IT MEAN TO BE A TWIN?

Lanaii: It means you always have someone to share your deepest feelings with. You know you can always count on your twin to be there. On the other hand, you might think you'd never have problems in a relationship with someone who is so much like you, but you do have problems sometimes.

Jill: If you are going through a difficulty in life do you turn first to your twin?

Lanaii: Yes. I might also turn to my older sister but first I always turn to my twin.

Jill: Laticia, what are your thoughts about being a twin?

Laticia: I consider Lanaii my best friend. If somebody at school asked me who my best friend is, I might mention other people who are also important to me. But when you get right down to it, Lanaii is the one I

(left to right) *Laticia and Lanaii*

can talk to about anything, even though it might backfire sometimes.

Jill: What do you mean?

Laticia: If we get in a fight she might use that information against me. (*both laugh*) But she is the one who knows me the best. My parents might think they know me best, but that isn't really the case. My twin is the person I turn to. I definitely can tell her things I wouldn't ever say to anyone else. Especially if I'm upset.

Jill: Can you tell me about the ways you are different from each other? I mean your personalities, not your appearance.

Lanaii: I'm a nonstop giggler and it sometimes gets me in trouble. I'm just more happy by nature.

Laticia: I'm more likely to show an "attitude." Lanaii's buttons are pushed more easily than mine, but I'm the one who is more likely to lash out if I think someone is on my case. She's quicker to feel, but I'm more likely to respond.

TWIN TALK

Dr. Pearlman

Eyi, 20-year-old identical twin sister of Yetsa

ON AND OFF THE FIELD—
EYI'S POINT OF VIEW

Dr. Pearlman:

You and Yetsa are both sophomores at Yale. Have you chosen career paths?

Eyi: I am not sure yet. I think I want to go to law school. Yetsa is premed.

Dr. Pearlman:

Have you always had different interests?

Eyi: Actually no. When I was younger, I thought I wanted to be a doctor. Yetsa and I did everything together until our senior year in high school. If I went to one camp, my sister went to that camp. If she went to medical school camp, I also went there. Actually the first time we were apart for an extended period of time was in the tenth grade. My sister did an exchange program for three weeks without me. I didn't think I would be that upset, but I was crying all the time. We talked every day on the phone.

Dr. Pearlman:

Did you talk to each other about her leaving before she went?

Eyi: Yes we did. I expected to miss her. But at the airport I was crying, crying, crying. Everyone said, "Why are you guys so upset, you're going to see each other in three weeks?" I don't think it was the fact that I wasn't going to see her for three weeks, it was that she was going somewhere and I wasn't going with her. We traveled a lot together when we were kids.

Dr. Pearlman:

Let's get back to your different career paths. When did you decide you didn't want to go to med school?

Eyi: All through high school I took a number of premed programs. I wanted to be an obstetrician. By the end of high school I realized writing was what I did best and that it was also most interesting to me.

Dr. Pearlman:

Was it hard for you to come to that decision and then to tell your mom and Yetsa?

Eyi: It wasn't hard for me to come to the decision, but it was hard for me to disclose my decision. I thought my mother and my father would be disappointed, but they weren't.

Dr. Pearlman:

How did Yetsa feel about your decision?

Eyi: She wasn't disappointed when I stopped being premed. But she was disappointed when I stopped running track. She often says she misses me in track—that it is hard for her to compete when I am not there. It was fun to run track with Yetsa because it taught me a lot about our relationship. People always asked, "Who is faster?" and I always said, "Me," because my sister had never beat me in a race. But actually, I think she should have beat me. I think she could have run faster than I in high school, but she always said she felt as though she honestly could not pass me. It

was weird. When we finished, we would always be so close to each other that I could never understand why Yetsa never got that half a second that it would have taken to beat me. She always said, "I felt like I should be just a little bit behind you." Nobody really understood why she said that. I understood why she said that. But nobody else did.

Dr. Pearlman:

What do you think she meant by that?

Eyi: I guess it always made sense to me because she was always right behind me, from the beginning. No matter what race it was, whether it was the 100 or the 200. Those are very short races. So if someone is always right behind you, it is very easy for someone to overtake you, yet Yetsa never did.

Dr. Pearlman:

So it appears that she monitored herself to stay just behind you.

Eyi: Yes! She had run track for so much longer than I, and she had run times that were faster than my times. Yet in our races together she was always right behind me. We were always first and second.

TWIN TALK

Dr. Pearlman

Yetsa, 20-year-old identical twin sister of Eyi

ON AND OFF THE FIELD—YETSA'S POINT OF VIEW

Dr. Pearlman:

Did you feel as though you have been labeled in a particular fashion?

Yetsa: I felt it a bit at school because people were always comparing us. People seemed to have a desire to label us—this is the athletic twin and this is the academic twin. Since I was a little more into sports and my sister was and still is a really good writer, I was labeled the athlete and my sister was considered the academic achiever. This was in spite of the fact that we both ran track and we both got good grades.

Dr. Pearlman:

So there were really only degrees of difference.

Yetsa: Yes. But people kept comparing us.

Dr. Pearlman:

Do you still run track?

Yetsa: Yes, but my sister quit.

Dr. Pearlman:

When you were running together, how was that experience for you?

Yetsa: It was competitive. Everything we do together is competitive—even school. We compete a lot. I guess it is inevitable, though we do try not to. In high school I was so depressed because Eyi would get straight A's and I would get straight A-minuses or something like that. Track was the same way. But the way we fixed the situation was by going into different events. When we did the same events we ended up fighting.

Dr. Pearlman:

Since you were labeled the athletic one, did you beat her most of the time?

Yetsa: No, actually in the sprints she beat me most of the time. I think it was psychological because I had believed since we were little that she was stronger than I was. I found myself not trying as hard when I knew she was going to be in the race because I felt she was going to beat me anyway.

Dr. Pearlman:

So you deferred to Eyi even though you may have been able to beat her?

Yetsa Yes. That's why she said she quit. She said, "I think you are faster than I am, but for some reason you don't run as fast when I am in the race."

Dr. Pearlman:

Were you aware of that psychological dynamic before Eyi talked to you about it?

Yetsa: No, not really . . . maybe I kind of knew. I could recognize when I was being competitive and when I was not. I was never aware that not running my fastest may have been a function of racing against my sister.

Dr. Pearlman:

You have said that there are many times that Eyi has gotten an A grade while you got an A-minus. Might you be holding back?

Yetsa: That might be the case with the writing class because I have always been a science and math person. I excel in math where Eyi finds it a little difficult and she is more of a writer. So in my classes that involve writing, like my seminars or English classes, I say it's okay if I don't get an A because I am not the writer anyway. I take it a little harder in my math and science classes because that is my thing. If Eyi didn't do well in the writing class, I think she would be upset.

TWIN TALK

Marco and Dino, 21-year-old fraternal twins

FIGHTING

Marco: I have to say we never really fought that much—never like a heated fight. I don't recall that many times when we would really get into it. I think part of it was there was always an understanding between the two of us that we are who we are, and we were not going to be able to change each other. I don't ever really remember Mom and Dad intervening. We had separate rooms, and that was really lucky. I remember one time I almost hit Dino. I pushed him really hard, and I was about to hit him and our mom flipped out. She did not like that at all. That was probably the maddest I've ever seen her. We were about fourteen, I think the last year in junior high school.

Dino: You know it's funny there would be so many times when I would get really mad at Marco, but I never wanted to hit him. It just felt stupid, like punching myself in the face. There's a movie called *The Big Night,* and there is a scene at the end where the two brothers [they are not twins] are fighting on the beach and they're yelling at each other, yelling nonsense. And the way they're fighting it's exactly what it's like to try to fight with your brother when you're really close. 'Cause they're hitting each other, but they're not really hitting each other. If I'm angry about something, it's always verbal—it was never physical. There is nothing that a punch is going to convey that I can't tell him.

Dino: When we were little kids we would fight over who was best friends with somebody, but that stopped pretty quick. We had a friend who was basically kind of like a brother to both of us. We would always hang out together.

Marco: I have to say, though, and Dino and I have talked about this, with the exception of this one other friend, we've pretty much always been each other's closest friend. We really never fought too much at all.

TWIN TALK

Dr. Pearlman

Amaro and Hermes, 11-year-old fraternal twins

THE JEALOUSY FACTOR

Dr. Pearlman:

What are some of the things you'd like people to know about being twins?

Amaro: There's the jealousy factor. Lots of kids are jealous of us because we have another person to play with.

Hermes: Basically the "up" factor of being twins is like Amaro said: We have each other to play with, and a lot of single kids don't. But the "down" factor is we have to share a room and stuff like that. A lot of people are jealous and they try to split us up—get us in fights and other stuff like that.

Dr. Pearlman:

What do you mean when you say people are trying to split you up?

Amaro: They'll tell me something and say, "Don't tell your brother." That's a way they try to get us in fights. Or they'll keep one person out of the game even though we're both their friend. Almost all the friends we have, except for our girlfriends, are both our friends.

TWIN TALK

Jill Ganon
Lanaii and Laticia, 16-year-old identical twins

FRIENDSHIPS

Jill: Do you have friends in common?

Laticia: We go to different schools and have different friends. But we have one friend in common who used to go to school with Lanaii but now goes to school with me. She is the friend we have in common for the longest amount of time.

Jill: Do you feel competitive about your shared friend?

Laticia: Lanaii might say, "She was my friend first." It is always a matter of who knew whom first.

Jill: Do you each seek out different types of people in your other friendships?

Lanaii: I get along with guys better than girls. I'm very friendly and some girls act like they are above me.

Laticia: I tend to be closer to girls than guys. But I have guy friends too. It is easier to talk to girls because I can't really tell guys my inner feelings. I had to give a speech the other night and I talked about how it is easier to open up girl-to-girl than girl-to-guy. The girls I hang out with are a lot like me. We tend to get along and be pretty happy.

Lanaii: I'd just as soon not talk about that inner stuff so I'm comfortable with guys. Also, the girls who are my friends are almost kind of my opposite. I tend to laugh a lot and I have a loud voice. So sometimes I really get going and that's when my girl friends say, "Okay. This is where you stop."

Jill: Do you have "best friends" in addition to each other?

Lanaii and Laticia:
Yes.

Jill: Is that difficult?

Lanaii and Laticia:
No.

Lanaii: It is a natural part of life to have other friends. Of course we are best friends because we are so much alike.

Laticia: I never really fuss with my sister over her having best friends other than me. She will always be there and we go through our everyday life knowing we are the most important to each other. To have other friends is just a natural part of life. Personally, I can't say I have any other friendship that I value to the extent of my relationship with Lanaii.

REFERENCES

CHAPTER 1

Agnew, C.L., et al. *Twins!: Pregnancy, Birth and the First Year of Life.* New York: HarperPerennial, 1997.

Arabin, B., et al. "Analysis of Prenatal Twin Behavior." Helsinki, Finland: International Society for Twin Studies, 1998.

———. "Intrauterine Behavior." In *Multiple Pregnancy*, edited by L. Keith et al. 331–349. New York: Parthenon Publishing Group, 1995.

Bessis, R. "Ultrasound Scanning Techniques." In *Multiple Pregnancy*, edited by L. Keith, et al. 195–213. New York: Parthenon Publishing Group, 1995.

Boklage, C.E. "The Frequency and Survival Probability of Natural Twin Conceptions." In *Multiple Pregnancy*, edited by L. Keith, et al. 41–50. New York: Parthenon Publishing Group, 1995.

Bomsel-Helmreich, O., et al. "The Mechanism of Monozygosity and Double Ovulation." In *Multiple Pregnancy*, edited by L. Keith, et al. 25–40. New York: Parthenon Publishing Group, 1995.

Bryan, E. *Twins and Higher Multiple Births: A Guide to Their Nature and Nurture.* London: Edward Arnold, 1992.

Creinin, M. "Conjoined Twins." In *Multiple Pregnancy*, edited by L. Keith, et al. 93–112. New York: Parthenon Publishing Group, 1995.

Derom, R., et al. "Placentation." In *Multiple Pregnancy*, edited by L. Keith, et al. 113–128. New York: Parthenon Publishing Group, 1995.

Landy, H.J., et al. "The Vanishing Twin." In *Multiple Pregnancy*, edited by L. Keith, et al. 59–71. New York: Parthenon Publishing Group, 1995.

Luke, B. "The Changing Pattern of Multiple Births in the U. S., Characterisitics, 1973–1990." *Obstetrics and Gynocology.* 84 (1994):101–106.

Luke, B. and T. Eberlein. *When You're Expecting Twins, Triplets or Quads.* New York: HarperPerennial, 1999.

Malmstrom, P.M. and J. Poland. *The Art of Parenting Twins.* New York: Skylight Press/Ballantine, 1999.

National Center for Health Statistics. *Trends in Twin and Triplet Births: 1980-97.* 47 (1996): 99–1120.

Piontelli, A. *From Fetus to Child: An Observational and Psychoanalytic Study.* London: Tavistock/Routledge, 1992.

———. "A Study on Twins Before and After Birth." *International Review of Psycho-Analysis.* 16 (1989): 413–425.

Segal, N.L. *Entwined Lives: Twins and What They Tell Us About Human Behavior.* New York: Dutton Books, 1999.

———. "Zygosity Diagnosis: Laboratory and Investigative Judgement." *Acta Geneticae Medicae et Gemollologiae.* 33 (1984): 515–520.

Dr. Pearlman was able to view many ultra-sounds from Alessandra Piontelli when she spoke at the American Pyschological Association, Division 39 Psychoanalysis, in Santa Monica, California, in 1994.

She was also able to view slides of ultra-sounds from Birgit Arabin of the Zeikenhuis, the Netherlands, in 1998 in Helsinki, Finland, at the International Society for Twin Studies (ISTS).

CHAPTER 2

Ainslie, R. *The Psychology of Twinship.* Northvale, N.J.: Jason Aronson, Inc., 1997.

Ames, L.B., et al. *Your Ten- to Fourteen-Year-Old.* New York: Dell Publishing, 1989.

Bowlby, J. "The Nature of the Child's Tie to His Mother." *International Journal of Psycho-Analysis.* 39 (1958): 350–373.

Bryan, E. *Twins, Triplets, and More: Their Nature, Development and Care.* United Kingdom: The Multiple Births Foundation, 1992.

Burlingham, D. "A Study of Identical Twins." *The Psycho-Analytic Study of the Child.* 18 (1963).

———. "The Relationship of Twins to Each Other." *The Psycho-Analytic Study of the Child.* 3 (1949): 57–72.

———. *Twins: A Study of Three Pairs of Identical Twins.* London: Imago Publishing Co., 1952.

Clark, P.M., et al. "Features of Interaction in Infant Twins." *Acta Geneticae Medicae et Gemollologiae.* 23 (1984): 165–171.

Collier, H. *The Psychology of Twins.* Engleton, Co.: TWINS Magazine, 1974.

DiLeo, J.H. *Child Development: Analysis and Synthesis.* New York: Brunner, Mazel Publishers, 1996.

Elkind, D. *Children and Adolescents: Interpretive Essay of Jean Piaget.* New York: Oxford University Press, 1970.

Flapan, D., et al. *The Assessment of Early Child Development.* Northvale, N.J.: Jason Aronson, Inc., 1975.

Gessel, A., et al. *Infant and Child in the Culture of Today.* Northvale, N.J.: Jason Aronson, Inc., 1995.

Greenspan, S.I. *Playground Politics: Understanding the Emotional Life of Your School-Age Child.* Reading, Mass.: Perseus Books, 1993.

Guifford, S., et al. "Differences in Individual Development Within a Pair of Identical Twins." *International Journal of Psycho-Analysis.* 47 (1966): 261-268.

Hay, D.A. "Speech and Language Development in Preschool Twins." *Acta Geneticae Medicae et Gemollologiae.* 36 (1987): 213-223.

Hay, D.A., et al. "The Role of Parental Attitudes in the Development of Temperament in Twins at Home, School and in Test Situations." *Acta Geneticae Medicae et Gemollologiae.* 33 (1984): 191-204.

Leonard, M.R. "Problems in Identification and Ego Development in Twins." *The Psychoanalytic Study of the Child.* 16 (1961): 300-320.

Lieberman, A.F. *The Emotional Life of the Toddler.* New York: The Free Press, 1993.

Mahler, M.S., et al. *The Psychological Birth of the Human Infant.* New York: Basic Books, Inc., 1975.

Mittler, P. *The Study of Twins.* London: Penguin Books, 1971.

Sandbank, A. *Twins and the Family.* United Kingdom: TAMBA, 1988.

Steinberg, L., et al. *You and Your Adolescent.* New York: HarperPerennial, 1997.

Stern, D.N. *Diary of a Baby: What Your Child Sees, Feels and Experiences.* New York: Basic Books, 1990.

———. *The Interpersonal World of the Infant.* New York: Basic Books, 1985.

Winnicott, D.W. "Birth Memories, Birth Trauma and Anxiety." *International Journal of Psycho-Analysis.* 26 (1949): 145-156.

———. "Dependence in Infant-Care, in Child-Care, and in the Psycho-Analytic Setting." *International Journal of Psycho-Analysis.* 44 (1963): 339-344.

———. *Playing and Reality.* London: Tavistock Publications, 1971.

———. "The Theory of the Parent-Infant Relationship." *International Journal of Psycho-Analysis.* 41 (1960): 585-595.

CHAPTER 3

Agnew, C., et al. *Twins!: Pregnancy, Birth and the First Year of Life.* New York: HarperPerennial, 1997.

Twin Care Handout Collection, Edited by P.M. Malmstrom. Rev. ed. Berkeley, Calif.: Twin Services, Inc., 1997.

CHAPTER 4

Bakker, P. "Autonomous Languages in Twins." *Acta Geneticae Medicae et Gemellologiae.* 36 (1987): 233-238.

Bryan, E. *Twins and Higher Multiple Births: A Guide to Their Nature and Nurture.* London: Edward Arnold, 1992.

Cassill, Kay. *Twins: Nature's Amazing Mystery.* New York: Atheneum, 1985.

Goshen-Gottstein, E.R. "The Mothering of Twins, Triplets and Quadruplets." *Psychiatry.* 43 (1980): 89–203.

Hagedorn, J.W., and J.W. Kizziar. *Gemini: The Psychology and Phenomena of Twins.* Chicago: The Center for the Study of Multiple Births, 1974.

Lytton, H., et al. "The Impact of Twinship on Parent-Child Interaction." *Journal of Personality and Social Psychology.* 35 (1977): 97–101.

Merriam Webster Dictionary. New York: Pocket Books, 1999.

Malmstrom, P.M. "Twin Myths." *Twin Services: Resource Series 500: #501.* Berkeley, Calif.: Twin Services, Inc., 1993.

Noble, E. *Having Twins.* Boston: Houghton Mifflin Company, 1991.

Pearlman, E.M. "Separation-Individuation, Self-Concept and Object Relations in Fraternal Twins, Identical Twins and Singletons." *The Journal of Psychology.* 124 (1990): 619–628.

Pearlman, E.M., and N.L. Segal. "Twin Myths." In E. Pearlman (chair), "Demystifying the Twin Experience," symposium conducted for the Extension Division of the University of California at Los Angeles, November 1993.

Sandbank, A. *Twins and the Family.* United Kingdom: TAMBA, 1988.

Savic, S. "Mother-Child Verbal Interaction: The Functioning of Completions in the Twin Situation." *Journal of Child Language.* 6 (1979): 153–158.

Segal, N.L. *Entwined Lives: Twins and What They Tell Us about Human Behavior.* New York: Dutton, 1999.

Vollmar, A.M. "How the World Views Twins." *The Twinship Sourcebook.* Englewood, Co.: TWINS Magazine, Inc., 1997.

Watson, P. *Twins: An Uncanny Relationship?* Chicago: Contemporary Books, Inc., 1981.

CHAPTER 5

Bryan, E. *Twins, Triplets and More: Their Nature, Development and Care.* United Kingdom: Multiple Births Foundation, 1995.

Greer, J. *Adult Sibling Rivalry.* New York: Crown Publishers, Inc., 1992.

Lytton, H., et al. "The Impact of Twinship on Parent-Child Interaction." *Journal of Personality and Social Psychology.* 35 (1977): 97–101.

Malmstrom, P.M., and J. Poland. *The Art of Parenting Twins.* New York: Skylight Press/Ballantine Books, 1999.

Sandbank, A. *Twins and the Family.* Great Britain: TAMBA, 1988.

Segal, N.L. "Cooperation, Competition, and Altruism in Human Twinships: A Sociobiological Approach." In *Sociobiological Perspective on Human*

Development, edited by K.B. MacDonald. 168–206. New York: Springer-Verlag, 1984.

Smilansky, S. *Twins and Their Development*. Rockville, Md.: BJE Press, 1992.

Twin Care Handout Collection, Edited by P.M. Malmstrom. Rev. ed. Berkeley, Calif.: Twin Services, Inc., 1997.

CHAPTER 6

Ames, L.B., et al. *Your Ten- to Fourteen-Year-Old*. New York: Dell, 1989.

Bakker, P. "Autonomous Languages in Twins." *Acta Geneticae Medicae et Gemellologiae*. 36 (1987): 233–238.

Batshaw, M.L. "Mental Retardation." *Pediatric Clinics of North America*. 40 (1993): 507–521.

Clark, P.M., and Z. Dickman. "Features of Interaction in Infant Twins." *Acta Geneticae Medicae et Gemollologiae*. 33 (1984): 165–171.

Conway, D., et al. "Twins-Singleton Language Differences." *Canada Journal of Behavioral Science*. 12 (1980): 264–271.

DiLeo, J.H. *Child Development: Analysis and Synthesis*. New York: Brunner/Mazel Publishers, 1977.

Engel, G.L. "The Death of a Twin: Mourning and Anniversary Reactions. Fragments of Ten Years of Self-Analysis." *International Journal of Psycho-Analysis*. 6 (1975): 23–40.

Flapan, D., and P. Neubauer. *The Assessment of Early Child Development*. Northvale, N.J.: Jason Aronson Inc., 1983.

Greenspan, S.I. *Playground Politics: Understanding the Emotional Life of Your School-Age Child*. Reading, Mass.: Perseus Books, 1993.

Hay, D.A., and P.J. O'Brien. "The Role of Parental Attitudes in the Development of Temperament in Twins at Home, School and in Test Situations." *Acta Geneticae Medicae et Gemollologiae*. 33 (1984): 191–204.

Hay, D.A., et al. "Speech and Language Development in Preschool Twins." *Acta Geneticae Medicae et Gemollologiae*. 36 (1987): 213–223.

LaTrobe Twin Study. *Twins in School*. Department of Psychology. La Trobe University, Melbourne, and Australian Multiple Birth Association, Inc., 1991.

Lytton, H. *Parent-Child Interaction: The Socialization Process Observed in Twin and Singleton Families*. New York: Plenum, 1980.

Lytton, H., et al. "The Impact of Twinship on Parent-Child Interaction." *Journal of Personality and Social Psychology*. 35 (1977): 97–107.

Malmstrom, P.M., and M.N. Silva. "Twin Talk: Manifestations of Twin Status in the Speech of Toddlers." *Journal of Child Language*. 13 (1986): 293–304.

Mittler, P. "Language Development in Young

Twins: Biological, Genetic and Social Aspects." *Acta Geneticae et Medicae Gemollologiae.* 25 (1976): 359–365.

Mohay, H., et al. "The Effects of Prenatal and Postnatal Twin Environments on Development." In *Research Issues in Child Development*, edited by C. Pratt, et al. Winchester, Mass.: Allen and Unwin, 1986.

Savic, S. *How Twins Learn to Talk.* San Diego: Academic Press, 1980.

Segal, N.L. *Entwined Lives: Twins and What They Tell Us about Human Behavior.* New York: Dutton, 1999.

Segal, N.L., et al. "A Twin Research Perspective on Reading and Spelling Disabilities." *Reading and Writing Quarterly: Overcoming Learning Difficulties.* 11 (1995): 209–227.

Smilansky, S. *Twins and Their Development.* Rockville, Maryland: BJE Press, 1992.

Tomasello, M., et al. "Linguistic Environment of One- to Two-Year-Old Twins." *Developmental Psychology.* 22 (1986): 169–176.

CHAPTER 7

Mahler, M.S., et al. *The Psychological Birth of the Human Infant.* New York: Basic Books, Inc., 1975.

Segal, N.L. "Cooperation, Competition and Altruism in Human Twinship: A Sociobiological Approach." In *Sociobiological Perspectives on Human Development*, edited by K.B. MacDonald. 168–206. New York: Springer-Verlag, 1988.

Twin Care Handout Collection. Edited by P.M. Malmstrom. Rev. ed. Berkeley, Calif.: Twin Services, Inc., 1997.

Winnicott, D.W. *Playing and Reality.* London: Tavistock Publications, 1971.

———. "The Theory of the Parent-Infant Relationship." *International Journal of Psycho-Analysis.* 41 (1960): 585–595.

CHAPTER 8

Bryan, E. *Twins, Triplets and More: Their Nature, Development and Care.* 1995. United Kingdom: Multiple Births Foundation.

Malmstrom, P.M., and J. Poland. *The Art of Parenting Twins.* New York: Skylight Press/Ballantine, 1999.

Samalin, N. *Loving Each One Best: A Caring and Practical Approach to Raising Siblings.* New York: Bantam Books, 1997.

Sandbank, A. *Twins and the Family.* Great Britain: TAMBA, 1988.

Twin Care Handout Collection. Edited by P.M. Malmstrom. Rev. ed. Berkeley, Calif.: Twin Services, Inc., 1997.

Wagner, H. *Child.* March 1999: 48–52.

CHAPTER 9

Gleeson, C., et al. "Twins in School: An Australian-Wide Program." *Acta Geneticae Medicae et Gemellologiae.* 39 (1990): 231–244.

Hay, D.A., and K. Taylor. "A Family-Focused Approach to Language Intervention With Multiples: Who Benefits and Why?" Paper presented at the Ninth International Congress on Twin Studies, Helsinki, Finland. 1998.

La Trobe Twin Study. *Twins in School.* Department of Psychology. La Trobe University, Melbourne, and Australian Multiple Birth Association, Inc., 1991.

Malmstrom, P.M., and J. Poland. *The Art of Parenting Twins.* New York: Skylight Press/Ballantine Books, 1999.

Preedy, P. "A National Survey of Multiples in Schools in England." Paper presented at the Ninth International Congress on Twin Studies, Helsinki, Finland. June 1998.

Preedy, P., and P. Tymms. "Do Multiples Start School at a Lower Point Than Singletons? Do They Make Less Progress?" Paper presented at the Ninth International Congress on Twin Studies, Helsinki, Finland. June 1998.

Schwarz, J.C. "Effects of Peer Familiarity on the Behavior of Preschoolers in a Novel Situation." *Journal of Personality and Social Psychology.* 24 (1972): 276–284.

Segal, N.L., and J.M. Russell. "Twins in the Classroom: School Policy Issues and Recommendations." *Journal of Educational and Psychological Consultation,* 3, (1). 1992. 69–84.

Segal, N.L., and T.D. Topoloski. "A Twin Research Perspective on Reading and Spelling Disabilities." *Reading and Writing Quarterly: Overcoming Learning Difficulties.* 11 (1995): 209–227.

Vander Sluis, K. "New Options for Multiples in School." *TWINS Magazine.* 16 (March/April 1999): 28, 29.

CHAPTER 10

Ames, L.B., F.L. Ilg, and S.M. Baker. *Your Ten-to Fourteen-Year-Old.* New York: Dell, 1989.

Dinkmeyer, D., et al. *Parenting Teenagers: Systematic Training for Effective Parenting of Teens.* Minnesota: American Guidance Service, Inc., 1998.

Elkind, D. *Child and Adolescents: Interpretive Essays on Jean Piaget.* New York: Oxford University Press, 1970.

Moilanen, I. "Psychic Vulnerability as a Sequel to Perinatal Morbidity." *Acta Paediatrica Scandinavica.* 344:77 (1988): 95–105.

Moilanen, I., and P. Rantakallio. "Living Habits and Personality Development of Adolescent Twins: A Longitudinal Follow-Up Study in a Birth Cohort from

Pregnancy to Adolescence." *Acta Geneticae Medicae et Gemollologiae*. 30 (1990): 215–220.

Sandbank, A. *Twins and the Family*. Great Britain: TAMBA, 1988.

Steinberg, L. *You and Your Adolescent: A Parent's Guide for Ages Ten to Twenty*. New York: HarperPerennial, 1987.

CHAPTER 11

Bryan, E. *Twins, Triplets and More: Their Nature, Development and Care*. United Kingdom: Multiple Births Foundation, 1995.

Malmstrom, P.M. and J. Poland. *The Art of Parenting Twins*. New York: Skylight Press/Ballantine, 1999.

Twin Care Handout Collection. Edited by P.M. Malmstrom. Rev. ed. Berkeley, Calif.: Twin Services, Inc., 1997.

CHAPTER 12

Barron, D.S. "Once There Were Two." *Health*. September 1996: 84–91.

Bryan, E., and F. Hallett. *Guidelines for Professionals: Bereavement*. United Kingdom: Multiple Births Foundation, 1997.

Fogarty, J.A. *The Grieving Child: Comprehensive Treatment and Intervention Strategies*. Arizona: American Academy of Bereavement, 1998.

———. "The Grieving Child: What to Do When Death Enters the Life of a Child." Seminar, Hollywood. April 1998.

Kubler-Ross, E. "On Death and Dying." New York: Simon & Schuster, 1997.

Martin, K. "Teen Grief." Seminar, POMBA Conference. Edmonton, Ont., Can. May 1997.

McInnes, S. "Death of a Twin." *The Twinship Sourcebook*. Englewood, Co.: TWINS Magazine, Inc., 1997.

Segal, N.L. *Entwined Lives: Twins and What They Tell Us About Human Behavior*. New York: Dutton, 1999.

Woodward, J. "The Bereaved Twin." *Acta Geneticae Medicae et Gemellologiae*. 37 (1988): 173–180.

———. *Joys and Sorrows: A Newsletter for Parents Who Have Experienced a Loss in a Multiple Pregnancy*, 4 (Fall 1996).

RESOURCE GUIDE

ORGANIZATIONS SERVING TWINS AND OTHER MULTIPLES

TWINS

The Center for Study of Multiple Birth
333 E. Superior St., Suite 464
Chicago, IL 60611
Tel.: (312) 266-9093
Website: www.multiplebirths.com
E-mail: lgk395@nwu.edu (Dr. Louis Keith, director)
A nonprofit organization providing information and professional and parental referrals regarding pregnancy management.

National Organization of Mothers of Twins Clubs, Inc. (NOMOTC)
PO Box 438
Thompson, TN 37179-0438
Tel.: (877) 540-2200 or (615) 595-0936
Website: www.nomotc.org
A nonprofit nationwide network of parents of multiples clubs providing information and resources. Publication: "Notebook," bimonthly.

The Twins Foundation
PO Box 6043
Providence, RI 02940-6043
Tel.: (401) 729-1000
Website: www.twinsfoundation.com
E-mail: twins@twinsfoundation.com
A nonprofit membership and research information center on twins with a national twin registry. Publication: "The Twins Letter," quarterly.

Twin Services Inc.
PO Box 10066
Berkeley, CA 94709
Tel.: (501) 524-0863
E-mail: twinservices@juno.com
Publishes parenting and educational materials.

TwInsight®
Eileen M. Pearlman, Ph.D., Director
1137 Second St., Suite 109
Santa Monica, CA 90403
Tel.: (310) 458-1373 or (310) 458-9723
Website: www.twinsight.com
E-mail: twinsight@aol.com
Consultations, workshops, counseling, and psychotherapy via telephone or in person for multiples of all ages and their families.

HIGHER ORDER MULTIPLES

Mothers of Supertwins (MOST)
PO Box 951
Brentwood, NY 11717-0627
Tel.: (516) 859-1110
Website: www.MOSTonline.org
E-mail: Maureen@MOSTonline.org
Provides information, resources and support network for families of triplets or more.
Publication: "MOST," quarterly.

The Triplet Connection
PO Box 99571
Stockton, CA 95209
Tel.: (209) 474-0885
Website: www.tripletconnection.org
E-mail: tc@tripletconnection.com
Information and support for expectant and new parents of larger multiples. Publication: "The Triplet Connection," quarterly.

TWIN TOPICS

Twin-Related Medical Issues

Twin Hope, Inc.
2592 W. 14th Street
Cleveland, OH 44113
Tel.: (216) 228-8887
Website: www.twinhope.com
E-mail: twinhope@twinhope.com
Provides support and information on twin-to-twin transfusion syndrome and other twin-related diseases. Publication: "TwinLines," biannually.

The Twin to Twin Transfusion Syndrome Foundation, Inc.
411 Longbeach Parkway
Bay Village, OH 44140
Tel.: (440) 899-TTTS or (440) 366-6148
Website: www.tttsfoundation.org
E-mail: TTTSFound@aol.com
Provides education and support to families diagnosed with TTTS.

Twin Loss (Bereavement)

The Center for Loss in Multiple Birth, Inc. (CLIMB)
PO Box 1064
Palmer, AK 99645

Tel.: (907) 746-6123
E-mail: climb@pobox.alaska.net
Provides support and information for parents who have experienced a loss of a multiple. Publication: "Our Newsletter: A Multiple Birth Loss Support Network," quarterly.

Twinless Twins International (TTI)
11220 St. Joe Road
Fort Wayne, IN 46835
Tel.: (219) 627-5414
Website: www.fwi.com/twinless/
E-mail: twinless@iserv.net
Provides peer support for twins of all ages and their families whose co-twin is deceased or terminally ill. Publication: "Twinless Times," quarterly.

TWIN MAGAZINES AND CHILDREN'S BOOKS

Twin Pleasures Publishing
Tel.: (800) TWINS-BKS/(800) 894-6257
Website: www.brownetwins.com
Books for and about twins.

TWINS 5 to 12
TWINS Magazine
5350 S. Roslyn St., Suite 400
Englewood, CO 80111-2125
Tel.: (888) 55-TWINS
Website: www.twinsmagazine.com
E-mail: TWINS.editor@businessword.com
Quarterly newsletter for parents of school-age multiples.

TWINS Magazine
5350 S. Roslyn St., Suite 400
Englewood, CO 80111-2125
Tel.: (888) 55-TWINS

Website: www.twinsmagazine.com
E-mail: TWINS.editor@businessword.com
Bimonthly.

DNA TESTING

Affiliated Genetics
PO Box 870247
Woods Cross, VT 84087-0247
Tel.: (800) 362-5559
Website: affiliatedgenetics.com
E-mail: btanner@burgoyne
Provides mail order genetic test (DNA-STAR)
to determine zygosity.

SOCIAL ACTIVITIES FOR TWINS

International Twins Association (ITA)
c/o Lynn Long or Lori Stewart
6898 Channel Road NE
Minneapolis, MN 55432
Tel.: (612) 571-3022
Social events for adult twins; annual Labor Day
convention.

Twins Day Festival
PO Box 29
Twinsburg, OH 44087
Tel.: (216) 425-3652
Annual festival for twins of all ages, usually the
first weekend in August, Twinsburg, Ohio.

Twins World (Debra and Lisa Ganz)
PO Box 6056
New York, NY 10128
Tel.: (800) RUTWINS or (212) 289-1777
Website: www.twinsworld.com
E-mail: Billywonka@aol.com
Owners of Twins Restaurant in New York City
and authors of *The Book of Twins*.

INTERNATIONAL ORGANIZATIONS

Australian Multiple Birth Association, Inc. (AMBA)
c/o The National Secretary
PO Box 105
Coogee, N.S.W. 2034 Australia
Tel.: 011-61-49-46-8030
Website: www.amba.org.au
E-mail: amba.national@yahoo.com.au
Network of clubs for parents of multiples.
Publication: "AMBA News," bimonthly.

International Society for Twin Studies (ISTS)
Professor Nicholas Martin
Queensland Institute for Medical Research
Post Office, Royal Brisbane Hospital
Brisbane, QLD 4029, Australia
Fax: 011-61-7-3362-0101
Website: www.ists.qimr.edu.au
Publication: "Twin Research," quarterly.
Multidisciplinary scientific organization.

Multiple Births Foundation (MBF)
Queen Charlotte's and Chelsea Hospital
Goldhawk Road
London W6 U.K.
Tel.: 011-44-181-383-3519
E-mail: mbf@rpms.ac.uk
Many services for parents and professionals
working with multiples. Publication: "Multiple
Birth Foundation Newsletter," quarterly.

New Zealand Multiple Births Association (NZMBA)
PO Box 1258
Wellington, New Zealand
E-mail: lizlake@xtraa.co.nz
Parent clubs and information. Publication:
"NZMBA Newsletter," quarterly.

Parents of Multiple Birth Association of Canada (POMBA)
PO Box 234
Gormley, Ontario, Canada LOH 1G0
Tel.: (905) 888-0725
Website: www.pomba.org
E-mail: office@pomba.org
Parent clubs and information, education and research. Publication: "Double Features," quarterly.

South African Multiple Birth Association (SAMBA)
46 Lockwood Road
Erindale, South Africa 5066
Support to parents of multiple births.

Twins and Multiple Births Association (TAMBA)
Harnott House
309 Chester Road
Little Sutton
Ellesmere Port CH66 1QQ United Kingdom
Tel.: 011-44-870-121-4000
Website: www.surreyweb.org.uk/tamba/
E-mail: tamba@information4u.com
Information and support network for families with twins and other higher order multiples. Publications: "Twins, Triplets and More Magazine," quarterly.

Twin Loss

Lone Twin Network (LTN)
PO Box 5653
Birmingham B29 7JY
United Kingdom
Support for twin loss.

OTHER TOPICS OF INTEREST

Bed Rest

Sidelines
PO Box 1801
Laguna Beach, CA 92651
Tel.: (949) 497-2265
Website: www.sidelines.org
Provides education and support for women across the U.S. and their families who are experiencing complicated pregnancies.

Postpartum Issues

Postpartum Support International
927 North Kellogg Avenue
Santa Barbara, CA 93111
Tel.: (805) 967-7636
Fax: (805) 967-0608
Website: www.chss.iup.edu/postpartum/
E-mail: thonikman@compuserve.com
Provides information, education and support for postpartum families.

Depression After Delivery, Inc. (DAD)
91 East Somerset Street
Raritan, NJ 08869
Tel. (800) 944-4PPD
Website: www.behavenet.com/dadinc
Provides support, education, information and referrals.

Bereavement—Parent Support

Centering Corporation
1531 N. Saddle Creek Road
Omaha, NE 68104-3696
Tel.: (402) 553-1200
Fax: (402) 553-0507
Website: www.centering.org

E-mail: j1200@aol.com
Nonprofit publishing company provides bereavement literature. Free catalog.

The Compassionate Friends, Inc.
PO Box 3696
Oak Brook, IL 60522-3696
Tel.: (630) 990-0010
Self-help organization for bereaved parents.

RTS Bereavement Services (formerly known as Resolve Through Sharing)
Gunderson Lutheran Medical Center
1910 South Avenue
La Crosse, WI 54601
Tel.: (800) 362-9567 x4747 or (608) 791-4747
Website: www.gundluth.org/bereave
E-mail: berserv@gundluth.org
Provides information, resources and/or referrals to local support groups and education to health care professionals.

SHARE: Pregnancy and Infant Loss Support, Inc.
St. Joseph Health Center
300 First Capitol Drive
St. Charles, MO 63301
Tel.: (800) 821-6819
Fax: (314) 947-7486
Website: www.nationalshareoffice.com
E-mail: share@nationalshareoffice.com
Provides support for parents experiencing the death of their baby. Also provides information, education and resources.

Psychological Services and Counseling

American Association for Marriage and Family Therapists (AAMFT)
1133 15th Street NW #300
Washington, DC 20005-2710

Tel.: (202) 452-0109
Fax: (202) 223-2329
Website: www.aamft.org
Provides information and referrals to local areas.

American Psychiatric Association
1400 K Street NW
Washington, DC 20005
Tel.: (202) 682-6000
Website: www.psych.org
Provides information and referrals to local areas.

American Psychological Association (APA)
750 First Street NE
Washington, DC 20002-4242
Tel.: (202) 336-5500
Website: www.apa.org
Provides information and referrals to local areas.

GENERAL HEALTH CARE

Asthma/Allergies

Asthma and Allergy Foundation of America
1233 20th Street NW, Suite 402
Washington, DC 20036
Tel.: (800) 7-ASTHMA
Website: www.aafa.org

Autism

Autism Society of America
7910 Woodmont Avenue, Suite 300
Bethesda, MD 20814-3015
Tel.: (800) 3-AUTISM x150
Website: www.autism-society.org

National Institute of Neurological Disorders and Stroke
National Institutes of Health

Bethesda, MD 20892
Website: www.ninds.nih.gov/patients/disor-
der/autism/autism.htm

Auto Safety

Auto Safety Hotline
Tel.: (888) 327-4236
Website: www.nhtsa.dot.gov
Sponsored by the Department of
Transportation. Provides free information on
car seats and auto safety for children.

Breast-Feeding

La Leche League International
PO Box 4079
Schaumburg, IL 60168-4079
Tel.: (800) 525-3243 or (847) 519-7730
Website: www.lalecheleague.org
Information and support on breast-feeding and
referrals to lactation consultants.

Cancer

National Childhood Cancer Foundation
440 E. Huntington Drive, Suite 300
PO Box 60012
Arcadia, CA 91066-6012
Tel.: (800) 458-6223
Website: www.nccf.org
Information about childhood cancer.

Cerebral Palsy

**United Cerebral Palsy Association, Inc.
(UCPA, Inc.)**
1660 L Street NW, Suite #700
Washington, DC 20036-5602
Tel.: (800) 872-5827
Website: www.ucpa.org

Childcare

**National Association of Child Care Resource
and Referral Agency (NACCRRA)**
Elaine Rank, Director
1319 F Street, NW, Suite 810
Washington, DC 20004
Tel.: (202) 393-5501 x123 or (800) 570-4543
Website: www.naccrra.net
E-mail: yvinci@naccrra.net
Organization of community-based child care
resource and referral programs for every state
in U.S., Canada and England.

Child Safety

National Safety Council
1121 Spring Lake Drive
Itasca, IL 60143-3201
Tel.: (630) 285-1121
Website: www.nsc.org
Information on safety issues.

Diabetes

Juvenile Diabetes Foundation International
120 Wall Street, 19th Floor
New York, NY 10005
Tel.: (800) 533-2873
Website: www.jdf.org
E-mail: info@jdf.org
Information on diabetes.

Emergency Preparedness

**Federal Emergency Management Association
(FEMA)**
PO Box 2012
Jessup, MO 20794
Tel.: (800) 480-2520
Website: www.fema.org
Information on disaster preparedness.

Epilepsy

Epilepsy Foundation of America
4351 Garden City Drive
Landover, MD 20785
Tel.: (800) EFA-1000 or (800) 332-1000
Website: www.efa.org
Information on children with epilepsy.

General Health for Children

American Academy of Pediatrics
141 NW Point Blvd.
Elk Grove Village, IL 60007-1098
Tel.: (800) 433-9016
Website: www.aap.org
For information, request the "Parents'
Resource Guide" for listing of brochures.

Hearing

Hearing Help Line (Better Hearing Institute)
515 King Street, Suite 420
Alexandria, VA 22314
Tel.: (800) EAR-WELL or (800) 327-9355
Website: www.betterhearing.org
Information on hearing problems in children.

Heart Disease

American Heart Association
1710 Gilbreth Road
Burlingame, CA 94010
Tel.: (800) AHA-USA1 or (800) 242-8721
Website: www.americanheart.org
Information and referrals to cardiologists.

Immunization and Health Screenings

National Immunization Information Hotline
1600 Clifton Road MSE-34
Atlanta, GA 30337
Tel./English: (800) 232-2522
Tel./Spanish: (800) 232-0233
Website: www.cdc.gov/nip
Information on vaccine-preventive diseases.

Learning Disabilities

Learning Disabilities Association of America
4156 Library Road
Pittsburgh, PA 15234-1349
Tel.: (412) 341-1515
Website: www.ldanatl.org
E-mail: ldanatl@usaor.net
Education and support for children with learning differences.

Orton Dyslexia Society
8600 LaSalle Road
Chester Building, Suite 382
Baltimore, MD 21286-2044
Tel.: (800) ABCD-123
Website: www.interdys.org
Education and support for children with dyslexia.

SIDS (Sudden Infant Death Syndrome)

SIDS Alliance, Inc.
1314 Bedford Avenue, Suite 210
Baltimore, MD 21208
Tel.: (800) 221-7437 or (410) 964-8000
Website: www.sidsalliance.org
E-mail: sidshq@charm.net
Research and parent support for Sudden Infant Death Syndrome (SIDS)

Back-to-Sleep Hotline
2070 Chain Bridge Road #450
Vienna, VA 22182
Tel.: (800) 505–CRIB or (800) 505–2742
Information on prevention of SIDS.

Vision

American Foundation for Vision Awareness
243 N. Lindbergh Blvd.
St. Louis, MO 63141
Tel.: (800) 927–AFVA or (800) 927–2382
Websites: www.afva.org and www.operationbrightstart.com
Information concerning children's vision health and development.

INDEX